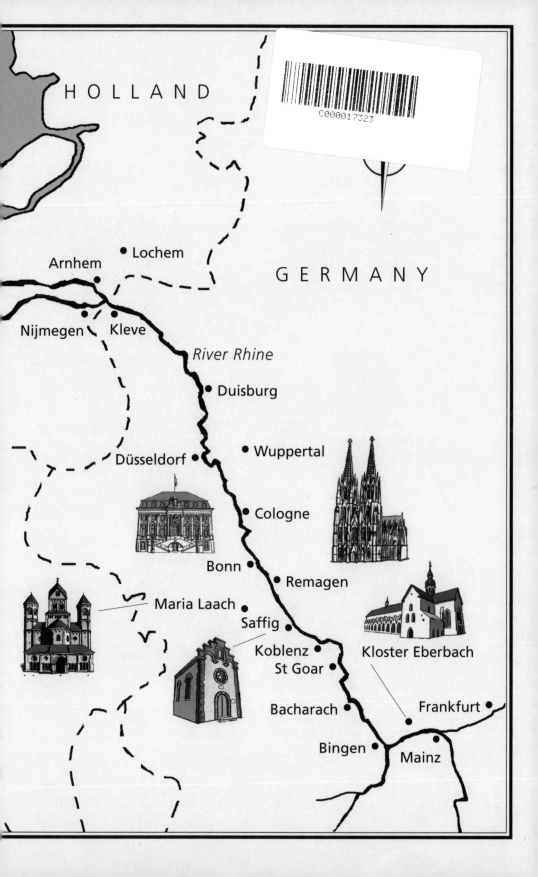

HOLLAND

GERMANY

Arnhem

Lochem

Nijmegen   Kleve

River Rhine

Duisburg

Düsseldorf

Wuppertal

Cologne

Bonn

Remagen

Maria Laach

Saffig

Koblenz
St Goar

Kloster Eberbach

Bacharach

Frankfurt

Bingen

Mainz

WALKING WITH THE LIGHT

From Frankfurt to Finchley

Rabbi Wittenberg's publications include

Three Pillars of Judaism: A Search for Faith and Values
(SCM Press)
*The Laws of Life: A Guide to Traditional Jewish Practice
at Times of Bereavement* (Masorti Publications)

The Eternal Journey: Meditations on the Jewish Year
(Joseph's Bookstore)

The Silence of Dark Waters: An Inner Journey
(Robin Clark Ltd / Joseph's Bookstore)

High Holiday and *Pesach* Companions
(Masorti Publications)

Walking with the Light

From Frankfurt to Finchley

JONATHAN WITTENBERG

QUARTET

First published in 2013 by
Quartet Books Limited
A member of the Namara Group
27 Goodge Street, London W1T 2LD

A catalogue record for this book
is available from the British Library

ISBN   978 0 7043 7279 5

Typeset by Antony Gray
Printed and bound in Great Britain by
T J International Ltd, Padstow, Cornwall

To my grandparents
Rabbi Dr Georg and Natalie Charlotte Salzberger
and to everyone who with compassion
for all living beings struggles against
suffering and persecution

Contents

And thou shalt command the children of Israel, that they bring unto thee pure olive oil beaten for the light, to cause a lamp to burn continually . . . from evening to morning before the Lord.

Exodus 27:20–21

It's my best time of day when I go to bed at eight, or at the latest at nine, and read. We only have electricity in two rooms and as the current is provided by a mill there isn't always light and when there is, it flickers a lot. We also have two petroleum lamps but we don't light them very often as petrol has become very expensive. Please send our greetings to all our relatives and tell them about us.

TRUDE

The last known letter from Trude Peiser, my father's aunt,
written in the ghetto of Ostrow Lubelski on
31 October 1941, from where she,
her husband Alex and their son Arnold
were taken in October 1943 and murdered.

With Gratitude

I would like to express my appreciation to everyone who helped me organise this walk, who assisted me in practical ways and who gave me so much encouragement.

My thanks go to: Doerte Letzmann, who worked with me so patiently and professionally on finding contacts, in making detailed route plans and in checking and rechecking all details; Claudia Meissner who helped arrange accommodation along the route; Dr Rachel Heuberger for her constant support, advice, help and guidance; Dr Wachten at the Jewish Museum in Frankfurt who answered my many questions, offered many helpful suggestions and showed us round the city; Frau Gudrun Hörner, who provided me with maps and who met me at Maria Laach; Professor David Ceserani who advised me on reading and research; Rabbi Professor Jonathan Magonet, who suggested people I might meet; Dr Clemens Nathan and Sir Erich Reich for their advice; Brian Berelowitz who so kindly drove with me through the night to reach Frankfurt on time and accompanied me on the first day's walk; Professor Andreas Lehnhardt who met me in Mainz and showed me the new synagogue; Dekan Pfizenmaier who walked with me through the hills and vineyards to Rüdesheim; Beate Goetz and the Arbeitskreis Jüdisches Bingen who looked after me there so well; Professor Wiese and Rabbi Leah Frey-Rabine and their students for welcoming me in Frankfurt; Dr Ries and Dr Kahn who welcomed me in Saffig and Koblenz; John Schlapobersky who joined me in Saffig and shared Shabbat with me in Koblenz and a wonderful day's walking; Dr Reinhard Schilling who took us to the Museum of the Rhine; Pater Viktor and Prior Petrus who were so welcoming at the Monastery of Maria Laach; Rabbi David Lazar who came specially from Stockholm to join me in Remagen; Professor Andreas Pangritz and his students who met me in Bonn; Michael Lawton, Günther Ginzel and his wife Sonja Güntner who, together with the community of Gescher Lamassoret welcomed me so warmly in Cologne;

the ladies of the Muslim women's centre in the city; Evelyn Friedlander for generously sharing with me the many contacts she and her late husband, my teacher and friend Rabbi Dr Albert Friedlander, had in common; Professor Bertold Klappert and his wife who welcomed with such kindness into their home in Wuppertal; Renata and Heinrich von Trott, and Katharina von Trott, who made me so welcome at Bad Hersfeld and in their home near Imshausen and who so generously shared their memories of their family, especially of their martyred uncle Adam von Trott zu Solz; Dr Michael Brocke who made contacts for me in Duisburg and Tanya Smolianitski and her friends who welcomed me there; Thomas Ruffmann and Wolfgang Krebs who looked after me and arranged an interfaith meeting in Kleve; Isidor Nathans who met me at Arnhem; Bert Oude-Engberink and Dan Daniels who met me in Haaksbergen and put me up in their home in Lochem; Emma Sevitt and her friends in Amsterdam; Dr Daniel Reisel who showed me round the internment camp at Barneveld; Rabbi Albert Ringer and his wife Aviva who were so kind to us on a cold and wet evening in Rotterdam; Ivo Godthelp from the mayor's office who showed us the site of the statue to the Kindertransport in Hoek van Holland; to everyone who showed us kindness along the way; to the many members of my community who encouraged me and followed my progress through my blog and some of whom came out to meet me, and especially to Claire Mandel, Rivka Gottlieb, Pauline Bravo, Michael Isaacs, Veronica Kennard and Eric Weigert all of whom helped me with countless practical details, and to my close friend and colleague Rabbi Chaim Weiner.

My especial thanks and appreciation go to Michael Kuhn of Querty Films for his huge generosity in sponsoring the film, and to director Guy Natanel and to Joe Cohen and Anna Wiehl who filmed the whole adventure and whose friendship and companionship along the way made it all an even better and richer experience.

My particular thanks go to David Elliott who has once again kindly and knowledgeably guided me through the process of turning draft writings into an actual book, and to everyone at Quartet Books for bringing the resulting work to publication.

My very special appreciation goes to Isca, my second mother, younger

With Gratitude

sister of my late mother Lore, who inspired this journey through sharing her many memories of Frankfurt; to my wife Nicky for all her love, encouragement and patience, and for coming out to rescue us at the end in Calais; to our children Mossy, Libbi and Kadya; and to Mitzpah the dog for the miles, the sunshine, the mud, the blankets and the biscuits we shared.

With gratitude to the God of all existence, who has kept me alive and brought me to this time.

Jonathan Wittenberg
December 2012
Kislev 5773

Introduction

I'm standing on the Freiherr-von-Stein Strasse in Frankfurt's West End. Which of these is the right door to the synagogue? The gentleman in the community offices round the corner told me quite clearly that the building was open and that I was perfectly free to look around. I go up the steps to the side gate; it's definitely shut. I walk back down the street to the small turning which passes directly in front of the main entrance; it must have been beneath this red-tiled portico that the community passed on Sabbaths and festivals. But all three gates are locked. I retrace my steps and notice another small door. Perhaps this is where the janitor lives? I try the bell but there is no answer. I turn back down the path and walk as far round the synagogue in both directions as walls and barriers allow. They said it was open, so maybe I missed something. This place was the centre of my grandfather's rabbinical life for thirty years but I'm unable to find my way in.

I'm on my second visit to Frankfurt, the first in preparation for my big walk. It will not be until my third trip that I finally get to see the inside of the synagogue and, weeping, read the inscription I will associate ever afterwards with its *Ner Tamid*, its Eternal Light: 'I shall not die, but I shall live and tell of the works of the Lord' (Psalm 118:17). It's a familiar verse from Psalms and overwhelmingly apposite. I stand here, the child of a family who lost everything and began again in a new country, a Jew, a follower in my grandfather's footsteps, seventy-two years after he took his lonely leave of the synagogue shortly before his flight to England and freedom just months before the start of the Second World War. I am indeed alive and have the privilege of telling the works of the Lord. Somehow, as a family, as a people, we have survived.

This is how my grandfather recorded his impressions at that time:

From the outside no sign of destruction could be seen. It was said

1

that the building had been spared in order to turn it into public baths. But inside, it offered a picture of terrifying devastation. The great candelabrum lay on the floor smashed into a thousand pieces. The benches, the lecterns, the pulpit where I had so often stood, the glorious organ, the cantor's prayer desk were all burnt. The Holy Ark was broken open; the Torah scrolls had been stolen. The sight pursued me like a nightmare long afterwards, until I was invited over a decade later to come from London to rededicate the newly restored house of God, in the presence of numerous representatives of both state and city, in a heart-rendingly moving service.[1]

The idea of walking from Frankfurt to Finchley came to me on the seventieth anniversary of Kristallnacht, when I reread my grandfather's memoirs. I was eighteen when he died and had always felt very close to him; to this day whenever I have to face a particularly testing challenge I think of his calm, wise face and feel inwardly stronger. I spent a lot of time with him when I was a teenager, but his experiences in the months before the family were finally able to flee Germany were a subject about which he rarely talked. Of his two terrible weeks in Dachau he determined that he would never speak at all. But he did write down his memoirs and they were published by the city of Frankfurt a number of years after his death.

From very early on my grandparents had been in no doubt about Hitler's intentions. My mother remembers lying awake late at night and overhearing them reading *Mein Kampf* out loud. But until after Kristall-nacht my grandfather, a leading rabbi in Frankfurt, had considered that 'the captain should be the last to leave the ship' and that his duty lay in remaining with his imperilled and beleaguered community. After the ninth of November this option was no longer open; the family had no choice but to flee or perish. He was arrested two days after the pogrom and taken to a gymnasium in the city where, alongside hundreds of others, he was made to perform humiliating exercises. From there he was deported to Dachau. It was a time of terror for thousands. People dreaded the arrival of the postman; many Jewish families were sent urns purportedly containing their loved one's ashes, accompanied by a curt note simply informing them that he or she had 'died'. For the receipt of these 'parcels' they were made to pay the sum of five reichmarks. While my grandfather was gone, the Gestapo came repeatedly to the family home in the middle of the night, banging on the door and demanding entry. They ordered them to 'do useful work for the first time in their lives'; this turned out to mean throwing the beautiful volumes of my grandfather's extensive library out of the window. Alone with three teenage daughters and fearing something worse, my grandmother, whose remarkable courage was ultimately responsible for getting the family out of Germany, told her children to comply.

The only path to safety lay in emigration. My grandmother was determined to find a way to get the family out of Germany. She followed up contacts abroad; she met with a British lawyer, whose first act in the Frankfurt hotel room where he held his interview with her was to bury the telephone in blankets, saying that he 'trusted nothing' in this country. She even went to the Gestapo offices, watching doors close behind her which had no handles on the inside by which she might possibly be able to open them again. On the strength of her efforts my grandfather was freed from Dachau concentration camp after two appalling weeks. He reached home sick with pneumonia but compelled nevertheless to report regularly to the Gestapo. After months of anxious waiting, the precious transit visas eventually materialised, permitting the family to reside temporarily in England before proceeding to the United States where a job had been found or created for my grandfather in a small provincial congregation. (In the event the war began and they remained in Britain.) Further terrifying weeks passed before all the papers were finally in order and the family was able to flee Germany, on 9 April 1939.

Some years ago my aunt gave me my grandfather's German passport, with the swastika and the Nazi eagle on the grey cover. In it was the stamp of the Frankfurt Bank indicating that all financial obligations to the state had been settled, no doubt at an exorbitant cost, as well as that of the authorities at Croydon Airport, where the family were met by friends and, for the first time in years, saw a policeman smile. Folded inside it was a small typed note advising refugees to avoid speaking

German in the street. Not many months after their arrival in Britain my grandparents would find themselves in the strange position of being labelled enemy aliens.

But this is to run ahead. On the morning after Kristallnacht my grandfather was summoned by the SA, the Sturmabteilung, a para-military part of the Nazi apparatus, to present himself at the synagogue on the Börneplatz with the keys, although, this being an orthodox institution and he a liberal rabbi, they must have known that he didn't possess them. He recorded walking through throngs of onlookers, none of whom was doing anything whatsoever to extinguish the flames which were devouring the remains of the building. There was no sign of any fire engines. But from among the crowd of Germans he heard comments like, '*Das wird sich rächen* – This will be avenged.' A sense of natural justice evidently remained; people still believed that God or destiny would not allow such a deed to pass unpunished. He also learned that the interior of the Westend-Synagoge had been destroyed, but that the *Ner Tamid*, the Eternal Light, continued to burn. '*Das nahmen Zuschauer als ein Zeichen von Gott,*' he wrote. 'Those who saw this took it as a sign from God.'[2]

It was when I read about this light, which neither the surrounding violence nor the encompassing darkness had been able to extinguish, that the idea was born in me of going to Frankfurt to kindle a torch from its fire and bring the flame back to London.

There was a further reason for my adventure: my community was building a new synagogue. In fact we'd been working on the project for no less than fifteen years, the relevant committees negotiating the many delays and difficulties, including a prolonged and frustrating battle for planning permission, with great stamina. The actual work of construction had finally commenced and it wouldn't be long before we could move into our new spiritual home. But what would prayer feel like in a synagogue which was entirely new? The problem was symbolised by the simple dilemma: how did one kindle a new Eternal Light? The combination of 'new' and 'eternal' sounded more like an oxymoron than a pair of spiritually compatible concepts.

But such a lamp might feel quite different if it was lit from a flame which represented a profound and challenging past, from a light which had burned through the deepest and most terrible of all periods of darkness experienced in the long and complex history of the Jewish people. Such a flame would indeed be fit to represent God's light.

These were the thoughts which came together, tentatively at first, in the plan to kindle a light from the *Ner Tamid* of the Westend-Synagoge in Frankfurt and walk with it back home to Finchley. I remember the first time I voiced my plans to Nicky, my wife, hesitantly, protecting myself with a 'maybe' and 'it's only an idea', well aware that I hadn't yet put this fantasy to even such a basic reality test as unfolding a map and taking a look. She was typically supportive, realising immediately that this was a project which I would find inspiring and sustaining. I also recollect when I first went to the bookshelf to get out the atlas. I turned with trepidation to the page with the map of Northern Europe: yes, the idea definitely was feasible; the distance didn't even seem impossibly great. Googlemaps quickly told me what it was: somewhat under four hundred miles from Frankfurt to Hoek van Holland, that is, if one travelled by car. But how far would this prove to be on walking routes, never straight at the best of times, and what kind of long-distance footpaths would exist to guide me across this unfamiliar landscape? How would I select a route? I looked again at the map and found that there was no real choice: the Rhine, that most ancient of watercourses across Northern Europe, would take me all the way from Mainz to the Dutch coast. To reach Mainz from Frankfurt-am-Main was a mere thirty miles along the river whose name both cities bore. A visit to Stanfords, that rambler's heaven in Covent Garden, procured detailed maps and descriptions of paths and cycle routes on either side of the Rhine from south of where I intended to join the river until at least as far north as Bonn. I had passed the point of no return; this had become a dream I was no longer prepared to forgo.

I have always loved walking. My first inter-city walk was a three-day affair we decided on after one of the children carelessly said, 'What would happen if we walked to granny and grandad's, instead of driving?' We took her at word, all sixty miles of it. Soon afterwards, Mitzpah, our ever eager borherder collie, set off with me on a 'hundred miles in a week' circuit round London, visiting hospitals, hospices, environmental projects, charities and places of worship, a whole range of organisations which together expressed my and my community's values. I was quite sure that the dog, who never put in less than three miles to my one, was up for such an adventure again and carefully updated his passport.

The plan thus became a promise first made to myself, then to my wife, to the dog, to the rest of the family and finally to the congregation. I had committed myself from the pulpit; this was something I was now under obligation to fulfil. What I did not yet have was any conception of the depth of stimulation, emotional, intellectual and spiritual, which I was to draw from the endeavour. Standing outside that locked synagogue in Frankfurt, I had no idea how many doors to places, people and knowledge, as well as to my inner sense of continuity with the history of my own family and people, this walk would eventually open.

The first decision I made concerned timing. I knew that if I waited for very long my diary would be booked up with lectures, weddings and other communal obligations and it would be impossible for me to get away from London for any significant length of time. I didn't want to make the hike a summer project; for one thing, I hate the heat and walking long distances is especially uncomfortable if it's too warm. For another, a lot of the people I hoped to meet would probably be away. It also seemed unfair on the family to force upon them a summer plan in which they'd had no say and, anyway, I didn't regard this simply as a holiday. I would go in October, after the Jewish New Year and the Day of Atonement were safely over, but not so late in the season as to extinguish the hope of walking through the last of the autumn's beauty. For obvious reasons it was important to me to commemorate Kristallnacht en route. I determined to walk for twenty days; in this manner I would be absent from my family and community for only two Sabbaths. This was as long as it felt fair to be away. I now regret that I did not take at least one more week: so many encounters seemed rushed and I often had the ugly sensation that I had failed to stay with people or in places for long enough to hear the hitherto unspoken stories they had to tell me. I blocked out the dates in my diary and, for once in my life, carefully delegated or deferred any commitments which threatened to get in the way. Then I set to work.

My idea had never been simply to walk along the Rhine with the dog as if we were on some rambling adventure *à deux*. I wanted to engage not only with the Jewish past but with its present, and with Christian and Muslim communities as well. In the following months I was frequently asked, often with considerable scepticism, about the overriding purpose of the walk: was it anything more than some pleasant private indulgence? Of what lasting value would it be to anybody? These weren't questions I found myself able to answer in a ready sound-byte. But the essential issue was *light*, political as well as spiritual: where did the light reside, both in society and in the individual human being? What brought moral darkness and what fostered spiritual and ethical illumination? It was never my intention to focus solely on the Holocaust; I was heedful of the words of my teacher, Professor Rabbi Jonathan Magonet, that it is all too easy for Jews to concentrate on the Shoah, avoiding the complexity, discomfort and moral ambiguity of more contemporary issues such as the treatment of asylum seekers and other outsiders in the Europe of today, the destruction of our environment, or the relationship between Israelis and Palestinians. It was not my aim in walking through Germany as a visibly committed Jew to provoke guilt or to elicit defensive apologies. The past, as I was to discover, is constantly present. It inhabits the very pavements and railway lines; it speaks out in memories of which the appropriate circumstances have never previously come together to provoke the expression; its consequences are enacted in the responses of children to what their parents did and said, or failed to do and say. It is inescapable. But I wanted neither to indulge in it nor to exploit it; rather to work with it, learn from it, and encounter the light and darkness within it.

The task of finding contacts proved far more difficult that I had supposed. I asked former teachers as well as scholars and writers for help. I followed up each and every one of the many leads I was offered. I discovered an article about my father's uncle Professor Aron Freimann and was reminded that he had catalogued and greatly expanded the remarkable collection of Jewish books belonging to the municipal library of Frankfurt and co-initiated the monumental project on German Jewish history known as *Germania Judaica*. A little research put me in touch with the present holder of his former position, now based at the university library, Rachel Heuberger. She was enormously helpful and unfailingly kind. When we met in London she told me that the date on which I planned to start my walk coincided with the centenary celebrations of the Westend-Synagoge, an event which was to give a new depth to the whole project. Through her good offices I was even invited to speak on that occasion. When the day finally came, after I said my piece from the pulpit which had been my grandfather's precisely a hundred years before, I found myself weeping without pause.

Slowly and with much assistance I was able to put together a full programme of meetings and encounters in virtually every place I visited in both Germany and Holland. Eventually, hearing of my imminent journey, people began to contact me of their own accord and I sometimes found myself in the awkward position of having to say no.

Thus the months went by, with a thousand other occupations and distractions competing with my preparations for this rapidly nearing adventure. My book bill was high, nearly all the money being spent on titles about European and German-Jewish history out of print for decades and imported from libraries in the States which had come to the sad conclusion that there were no longer any borrowers interested in these forlorn volumes and that they might as well be sold off. The summer passed; it was time to count down the weeks and enter a final, but thorough, phase of preparation. Did I know exactly which way I was walking each day, with whom I was meeting and where I was staying each night? (For the latter I had three stipulations: the place must take dogs, have Internet access so that I could send a daily blog to my community, and provide good coffee. Unexpectedly, it proved to be the second of these three conditions which was most often not fulfilled.) What maps were still missing from my growing pile? Had I actually looked carefully and checked whether my weak orientation skills would be up to the task of reading them accurately? I put into one single folder every address, phone number and email I thought I could possibly need for the whole of the walk, duplicating everything on a memory stick which, except for my passport, was now the single material item I was most afraid of losing.

It was at this point that the plan to film the journey was finalised. I met Guy, the director, for the first time over a quiet Sabbath lunch at my home and liked him at once. But I understood absolutely nothing about filming and had not the vaguest idea about what it would entail. It wouldn't be long before I began to learn.

Meanwhile, the time to set off had drawn excitingly, and worryingly, close.

Last-Minute Preparations

A candle by my foothold is your word,
and a light upon my path.

Psalm 119:105

The necessaries for the journey began to pile up in the bedroom, the kitchen and my study. All but the thinnest of books had to be eliminated; I painstakingly copied on to my memory stick the key quotations, quirky facts and essential historical data I felt I would need, both for writing my blog and in preparing the various talks I had been asked to give along the way. The subjects varied from reflections on the meaning of light to Jewish law and life today. Several inter-faith dialogues were also planned. I acquired basic medical supplies, surgical spirit to toughen up my feet (the dog hated the smell so much that he hid under the bed as soon as he saw me go near the bag in which I kept the bottle), blister plasters and enough pills for my diabetes to last a good month. My walking boots joined the stack, as did several pairs of outer and inner socks and a storm-proof anorak borrowed from my son. The dog also needed his essentials: cream for his paws, a pair of boots (experimentation had already proved them totally useless since I couldn't persuade him to keep them on for more than half a minute, but I included them anyway in the hope of faring better should an emergency arise such as one of his pads receiving a cut), towels, urgently required to cover the bed in the short interval between opening the door of our hotel room and his jumping on to the clean white duvet, a decent supply of his regular food and treats (to prevent the unfortunate effects of an unfamiliar diet), an ample quantity of small plastic bags for purposes best not described in detail, and, most important of all, his passport, duly stamped and with all inoculations up to date. His travel arrangements had been worrying me for a while, but everything seemed to be more or less in order. My blog, which I started a couple of weeks before setting out (blog entries are marked throughout with a ❖), testified to my ignorance of the actual difficulties which were to follow:

❖ A small dilemma faces Mitzpah, or rather his owner, as he himself remains blissfully unaware of the concern. The issue is this: in order to arrive at the centennial commemorations of the Westend-Synagoge in Frankfurt on time, the only way we can travel out to Germany is by plane. This goes against the grain; for environmental reasons I would much rather take the train or ferry, as we plan to do on the return journey. But in this case I have no option. I have to spend the Sabbath with my own community in London and cannot therefore leave until Saturday night. The service in Frankfurt begins the next morning at 11.00. Lufthansa, the only airline to do a 6.20 a.m. flight on a Sunday morning, does carry dogs. They travel in an air-conditioned compartment of the hold, which I'm assured is perfectly safe. The books tell you to leave a familiar toy with your pet so that he doesn't feel abandoned. On enquiring about the cost of a dog ticket, I learnt that one pays per kilo, just like for excess baggage. Mitzpah is heavier than he looks and a succession of Yom Tov (festival) snacks has hardly helped. So the question is: would it be cruel to put him on a gentle diet, just to remove a kilo or two? Perhaps the fair thing would be to do the same myself?

Mitzpah's companionship on the journey was going to be very important to me. A scene came to mind from Aharon Appelfeld's autobiography, in which he described how, during his months of flight and hiding in Nazi Europe as a young boy, he would often find refuge among the farm animals. There with the sheep, cows and puppies he felt safe; they would never betray him. Curled up next to them he could sleep once again the sleep of a child.[1] What a troubling testament to how poor our own kind is at trust, at offering each other unequivocal protection when in need, without the hovering presence of suspicion, fear, ambivalence and the threat of sudden betrayal.

It's to the discredit of our species that treachery is associated exclusively with humankind while faithfulness is attributed to the beasts, to the dog, the donkey and the horse. Above everything else I hope I shall never betray what it means to be a human being. I pray to be spared the terrors and temptations which induce or force people to do so, for this would truly be an extinguishing of the light within.

A further problem, which had been troubling me for some time, was how I would actually transport the light. I dismissed at once the notion of carrying a naked flame; I simply couldn't see myself as a slow-motion version of an Olympic runner, trying to hold a burning brand in one hand and the lead with the dog tugging at it in the other, being told wherever I went, 'Regrettably we don't admit animals, and we can't permit bonfires,' and with the police on my tail within half an hour, challenging me to prove that I wasn't some kind of crazed religious terrorist. I would have to use an electric torch, anodyne symbol as this was. But how would I find the correct kind of instrument with batteries which wouldn't have to be renewed twice a day, creating an unconscionable quantity of waste?

In the event I was presented with a beautiful torch which could be left on for up to five days before the battery required recharging. A friend also gave me a solar lamp which absorbed energy by day and shone by night. In answer to the many people who asked me, I made it clear that I was not planning to attach the torch to either the tail or collar of poor Mitzpah the dog. (Little did he know what he'd got coming to him.)

Carrying a light was a great responsibility. Symbolically this flame would be one small way in which to take the Jewish past, a long, haunting, complex and sometimes tragic past, into the present and future of the new synagogue. I hoped that it would inspire further journeys and different ways in which others could also bring their own treasures and lights from that history into the shared communal home we were shortly to consecrate. For how else, except through the presence of the past and the dedication of the future, could one sanctify the new?

The Torah describes the light of the Menorah as *tamid*. It isn't easy to translate the term: does it mean 'eternal', 'everlasting', 'constant' or 'regular'? According to the mystics its illumination exists not only outside us as a flame in front of the sanctuary, but also within us as God's light inside the soul, for 'A lamp of the Lord is the human spirit, searching all the chambers of our being' (Proverbs 20:27). Perhaps it is this light inside us, obscured so much of the time by our constant occupations and preoccupations, which is privileged in spite of our mortality to recognise and feel wonder at what is eternal all around us: beauty, and a secret unity which fills and courses through all life, the great oneness to which we belong and to which, in our best moments of love and prayer, we testify.

I was delighted that Isca decided to accompany me for the opening day in Frankfurt. Isca became my second mother after Lore, her elder sister, died when my brother and I were very young. It was she who really brought us up. Countless times when I couldn't sleep as a child she would come to our room and read to us. But what I liked best, and what I always begged for, were stories about when she was a child in Frankfurt. She told me how in the Nazi years she would go to bed with her head covered by her pillow for protection, uncertain if she would wake up safe the next morning. She explained how the Philanthropin, the oldest Jewish school in Frankfurt, founded in 1804, employed two young teachers from Britain who made English the language of instruction so as to prepare the girls for emigration, and who constantly went back and forth to London trying to persuade the authorities there of the urgency of their pupils' plight. She described the long walk she undertook through the dangerous streets of her home city to the hotel where they met with the English lawyer who was to help the family obtain visas. It fell to her to accompany my grandmother because she spoke the best English, the safest language to use whenever there were Nazis within earshot, and on this particular day the SS were stopping people at every street corner. She also went on behalf of the family to the British Consulate, an island of kindness in a sea of hatred. The Consul-General, Robert Smallbones, and his assistant Arthur Dowden, took pains to ensure that the basic human needs of the terrified people who thronged to their offices day by day were met. 'The first thing they asked me at the Consulate,' one woman recalled, 'was, "Have you had anything to eat today?" And before they did anything else, they fed me with coffee and sandwiches.'[2] Isca was surprised by this reference to coffee. 'It was tea they gave us,' she remembered. 'That's where we learnt to drink tea.'

The visas eventually arrived on Isca's birthday, 4 March 1939. Without those papers my brother and I would not have been born.

Isca decided, too, that she would like to donate the new *Ner Tamid* to the synagogue. This touched me deeply for she had borne the light of the family's culture and values from Germany to Britain. Here in England life had been hard in many different ways; within weeks of arrival she found herself in Yorkshire, far from her beloved parents and sisters, doing night shifts caring for babies in a grim establishment where mice ran up and down the curtains. It wasn't until years later, when she was in residence as a student in a Quaker hall, that she felt truly at home. Both here and in Germany the Quakers acted with profound and simple humanity. My grandfather wrote in a deposition about life in Frankfurt in the Nazi period that 'the spiritual and intellectual leadership failed'. But he then qualified this judgement: 'Those who were truly helpful and empathic were the Quakers; many Frankfurt Jews owe them their lives.'[3] He also added the names of a number of individuals who had behaved with exceptional courage and kindness.

Many times I heard Isca say that what she had learnt above all else from her terrible experiences was the importance of building bridges. This she achieved through her work as a psychotherapist, fostering understanding not only between individuals but also among whole groups of professionals, especially social workers and teachers, and by creating connections across different disciplines and between fellow therapists in many countries and continents. On a more personal level she had also carried the light between the generations; she would often describe herself humorously as known in some circles as the rabbi's daughter and in others as the rabbi's mother.

Thus my concerns moved backwards and forwards between the spiritual and the practical, between theology and the medicine bag. The departure date was now only ten days away and a sixth sense made me call Lufthansa once again to check if the arrangements for the dog (and for Isca and myself) were still in order. I was duly assured that everything would be fine. I needn't even worry about finding a travel crate for Mitzpah; the company would be happy to lend us the requisite item. Somehow, though, it all sounded a little too good to be true and something told me not to believe what I was being told. A further phone call confirmed that my scepticism was well founded; we would most definitely have to supply the requisite crate ourselves.

Panic followed. How were be to obtain this essential item at such minimal notice? How could I be sure that it would comply with all the detailed specifications demanded by the airline company, and, even supposing I was to find such a blessed box, what was I going to do with it at Frankfurt Airport? At least a metre long and high by half a metre wide, it was scarcely the kind of unobtrusive object I could simply ditch in a corner of the arrivals hall or the car park without attracting the attention of the airport security team. Matters were not looking good. My blog reveals, to my shame, that it was Nicky who was doing all the research while I was burying my head in complex elucidations of a favourite passage of Torah.

❖ I was at my desk at about half past eleven at night, trying to decipher the small print of an abstruse commentary. Everyone is stirred by the words of the priestly blessing, Christians as well as Jews; it's widely known that St Francis of Assisi loved them.

> May the Lord bless you and keep you;
> May the Lord make his face shine upon you and be gracious
> to you;
> May the Lord turn his face towards you and give you peace.
> (Numbers 6:24–6)

Somehow, the middle sentence touches me most. According to rabbinic tradition, it refers to the blessings of the spirit. It makes me think of those special people I know whose faces are radiant, as if God's presence were not only shining upon them from above but also outwards from inside them through their goodness and kindness.

In his mystical commentary the *Kli Yakar*, Rabbi Shlomo Ephraim of Lunschitz (1550–1619) describes the relationship between God and Israel in the first verse as like that of mother to daughter, from above to below, whereas in the middle verse it is like that between sisters who stand together on the same level:

'May the Lord make his face shine upon you' – as if God were standing opposite you face to face, just as the moon receives its light from the sun by standing opposite it.

The rare and tender femininity of this image moved me, the thought that we are like God's younger sisters, absorbing his blessings like the moon.

At that moment the phone rings. It is Nicky (my office is in a converted part of the garage and she works at the top of the house, so we sometimes resort to this method of communication). 'Pop upstairs, I think I've solved the problem.'

Nicky (and Pauline at the synagogue) had spent gracious hours searching through websites to ascertain exactly what kind of crate Mitzpah required. They'd tried Skydog, Flydog and Highdog – you wouldn't have thought such organisations existed. Eventually Nicky found BA's excellent guide to flying with your dog. Crates, it transpired, came in all sizes and you had to get the dimensions right or the dog wouldn't be permitted on board. You entered a range of measurements and the computer told you what kind of cage you required. So Mitzpah was hauled upstairs from his beauty sleep (on our bed) and, holding him still with one hand while trying to operate the measuring tape with the other, I worked out his vital statistics and called them out to Nicky who typed them into her computer: tip of nose to base of tail, top of ears to pad of paws, floor to elbow joint. He was quite thin (eight inches at his widest) but extremely long, and the bad news was that he fell into the category of 'extra large'.

We searched the Internet for special offers, looked on eBay and put out an advert on the weekly community email. Just after we'd finally resigned ourselves to the fact that we would have to spend a hundred pounds on the essential item, we heard that a friend who lived only a few streets away had a cage of exactly the right dimensions stored away in her garage since the one and only time she had ever used it. But that was not, of course, the end of the matter. One issue led to another: in the end it transpired that the combined weight of dog and container was too heavy for Mitzpah to be allowed to travel other than as cargo.

'You'd better leave him at the airport the day before,' the man in the relevant department advised me. He was kind, but evidently no dog owner; there was simply no way I was prepared to do any such thing. How could I trust that Mitzpah would be safe there all on his own? He would feel hungry and terrified. He would miss the holy Sabbath, and what would he do without his Friday-night treats? Further, I was warned that he mightn't even get on to the same flight as his human family. Finally the whole unreliable operation would have cost so much that I could have taken a long holiday in New Zealand and had something to spare. No; I would have to abandon the whole idea of flying.

Trains were sadly not an option. Eurostar doesn't take dogs. The Stena Line, which runs the ferry service between Harwich and the Hook of Holland, and by which I intended to return, did. But from the Hook to Frankfurt was still a long way and, fast as the trains were, I wouldn't get to Frankfurt early enough for the service. There was no alternative; I would simply have to drive. This I was prepared to do, if necessary, but I didn't particularly want to undertake the all-night journey on my own.

I still remember the exact moment when I called my friend. 'Brian,' I said, 'I need to ask you a favour, a very big favour.' 'Sure,' he replied, 'Just tell me what it is.' 'Will you drive with me through the night, so that we can get to the synagogue in Frankfurt on time?'

Sorting out the details with Eurotunnel was simple compared to all the complexities of the dog-crate fiasco. Mitzpah would be able to enjoy his journey from the lazy warmth of a blanket on the back seat of Brian's car. A short run around two a.m. would keep him comfortable and we'd all arrive in Frankfurt on the morning of 24 October in time for the synagogue service feeling every bit as fresh as daisies. 'When do you think you'll get here?' the receptionist at the hotel asked me over the phone. 'Between three and four a.m.,' I answered optimistically. In the event, the driving took us longer than we thought. We rolled into Frankfurt at six and rolled straight into bed after that. We lost one hour owing to the time change; the disappearance of a second hour remains a mystery to Brian and me to this very day. Mitzpah, spared the trauma of queues, crates, weighing in, waiting, and the unfamiliar sensations of take-off, flight and landing in an aircraft hold, evidently felt that it all lay happily within his accustomed comfort zone.

Though practical matters predominated, I harboured other anxieties as well. I was concerned to prepare properly for the many encounters planned en route. But there was one for which there was little I could do to get ready and about which I knew I would be asked: 'What kind of God do you think you're going to meet on the journey?'

Before me on my desk lay a memory of the Holocaust which I'd received a few days earlier from my friend, the artist Roman Halter, a survivor of the camps (who has sadly since died).

> After an inspection of our pitiful state by Dr Mengele, who decided that everyone on the train – 2800 of us – was only fit for the gas chambers, we were lined up and told to march slowly towards the crematoria. I was next to a man who kept on repeating Hebrew words over and over again. I asked him what he was saying; he told me that he was quoting Psalm 31. Years later, in England, I asked [a friend] what the man had said. He translated for me: 'Into your hand I submit my spirit; you have redeemed me, O Lord, God of truth.'

It turned out that I was the 'friend'. Next to this account, Roman had sketched the tower at the entrance to Birkenau underneath which the railway line enters. But, unlike in the iconic image when the viewer looks at them from the outside, these buildings were depicted from within the camp.

Everything I might write or say about God had to pass through the filter of such scenes. It had to honour the faith of those who maintained, or even discovered, it in the very teeth of persecution, torture and murder. Yet at the same time it needed to respect the incomprehensibility, the impossibility, of faith in the face of precisely such horrors. It's unconscionable to base what we say about God purely on dogmatic conviction or creedal convenience; it is of value only if spoken with a bare, scoured-out integrity of heart.

❖   I sometimes find myself reflecting on the Mishnah, that remarkable second-century rabbinic code and compendium of Jewish life and law which stipulates that if a prayer-leader says from in front of the Ark, 'Your mercies, God, extend to the bird's nest,' one has to silence him. (Mishnah Berachot 5:3). The Talmud asks the obvious question: what could possibly be wrong with so sweet and innocuous a sentiment? Its first answer is sadly familiar: it makes the rest of creation jealous and what are the fishes going to feel? It's the Talmud's second response which is truly disturbing: don't start attributing intentions to God, because what will you say when something really terrible happens? Will that too have to be defined as 'an act of mercy'? Rather, let God's actions simply remain inscrutable decrees (Talmud Berachot 33b).

I often think about the elderly member of my community, no longer alive these last several years, who came to Britain with the Kindertransport and whose first wife was a Holocaust survivor. 'I struggle with God,' he once told me, 'and the only resolution I can find is to think that God is not just creator but also destroyer.'

I know that I will encounter the effects of that destruction everywhere on this walk. From Mainz to Cologne my route follows the path of the First Crusade, which took place in 1096. The Jewish communities were simply obliterated and the accounts of those appalling events can only be compared in the annals of Jewish history to the documents about the deeds of the Einsatzgruppen in Eastern Europe. Testament to the Shoah will be everywhere. A friend sent me an article: 'Only four Jews came back to Frankental,' it begins. A comment which sustained me in moments when I thought I was simply being an idiot to pursue an idea like this came from a Holocaust survivor whom I'd never before met, 'I'm glad you are making this journey; it means a lot to me.'

But I hope to find another, very different, manifestation of God as well: God who is discovered, despite everything, in the depths of the heart. One of the leaders of the Jewish community of Koblenz wrote to me: 'I will take you to the monastery of Maria Laach where you can hear some of the accounts of the monks who saved Jewish lives during the war.'

I don't believe in proofs of the existence of God, or in magic formulae adduced by mixing and multiplying the numerical values of the words on some sacred page. But I do believe in testament. The greatest of all such testament is what human beings manage to do with their time on earth because they are inspired by God's presence in the dignity, tenderness and vulnerability of human life.

The last few days flew by. The film team, Guy, Joe and Anna, came to photograph me doing my normal 'stuff' around the house. They had long interviews with Isca. The dog arrived at the happy realisation that, whatever was in the offing, it most certainly included him.

❖   He watched me pack a bag for him: a huge box of his regular food (there's no point upsetting his stomach), dog chews to keep his teeth clean and his breath fresh, poo bags in plenty, his brush, his toothbrush (under-used, but my fault), shampoo (just in case he rolls in anything awful, which, I have to say, he almost never does), a ball, his lead . . . So he knows there's something coming up soon, but what exactly it is remains a cheerful mystery. I'm fearful of the day when, after all this is over, I say the word 'walk' and he thinks to himself, 'Never again!' and disappears off to hide under the bed.

I think it was at this point that I made two further minor decisions. First, Mitzpah would write his own blog. ['Everybody's talking about it,' I was told when I phoned home on the third day. 'He's got a lot more readers than you have.'] Secondly, he would have his own sponsorship; or rather I would devote a modest percentage of what we raised together to a suitable canine cause. The training of guide dogs in Israel seemed an obvious choice; I had visited the centre and was deeply impressed.

Countless people asked me after we returned how the dog had managed, whether he was exhausted and if he was enjoying his well-earned rest. If human observations are anything to go by, it struck me that he was rather disappointed to be home and that he missed his long walks, his big river and his uninterrupted special time with his human companion. He certainly wasn't tired and at night when he lay half asleep on the bed I could see his paws twitching and making the motions of walking, as if he was reliving his adventures just to remind himself that they really had occurred. The trailer for our film arrived via email and I sat him on my lap in front of my computer to watch it. He most definitely was the star, but he showed no interest at all. I don't know what dogs are able to see on screens but I'm sure that he retains the memory of our route in his muscles and in a thousand smells he would recognise at once if only I would take him back, soon please, to that long and exciting path.

*   *   *

The house was quiet during the week before my journey. Nicky took our daughter Libbi to Venice as a pre-birthday treat but they were back home in time for Shabbat so that we could spend it together. Though we often have thirty or forty guests for the Sabbath dinner, this Friday night was kept strictly for family only.

That morning at synagogue we celebrated the Bar Mitzvah of a boy whose mother's parents had both been hidden as children in Eastern Holland near Arnhem. Remarkably, they survived together with their parents. 'Growing up in Holland, I was the only child who had all her grandparents,' the boy's mother told me. I was to meet her father on my walk and he would show me round the beautiful synagogue where he had celebrated his own Bar Mitzvah, aged fourteen, just one year later than usual, after the war. A skilfully constructed glass partition divided it into two halves; its original size had become a hindrance to creating a sense of spirit among the now small congregation. I recalled how we had marked the Bar Mitzvah some years earlier of a boy whose grandfather had survived Birkenau. I remembered saying, after first asking his permission to refer to those experiences, that once he had stood before the gates of Auschwitz but that now he stood in celebration with two new generations of his family in front of the open Ark of God's presence.

It is easy to forget how lucky we are to have life around us, children, hope. It can all so easily be taken away.

I reserved the last few hours of that Sabbath for the family alone. Sadly, term dates meant that none of the children would be able to join me on the walk. I had previously always avoided being absent for this length of time. I blessed them each in turn, asking, in the words familiar from the Book of Numbers so beautifully explained by the *Kli Yakar*, that the light of God's countenance be shed upon them and within them. A quarter of an hour after the close of the Sabbath, Brian arrived to pick me up. I spread out the blanket on the back seat of his car and Mitzpah promptly curled up on that section of the upholstery which it wasn't sufficiently extensive to cover. A further fifteen minutes found us snugly stuck in a traffic jam on the North Circular. At least this part of the route was familiar; we were on our way.

❖   Brian and I drive through most of the night, arriving in Frankfurt at six a.m. For part of the journey we listen to a CD of the remarkable Radio 4 programme introduced by Alan Dein, *I Did Not Interview the Dead*. In it Alan considers the work of Dr David Boder who spoke with survivors of the Shoah in Displaced Persons' Camps across Europe in 1946. This is therefore some of the first recorded testimony about the Holocaust in existence, preceding the many volumes by historians and the personal narratives with which we have now become familiar. Thus, as we travel through the midnight hours towards Germany voices address us out of the dark: 'I was frightened of that small room. In it there were fingernails torn off, ripped-out hair; there was lots of blood on the floor. They pierced my tongue with nails' . . . 'I had been used to luxury; now I had to give birth to my child in this tiny space with all those people around me. My husband said that I should give my baby daughter to a Gentile; maybe that way at least she would survive. The woman was afraid. "Leave the baby there in the snow," she said "Afterwards I'll pick her up." I suffered for twenty-six hours giving birth to her; now I'm going to suffer for the rest of my life. The baby did not survive.'

Thus we cross Europe through the darkness.

Day One – In Frankfurt: Lighting the Torch

If I were to say, 'Surely the darkness will crush me, and the light around me shall be night,' even the darkness is not too dark for you, and the night shines like the day; the darkness is as the light.

Psalm 139:11–12

I remember well that first morning in Frankfurt. It was my third visit to the city and I felt calm and strangely at home. I took Mitzpah down for a short walk in the beautiful autumn sunlight. As he lifted his leg against a shrub in the small front garden of a terraced home I asked myself for the first time the question which would turn everything I looked at into a double image: was any of this the same when my grandparents lived here? On those long walks home from the synagogue, when, popular with all the teenage girls, my grandfather would stroll back answering their no doubt exclusively theological questions, did he sometimes pass by this street, this very house?

Or was it here that, sometime after 1933, he witnessed that minor incident which affected him so deeply. Two young schoolboys were threatening their friend, fists at the ready: 'You were talking to that Jew!' they accused him, while he, weeping bitterly, denied having committed such a sin.

The Palmengarten was only a short distance down the road, the beautiful gardens where my mother and her sisters were taken for walks when they were small. It was there that my grandfather judged it safe to speak with the famous Protestant theologian Rudolf Otto, author of the *Idea of the Holy*, who had written to him from the University of Marburg asking for a private meeting at which they could talk openly. Otto died in 1937 of pneumonia after sustaining serious injuries when he fell twenty metres from a tower; some think that it was an attempt at suicide. Many years later my grandfather could still recall the exact details of the encounter. Otto took him to a remote corner of the park, from where they could not be overheard, and said that he'd come to bring him courage

> so that you can give courage to your co-religionists. A most terrible fate has descended upon you all. But there exists a God in whom we, Christians and Jews, believe, and what is happening today, especially what is being done by that Mephistopheles Goebbels, will one day exact its bloody vengeance.[1]

Another Protestant professor from the same university regularly brought his students to Frankfurt and on each occasion asked my grandfather to give them a lecture on the subject of Judaism at the Westend-Synagoge so that they could be properly informed. This was no minor act of defiance in such a time of terror.

I met Isca in the hotel foyer, relieved that she had arrived safely after a very early morning flight which she had now been forced to negotiate on her own. I was glad that we were sharing this day; later, as I sat in the synagogue, I kept asking myself why I hadn't tried harder to persuade my brother to come. It was as if history, ever recalcitrant, always stealing the present away to hide it in its locked chambers, had opened those doors very slightly, more than it would ever do again, and in faint colours refracted through wars and exile, our grandparents together with all the *dramatis personae* of their lives and the Frankfurt they so much loved were dimly visible.

❖ As I stand with Isca outside the Westend-Synagoge before the service to mark its centennial year, I find myself thinking about my grandparents, trying to imagine them as they must have been when they were young. I picture to myself a wedding in the spacious forecourt, maybe in the 1920s, my grandmother elegant and beautiful as she always was, my grandfather talking to the guests. I recall them telling me how sometime in 1914 they sat in the empty synagogue prior to becoming engaged and discussed whether the love they felt for one another was '*objektif oder subjektif*', before allowing themselves their first kiss.

The streets are full of people arriving for the service. I am moved to
see how many come in wheelchairs or with frames to help them walk;
all of them are kindly and thoughtfully assisted up the few steps or
the short ramp into the rather grand synagogue hall. Isca, Brian and
I are warmly welcomed. Sitting in the front row I feel the presence
next to me of all my family: my father, my mother, my grandparents,
as if the passage of time which has taken them all to their graves has
been repealed and we exist together in some extra-terrestrial domain.
Or perhaps it is precisely that which Judaism creates: a liturgy,
melodies, spiritual and ritual associations in which we encounter
each other across the generations, transcending the destruction
wrought by time.

Through the good offices of Rachel Heuberger, scholar and curator of
Jewish books at the university library, I had been invited to speak at the
service. 'Don't be too brief,' she told me. 'Remember that you'll be the
only speaker who has such close family connections with the Frankfurt
community of this synagogue as it was before the war.'

My grandfather had loved Frankfurt. He had travelled here from
Berlin in the summer of 1910 to take up his first rabbinical appointment
after completing his studies at the liberal rabbinical seminary, the
Hochschule für die Wissenschaft des Judentums. This was the very
year the Westend-Synagoge was dedicated. Had my grandfather been
present on that remarkable occasion?

I reread the relevant chapter in his memoirs, for which he had chosen
the superscription from the Book of Kings, 'Be strong, and so become a
man,' since it described his first ventures in the practical rabbinate. He
had fallen in love with Frankfurt the moment he arrived. For one thing,
it was the town of his beloved Goethe's birth; he described his many
visits to the house where the great poet was born, how he stood in
veneration before his desk and even enjoyed looking at his puppet theatre.
Only afterwards did he mention Frankfurt's synagogues, noting that 'the
fourth, a liberal synagogue, was still under construction'.[2] The dedication
ceremony took place shortly before the High Holydays of the same year
and my grandfather was most certainly present. He even wrote about the

lighting of the *Ner Tamid*. At the critical moment, just as the choir was singing music from Beethoven on the very theme of illumination, all the lights in the new building went out and the entire congregation was left sitting in the dark. He refrained from comment, but I wonder whether he came, many decades later, to see this as an omen.

He also noted wryly that after the service the mayor of Frankfurt asked a leading congregant why Jews always built their synagogues in the styles of their persecutors. (The Westend-Synagoge was apparently constructed after the Babylonian-Assyrian manner.) The man was tempted to reply by enquiring of the honourable gentleman if he could name a nation which had never been counted among our oppressors.

My grandfather was also present at the rededication of the synagogue after the Holocaust, in September 1950. I believe this was the first time he returned to Germany since fleeing the country eleven and a half years earlier and I wonder what he must have felt on that occasion. I would also love to know what he said, but was told in response to my enquiries that sadly no transcript appeared to have survived. A Midrash or rabbinic interpretation teaches that five people 'saw a new world' in their own lifetime. Among them were Noah and Job, figures scarcely to be envied. The latter's book ends with the somewhat surreal description of how God provides him with a new and apparently even nicer family, as if this were some kind of divine compensation for all he had suffered and the children he had lost could simply be replaced. My grandfather's 'new world', like that of Noah after he landed in the endless desert of post-diluvian mud, must have been haunted by the presence of vanished faces staring at him with pain and anguish at every street corner and from every pew.

Through a further strange coincidence, only three weeks earlier I had spoken at the dedication of the new building of the Belsize Square Synagogue in London, which had been founded by refugees from Germany in 1939 and of which my grandfather had been the first rabbi. On that occasion I said:

This community has a unique and deeply important identity. Its beginnings lie in the raw hearts of refugees, a remnant of great continental congregations, who left everything behind, grateful to find shelter in this country with their lives and, if they were fortunate, with some at least of their loved ones. It grew out of the need for comfort, for the companionship, when so much had been lost, of familiar prayers and melodies, for words of Torah spoken in German and a place for exiles to meet and help each other to create a new home. No doubt that was what led my grandfather to choose the words from Isaiah read on the Sabbath of Consolation, 'The word of our God endures for ever' (Isaiah 40:8), which still remain inscribed at the base of the doors to the Holy Ark. Over the decades this congregation has journeyed from survival to renewal and creativity, with a strong spirit of music, joy and humour. It stands as an inspiration to other groups of refugees struggling to build a new home here and make a contribution to this country.

Because of this history, every act of building, whether in cement and bricks, in bonds between people, in ideas or through celebration, is a spiritual victory over the Nazi devastation of Europe, over the ninth of November 1938, when the synagogues from which so many of the founding families came were smashed and burnt, and over the years of persecution which preceded that night, and which followed it with ever increasing cruelty.

Three weeks later in the Westend-Synagoge I said:

When for the first time I entered this beautiful sanctuary, I looked up at the *Ner Tamid* and saw the words of the Psalm: 'I shall not die, but live, and declare the works of the Lord.' Only silence and tears can describe what I felt then. That we, as a world, as a people, as a community, as a family should have survived all that came to pass and should be privileged to stand here today to 'declare the works of the Lord' is almost impossible to believe.

Nothing can be of greater importance to us than that light which continues to burn despite all the darkness. This inextinguishable light constitutes our hope. There are times when an all but despairing humanity believes that it no longer shines. There are times when it survives in secret only, in the hearts of a few courageous individuals.

But today the eternal light burns bright and clear.

I actually lit the torch in a simple service together with a small group
of congregants from London led by my colleague Rabbi Chaim Weiner,
in the company of a few friends from the local community. We began by
reading the words from Psalm 139: 'If I were to say, "Surely the darkness
will crush me, and the light around me shall be night," even the darkness
is not too dark for you, and the night shines like the day; the darkness
is as the light.'

Then I pointed the torch towards the *Ner Tamid*, high on the eastern
wall above the Ark, and, as if it was drawing its illumination from that
flame, turned it on. As I did so, Jacky Chernett sang the opening verse
of Psalm 27, 'The Lord is my light and my salvation.' Six and a half
months later she sang the same words as Isca switched on the fuse
controlling the Eternal Light in our new synagogue in London, while I,
who held that same torch focused on it until it began to burn, turned
it off, and felt at once a sense of loss which has never since entirely
left me.

Later that night, while Mitzpah lay comfortably sprawled across the
bed in our gleaming hotel room, I wrote:

❖ Now the small but hopefully long-lasting light burns on the
desk beside me. I realise that it is not yet completely lit, nor ever
shall be. Every flicker of half-hidden light, every illumination of every
act of kindness, especially when cruelty rules on all sides, the insight
and the inner strength of every heart, will add to the depth and range
of its brightness. For the light itself, as the Kabbalists teach, resides
everywhere. In Koblenz, when I meet four people each of whom
survived the Shoah in a different place and as the result of a different
coming together of circumstances, and in Cologne, when I go with
others from our community to the services of Gescher Lamassoret, a
progressive congregation which, I believe, meets in a room once
used by the Nazis, in order to replace terror with prayer and music,
I shall witness more light and the torch will burn more powerfully.

It was only much later that I realised when studying the verse carefully
that the words from Psalm 137 could be translated to mean either 'the
light about me is night' or the very opposite, 'the night about me is

light'. Through our deeds, and our faith, we can either bring illumination into the darkness or turn the very daylight into a dungeon.

*   *   *

It is impossible to understand either the political or the religious development of German Jewry without reference to Moses Mendelssohn (1729–86), the self-taught scholar from Dessau, to whom the saying was applied: 'From Moses [Maimonides] to Moses [Mendelssohn] there arose none like Moses.' By virtue of his unique personality, the range of his scholarship, his tact and perspicacity, as well as the course of his career and the people with whom he came to interact, he created an entry for Jews into the world of German letters which many were to emulate but none were to follow with his depth of learning, commitment to Judaism and political sagacity. Nor was there any other figure who so blazed the trail for the future of Jewry as a whole in Germany. It was not his intention to pave the way for integration, let alone assimilation, only to do his best to support his fellow Jews in their just claims to due consideration by the government, and ultimately to fellow citizenship founded on the principles of religious toleration and the separation of Church and State. Behind his views on both this-worldly and other-worldly authority lay a crucial understanding of, or perhaps in the light of hindsight one should say misplaced faith in, the centrality of reason in human affairs which characterised both his own age and most of the century to come.

'I am fortunate enough to live in a state where these my ideas are neither new nor remarkable,' wrote Moses Mendelssohn in his *Jerusalem*, published in 1783.³ He was referring to the Prussia of Frederick the Great and no doubt the words were carefully chosen as Frederick was an authoritarian, if enlightened, monarch. But behind them lay not ingratiation but conviction and a profound understanding of the historical moment through which the world was passing. As his biographer Alexander Altmann noted: 'The boldness with which Mendelssohn stated his plea for liberty of conscience, unrestricted toleration, and civic equality irrespective of creed makes *Jerusalem* a classical document of the new age that was ushered in by the American

Revolution and was about to stir in France, while Germany was a mere onlooker.' [4]

Mendelssohn's argument was unconditional: Jews should be made equal citizens of the state without anything further being expected of them other than that they should be virtuous and obedient citizens. They should not have to yield any of their religious particularity. On the contrary, he boldly asserted that, were acceptance as a Prussian citizen to involve any infringement of the ability to practise Judaism, he would sadly have to forgo the opportunity in favour of loyalty to God's law. This was a moral choice which many of his co-religionists would have to face within scarcely more than a generation, a significant number of them making, some for pragmatic and some perhaps for idealistic reasons, the opposite decision.

Mendelssohn argued that it was not the concern of the state to legislate over opinions, nor was it to the benefit of a basically secular authority to confer advantage upon one religious group over another. He thus quotes with approval the words of a reviewer of his own *Preface to Rabbi Menasseh*: 'With respect to civil rights, the members of all religions are equal, with the sole exception of those whose opinions run counter to the principles of human and civil duties.'[5] Whereas the aims of state and religion were perfectly compatible, indeed harmonious, being the happiness of humankind through the maintenance of moral rectitude, the nature of the power wielded by each was distinct and this difference rendered them not only compatible but mutually reinforcing: 'The state gives orders and coerces, religion teaches and persuades. The state prescribes *laws*, religion *commandments*. The state has *physical power* and uses it when necessary; the power of religion is *love* and *beneficence* . . . '[6] Mendelssohn strongly opposed religious coercion, arguing that it was neither an original nor a necessary feature of Judaism.

Towards the close of *Jerusalem* he addressed his Christian readers in the hope that they would accept his argument, but that, failing this, they would at any event: 'Regard us, if not as brothers and fellow citizens, at least as fellow men and fellow inhabitants of the land.' Whatever the outcome, it behoved him and his co-religionists to 'love you, nevertheless, as brothers, and to beseech you as brothers to make our burdens as bearable as you can'.[7]

Kant wrote approvingly to Mendelssohn on 16 August of that year (1783):

I consider this book the herald of a great reform which, though slow in starting and advancing, will affect not only your nation but others too. You have known how to reconcile your religion with such a degree of freedom of conscience as one would not have imagined it to be capable of, and as no other religion can boast of.[8]

Behind Mendelssohn's analysis of the role of the state lay an equally significant view of the nature of religion, no doubt deeply influenced by the rationalist and universalist tenor of his age. Its essential truths were not based on revelation as opposed to reason; on the contrary,

Eternal truths . . . in so far as they are useful for men's salvation and felicity, are taught by God in a manner more appropriate to the Deity; not by sounds or written characters, which are comprehensible here and there, to this or that individual, but through creation itself, and its internal relations, which are legible and comprehensible to all men.[9]

In other words, the key insights of religion could be derived through observation and reason. An uncompromisingly traditional Jew throughout his life, Mendelssohn did not deny the importance of revelation to Judaism. Rather, he argued that what was revealed at Sinai were not the first principles of religion but the rules of religious practice, by which Jews were still obliged to abide.

Mendelssohn's hopes for full citizenship for his people in the Prussian state and throughout Germany were to suffer the vicissitudes of history, advancing with Napoleon's victories, all but collapsing with his defeat, flourishing after the revolution of 1848, but not fully realised until the 1870s when Germany was united by Bismark.

His influence on Judaism in Germany is hard to measure; what followed there and across the Austro-Hungarian Empire was the result of multiple currents of thought and events and did not occur in the even manner which he envisaged. But his writings helped to open the door for

Jews to see Judaism and the European Enlightenment as essentially guided by a similar world view. It was this which allowed the Reform Movement to take root in Germany and flourish there throughout the nineteenth century. Departure from the ritual practices of Judaism was not perceived as the abandonment of the essential Jewish moral and eschatological vision. For was not society as a whole, or were not at least its *Gebildete*, its ethically and culturally refined classes, proceeding towards the same goal of universal harmony preached by both Judaism and Christianity? Thus the Jew, especially the *liberaler Jude*, the progressive Jew, could embrace the zeitgeist with genuine faith in the future. Even such rabbis as Samson Raphael Hirsch (1808–88), arguably the founder of Modern Orthodoxy, while attacking Reform and preaching strict fidelity to the law of God in the face of the erosion of traditional Jewish observance by new cultural choices and opportunities, felt a genuine love for German culture. He thus interpreted the much-quoted rabbinic phrase *Torah im derech-eretz* (Torah together with the way of the world), which in most of its early contexts signifies the importance of balancing the serious study of Torah with making a living off the land, to mean that one could be completely faithful to the demands of Torah while participating fully in the life and culture of the country in which one was resident.

The First World War gnawed away at the foundations of such hopes; the Holocaust turned them to ashes.

Yet I can't help feeling that there was something in those universalist nineteenth-century dreams which should be honoured. Nor am I convinced, despite all the terrible experiences since and the justified scepticism which they have engendered, that we have a significantly better ideology to put in their place today.

*   *   *

❖   During the afternoon Dr Wachten, the charming and immensely knowledgeable director of Frankfurt's Jewish Museum, is due to take us, together with a group from London who had joined us, on a tour of Jewish Frankfurt. Amidst profuse apologies the coach driver explains that he is not allowed to carry dogs, so Mitzpah and I have to make our own way around the city. We are left standing in the street with freezing feet by the site of what had once been Frankfurt's largest synagogue in the Friedberger Anlage. It was built in 1907 and belonged to the Austrittsgemeinde, the separatist orthodox congregation established by Rabbi Samson Raphael Hirsch. Burnt to the ground on Kristallnacht, it had been converted into a huge bomb shelter, which now housed exhibitions about the Jewish past.

But nothing is without its gains; I owe to being left behind a series of fragmentary but stirring encounters. An elderly couple carrying bags of rubbish to the recycling bins stop next to us; Mitzpah sniffs at the contents of their carriers.

'Are you Jewish?' they ask.

'Yes.'

'So are we,' they say with big smiles. 'From the Ukraine,' and they walk cheerfully on, evidently pleased to see someone openly Jewish and wearing a kippah on the streets. I am left wondering what they and their families may have been through for the sake of their faith and identity.

Another man approaches me. 'Can you explain to me,' he asks, 'the difference between a synagogue and a *Betstube*, a prayer room?' After we've discussed the question for a couple of minutes he says, 'I'm not actually Jewish. I'm a therapist. But I'm very interested in Judaism.'

During the whole of my time in Germany I was met with friendliness and curiosity and was fortunate to receive not one single overt hostile comment.

I turned back to stare at the ruins of this once great house of prayer. I discovered much later that my grandfather had come here from the Börneplatz on that dreadful morning of 10 November, recording that he had found 'the beautiful synagogue in flames'.[10] Relations had always been tense between the Einheitsgemeinde, the overall community, which included both orthodox and liberal denominations who cooperated with one another in numerous civic and welfare concerns, and the separatist Austrittsgemeinde, so-called because they had determined to leave the general fold in the late nineteenth century in objection to what they saw as the excessive influence of the liberals. It wasn't until after Kristallnacht that, compelled by the Nazis, the heads of the Austrittsgemeinde finally began to work together with the leaders of the rest of the community, meeting in a flat adjacent to the charred and ruined interior of the Westend-Synagoge. In the end, one fate overtook them all.

❖ Mitzpah and I eventually catch up with the rest of the group outside the house which had once been Franz Rosenzweig's home. A modest plaque explains: 'Here, together with Martin Buber, he became a pathfinder . . . ' Here Rosenzweig lived after coming to Frankfurt in 1920; here for many years he lay ill and increasingly paralysed in his room while continuing nevertheless to write and teach; here he undertook in this impoverished state of health to translate the entire Hebrew Bible into German together with Martin Buber (an endeavour the latter finally brought to completion in Jerusalem in the 1960s, where, at the celebration to mark the occasion, the great scholar of Jewish mysticism Gershom Scholem declared it nothing more than a memorial to the once great culture of German Jewry which was now dead and gone); here in 1929 Rosenzweig died.

I am gripped by a sense of awe.

It was Franz Rosenzweig who, arguably more than anyone else, led a lost generation of Jews back to their heritage.

In a letter to Eugen Rosenstock, he described the beginning of his own journey back into himself to rediscover his Judaism:

It's the problem of a generation, or possibly of a century: how 'Christian' Jews, national Jews, religious Jews, Jews from self-defence, sentimentality, loyalty, in short 'hyphenated' Jews such as the nineteenth century has produced, can once again, without danger to themselves or Judaism, become *Jews*.[11]

In a famous speech at the opening of the Freies Jüdisches Lehrhaus in 1920, a novel development in Jewish education, but soon replicated in many cities across Germany and deeply influential elsewhere even decades later, he declared that a new kind of teaching was urgently required. Until now study since the spread of assimilation had been 'from the inside, out', that is, those with Torah knowledge had endeavoured to appeal to the often uninterested masses. But from now on what was needed was 'from the outside, back in', that is, a fresh approach which would point the way back from a secular existence into the heart of Judaism:

> It is a learning in reverse order. A learning that no longer starts from the Torah and leads into life, but the other way round: from life, from a world that knows nothing of the Law, or pretends to know nothing, back to the Torah.[12]

Only those who were themselves alienated could be the teachers on such a path, he declared. Indeed, the more alienated the better.

Rosenzweig was not alone in his thinking. Weimar Jewry, that is, the Jewry of those two brief decades which we tend to think of solely as overshadowed by the rise of Nazism, was immensely creative in every cultural field. Not least, it was a Jewry of dis-assimilation, which consciously revisited the inadequate compromises and watered-down sense of its own culture which it felt it had received from its Wilhelminan ancestors and sought to restore a vital, informed, spiritually engaging Judaism. (Thus Rosenzweig: 'The Jew in oneself is not a circumscribed territory bounded by other circumscribed territories, but a greater or lesser force flooding one's whole being . . . It is not what the century of emancipation with its cultural mania wanted to reduce it to.')[13]

I remember how my grandfather took pride in his contribution to bringing Rosenzweig to Frankfurt. So I was amused to come across a reference among Rosenzweig's letters to Rabbi Salzberger as someone whom he had reluctantly included among his teachers at the Lehrhaus because he needed one or two 'official rabbis' and because 'he is a nice person . . . he belongs to us, just as a solid editor of the local news belongs to an international newspaper'.[14]

Back home in London, I spent a long time pondering my grandfather's Judaism. He might well have been hurt by that rather offhand reference to him in Rosenzweig's letter (I have since discovered another, in a similar tone). To what degree were the two teachers really on the same wavelength, both with regard to their Judaism and in their relationship to German culture?

On my desk sit the five volumes of my grandparents' edition of *Lessings Werke*, the collected works of Gotthold Ephraim Lessing (1729 –81), dramatist, hero of the German Enlightenment and close friend of Moses Mendelssohn. I carefully open the small, beautifully bound volumes, looking for the text of his famous play *Nathan der Weise* (*Nathan the Wise*). The colophon tells me that the books were printed in Stuttgart in 1874. My grandparents could surely not have included them among the few precious possessions they were allowed to take, just one suitcase each, when they fled Germany in April 1939. I wondered if they had acquired them later, perhaps as a gift from a fellow refugee in London similarly concerned to recreate if not a lost culture then at least a lost corner of its poetry. Isca thought that the books might have been rediscovered in Frankfurt after the war, from where they somehow found their way back to their true owners. It seemed to me that there could no longer be any way of knowing for certain. All through my childhood the volumes sat on my grandmother's shelves alongside the works of Goethe, Schiller, Heine, Mörike, Schopenhauer, and the more recent poetry of Rainer Maria Rilke, which I especially loved and which I would often take out to read with them in their old age. A bookcase is a world in lieu, a universe of heart and soul the significance of which, especially in the life of a refugee, is often far greater than the view outside the window or the name and language of the city in which its owner happens to be living.

Yesterday I opened the small blue jewellery box which we found among my aunt's effects after she died. It contained my grandfather's wedding ring; I knew for certain that it was his because my grandmother's initials were inscribed on the inside together with the date of their marriage, 31 May 1917. Almost three years into the First World War my grandfather finally took a furlough from the army and married his beloved Natalie Charlotte Caro, to whom he had by then been engaged for three years. The fighting had not been over by that first Christmas, as the Kaiser had assured his people, nor by the subsequent one, nor by the Christmas after that. So in the late spring, on the Hebrew date of the 10th of the month of Sivan 5677, just after the festival of Shavuot (Pentecost), my grandparents were married in Posen, the town were my grandmother had spent her idyllic childhood, spoilt by her father, going swimming in the river and eating pickled cucumbers rather than the sweets preferred by all the other children during the morning break at school. The tables were decorated for the occasion with *Maiglöckchen*, lilies of the valley, which remained throughout her life my grandmother's favourite flowers. My mother Lore was born seventeen months later, on 27 October in the final year of the Great War, at the conclusion of which my grandparents found themselves on opposite sides of the new border between Poland and Germany, so that even after the end of hostilities many weeks of anxious and frustrating waiting went by before my grandfather could at long last see his baby daughter.

During my upbringing I heard frequent reference to the story of *Nathan der Weise*, and to Nathan himself, the shrewd and tolerant Jewish hero of Lessing's famous drama. The character of Nathan is generally understood to be based on Moses Mendelssohn. Fellow men of letters, their common ideal of the tolerant state supported by a rational approach to religion united Lessing and Mendelssohn far more deeply than their different faiths divided them. '*Nathan* without Mendelssohn would have been like *Hamlet* without the Prince of Denmark,' wrote Mendelssohn's biographer, the rabbi and scholar Alexander Altmann.[15]

My grandparents told me nothing about the actual plot of the play; I was left to discover that it was set in the Crusader period in the court of Saladin and involved, beside the wealthy Jew Nathan, his daughter Recha, a Knight Templar, various advisors and the Sultan himself. What they always referred to, what truly mattered to them about the play, was not the overall unfolding of the drama but the scene in which Nathan tells Saladin the story of the ring. The parable itself was not original to Lessing; he would have encountered it in Boccaccio's *Decameron*, as well perhaps as in Solomon ibn Verga's *Shevet Yehuda*, about which he might have learnt from Mendelssohn. But he deployed it in a unique and striking manner. From generation to generation a ring is passed down from father to favourite son as a token of preferential love. In the ring is set a remarkable opal stone, imbued with the power to make the bearer beloved of both God and humankind. The ring eventually comes into the possession of a parent who loves each of his three sons equally;

unwilling to choose between them, he has two identical copies made by a craftsman whose work is so skilled that even the father can no longer tell the original apart. As his death approaches he calls his sons to him and, one by one and in private, gives each of them *the* ring. After his death they all claim that they must be the favourite, supporting their case by presenting the enchanted object, only to discover that they are each the equal possessors of indistinguishable rings.

> They quarrel,
> they complain. In vain! Which is the true ring
> is incapable of proof.

Nathan pauses for a moment to assess the Sultan's response before he, a Jew in a Muslim court and in the presence of a Christian knight, delivers the punch-line:

> Almost as incapable of proof as
> for us today the true faith.

Each of their three faiths, he argues, relies on history for verification and each of us is inclined to credit most the narrative we have learnt from our ancestors: 'How can I believe my own fathers less than you believe yours!' Hence there are no real grounds here to prefer any one truth claim over another.

The case is brought to court and the three brothers stand before the judge. Saladin urges Nathan to continue with his parable; he is anxious to hear what the decision will be. The judge is tempted to dismiss the case; he can scarcely keep the court waiting until the true ring grows a mouth and speaks for itself! But then he recalls that the power possessed by the opal set within it lies in its capacity to render the wearer beloved of both God and man.

> That must
> Decide! For the false rings will surely
> Lack that power. – Now, which one of you do the other
> Two of you love most? Come on, say!¹⁶

In other words, the genuineness of the ring can be proved not by any examination of the object itself, or thus of the faith in question, but only through the deeds of its bearer. Perhaps, continues the judge, what motivated the recently deceased father to act as he did was his inability to tolerate any longer the tyranny of the one sole ring. Loving all three sons equally, he could not contemplate the thought of any of them being oppressed. In this audacious manner, Lessing suggests that it is time for the state to be separated from the Church and recognise equally the claims of the three great Abrahamic faiths. The judge proceeds to dismiss the brothers, instructing them each to prove the worth of the stone set in their particular ring through deeds of goodness, gentleness, humility and peace. Let them return with the evidence of their own actions in a thousand, or a thousand thousand, years.

Lessing's decision to set the play in the court of Saladin, who presumably represents Frederick the Great, the contemporary king of Prussia, upon whom he thus confers the great Muslim ruler's reputation for both wisdom and compassion, is as bold and engaging as his choice of the Jew Nathan to be the mouthpiece for this profound advice.

(In reading for the first time Lessing's description of the ring's secret power 'to make [the wearer] pleasing before God and man', I could not help but think of the verse from the Book of Proverbs to which these words so closely approximate: 'You shall find grace and good understanding in the sight of God and humankind' (Proverbs 3:4). Was this part of the reason why my grandfather selected that quotation as the inscription on my mother's gravestone? She died, aged forty-four, on the afternoon of his eightieth birthday. Was this choice a testament not only to Lore's intelligence and grace, but also to the German literary culture which she too, completing her PhD on the poetry of Hölderlin in Oxford in 1949, had studied and loved?)

Lessing's parable served to epitomise what my grandparents always believed were the true core values of that stratum of German society in which they lived and which was defined by the concept of *Bildung*. The term, which is untranslatable, indicates at once educational and cultural refinement and moral worthiness. This Enlightenment ideal was both rooted in and nourished by ideas of religious tolerance, the faith that Judaism and Christianity could together create and sustain a shared culture in which art, morality and religion forged a common path along which humanity would progress to ever greater levels of ethical, spiritual and aesthetic refinement. The very friendship between Lessing and Mendelssohn itself came to symbolise that hope of a harmonious relationship between Jews and Christians epitomised in the figure of Nathan. For my grandfather, neither the First World War nor the rise of Nazism nor even all the terrors revealed in the wake of its bloody defeat ever completely shattered this vision. 'Never confuse Hitler and Nazism with the glories of German culture,' he taught us. For him not only the artistic and philosophical achievements of Germany remained intact but, more remarkably, so did the ideals which nourished them. When, in his late eighties, he received the Buber-Rosenzweig Medal for his work in Christian–Jewish understanding in postwar Germany he spoke of his threefold loyalty, to Judaism, his spiritual home, to Germany, his cultural home, and to England, which had saved his life and the lives of his family.

I looked again at the works of Lessing lying in front of me on my desk, hoping that maybe my grandfather might have left a letter, or at least some notes in his beautiful Gothic handwriting, inserted some-where between the pages of one of the volumes. But there was nothing to tell me which particular lines most struck him or in which sermon and on what festival he had quoted them, as no doubt he often did. On the contrary, I noticed translations into English scribbled in pencil in the margins. My grandfather would never have committed such an act of desecration; that was proof positive that the books were acquired second-hand after the war.

I wonder if my grandfather knew about Franz Rosenzweig's critique of his hero. Nathan is all very nice, he apparently said, but there's nothing left of the man that's Jewish. For Rosenzweig, he represented not the model *gebildeter Mensch*, universal cultured man, but rather that steady erosion of Judaism throughout the nineteenth century by German culture which had in the end left it so utterly devoid of content that it was no more than an empty vessel, an identity in nothing more than name. In 1919 Rosenzweig delivered two lectures on *Nathan der Weise* in the theatre in Kassel. Sadly we do not have the full text, only his notes. 'Not: "because you are Edom may I be Yaakov," rather: because we are all the same,' he argued.[17] Though the sentence is somewhat cryptic, his point is probably that true respect should not have to conceal the reality of significant difference. There is a watery quality to a tolerance which can only exist on the premise that we're all really the same. But just that, argues Rosenzweig, is the ideology implied in the play: 'because we are all the same, therefore let us mutually concede to each other the harmless difference of dress, food, and drink'. Religion is thus robbed of all genuine content. 'The friendship between Mendelssohn and Lessing was too messianic,' he concludes. 'It lacked the blood of the present time.' His meaning is made all too clear in the parentheses which follow: '(Proof: the Mendelssohn family [i.e. all]were baptised)'.[18] Like so many others through the nineteenth and early twentieth century, they allowed their Judaism to be washed clean out of them. To Rosenzweig, the price of entering German society was paid for by too many Jews with the essence of their own identity. What is worse, and this goes to the heart of his polemic as an educationalist, is that so many paid it so willingly.

But there is another twist to the story of *Nathan der Weise*. When in 1933 Jewish artists and musicians were dismissed from their positions throughout Germany by the Nazis, and the Jüdische Kulturbund was formed both to provide them with work and to offer Jewish audiences cultural nourishment to sustain them in the terrible predicament in which they were ever more hopelessly trapped, Lessing's famous work was chosen to be the first production. 'We do not want to set up a new ghetto,' wrote the Berlin dramatist Julius Bab about the vision behind the Kulturbund, 'Through our work we want to keep the German Jews in vital contact with the great life of Western culture in which they have become so deeply rooted over one and a half centuries! And therefore: Lessing, Mozart and Shakespeare!'[19] Yet significant changes were made to the key character. Nathan came on stage singing a Hasidic melody and greeted the audience with the words, '*Baruch Haba!*' ('Welcome!') In the final scene in which, as a result of the Sultan's warm response to his parable, everyone is reconciled, Nathan himself was left standing to one side, alone and apart. The message was clear: the Jew no longer belonged within the same society. Thus the play both made its point and undermined it at the same time.

The Zionists condemned the Kulturbund's choice as unsuitable to the times; what was needed was rather something which truly affirmed Jewish identity. Others made the opposite criticism; the very universalism of the play, its core message, had been distorted. Yet perhaps there were deeper, even unconscious, reasons for the selection: 'Lessing's Nathan was a symbol of tolerance in a time of intolerance,' wrote Michael Brenner. 'Therefore, to perform this play was to produce a moral and intellectual outcry against the injustice and discrimination outside the theatre hall.'[20]

The performance was staged in Berlin, so it is almost certain that my grandparents did not see it. But I wonder what they would have thought of this subversion of their hero. Or did he survive in their hearts as the same Nathan they believed Lessing had intended him to be, because for them it was precisely by this universalist ideal that the treachery of Nazism could truly be measured and by this ideal alone that the world could be reconstituted after the horrors perpetrated by Hitler were finally over?

*   *   *

That evening in my hotel room I began a process which was to become a central focus of these three weeks: I wrote an extensive blog. I did so because it helped me to place in focus the events of the day; because without writing I couldn't digest what was happening and what I was feeling; because the companionship of those who told me that they wanted to follow what I was doing mattered to me and helped me on my journey. Sometimes I stopped walking in the middle of the day and caught up with events over a coffee and cake. (Cake was a boon; as soon as I was diagnosed as diabetic I ceased to be a person who survived off buns and biscuits. But the amount of walking I was now doing necessitated a certain input of sugar and the occasional slice of cheesecake or *Apfelkuchen* felt justified, especially if I shared it with Mitzpah, an agreement to which he had little objection.) But mostly, I wrote very early in the morning or late at night. I was never too tired; on the contrary it was on those days when I failed to make time to write that I felt overwhelmed and exhausted.

I remember going to my bed at an extremely late hour only to find it, as I would on every subsequent night, already occupied. It's amazing how a dog can extend himself in such a way as to make it impossible for anyone else to grab even a modest corner of the duvet. 'Sorry,' I said, and carefully reoriented him so that his body was vaguely parallel with the length of the bed. Mitzpah had evidently been a little less tired than I'd realised when he'd turned himself in. I'd carefully spread out two old towels so that he could lie down without getting everything muddy or dirty. (The notion that he might be content with sleeping on the floor simply never entered my mind.) But he would have none of it. He'd stretched himself out in proper comfort with his head on the pillow and the rest of himself across the entire bed. All that was missing was a little notice saying 'Please do not disturb'.

This night, and every other on my journey, I hardly read in bed at all. The next thing I knew was the sound of my alarm clock.

From Mitzpah's Blog

Something very exciting has happened to me. Yesterday was that funny day in which I never go anywhere by car but get lots of treats and my family eats too much. Well, when it was over they put me in daddy's friend's car. I've been in cars lots and lots of times, but this car did something different – it went on a train. After that we drove a very long way. But we stopped many times and I had lots of night walks and little snacks and now we're in a different country where I've never been before. The cars go on the wrong side of the road, which I find very frightening. Everybody speaks a strange language and they keep calling me '*Hund*'. But the wonderful thing is that my daddy's allowed to take me in to breakfast. I hope he has a roll and butter because I like them very much. Or do you think it would be all right if I went to that pretty table and helped myself?

PS Daddy's promised me that we'll be going on lots of long walks, but I don't really believe it. He's always saying that. Are rabbis allowed to lie to their dogs?

Love, Mitzpah

Day Two – From Frankfurt to Mainz

❖   I wake up tired; the effects of driving through the night have caught up with me. But weariness is quickly overcome by coffee and excitement. This is the first day of real walking and I'm itching to be underway. The plan is to follow the Main River until it meets the Rhine just outside the city of Mainz, or if the distance proves too far to complete before sunset, at least until a convenient point on the road. Brian is walking with me and I'm appreciative of his company. Life is also made much easier by the presence of the film crew. First of all, I don't have to plan my route each day so that it ends at a convenient railway station or bus stop. Nor will I have to fork out huge sums on fares for cabs to pick me up from the middle of nowhere. I can simply call Guy, Joe and Anna from my mobile phone, work out where they are and arrange a suitable place for us all to meet up. Secondly, I don't have to carry all my gear; every morning I sort it into two halves; what I need for that day's walk and teaching and what can happily wait in the boot of their car until I retrieve it late at night.

I carefully check the portion which goes into my rucksack: some food, a change of clothes, first-aid kit, wash things, my laptop, water, a thermos flask freshly filled with boiling water, teabags, a small container of milk, my prayer book together with any essential reading for the day, a dog towel. Mitzpah watches me pack a generous portion of his food; throughout the journey all I will have to do to get his attention is take my rucksack off and open the pockets. I know I'm teaching him bad habits, but we generally share; if I eat, I give him a little bit to try. This also makes me feel less guilty about breaking the stringent rules I've established for myself since being diagnosed as diabetic: no cake, no biscuits, black or diabetic chocolate only very rarely, except if I feel a sudden drop in blood sugar. But here I'm getting so much exercise that I even allow myself an occasional slice of something sweet, a third of which disappears down the gullet of my canine companion, satisfying his dignity and assuaging my conscience at the same time.

I'm actually quite worried about how Mitzpah will manage. The issue has nothing to do with distances or tiredness; he can out-walk me by a factor of at least twenty to one. The problem is rather that we're going to have to pass through extensive urban areas; today, for example, we'll begin in the very centre of Frankfurt. Something Mitzpah hates is when traffic approaches from behind him so that he can hear it coming but cannot as yet see it. Often he simply freezes and refuses to budge until the offending vehicle has passed. My aim is to keep on paths as much as possible, but inevitably a proportion of the route will be along the pavements of busy streets where Mitzpah's habit is likely to slow us down. I know from experience that there are two choices: to give him an encouraging tug, which is an unpleasant thing to do to a dog very often, or to pick him up and carry him (which, incidentally, he loves). Both options have their limitations, the latter twenty-one kilos worth of them. But during a discussion of this minor matter with a group of friends in London someone comes up with the perfect solution: 'Buy him an iPod and plug it into his ears!' Brilliant! But what should it play? The discussion goes back and forth: music, birdsong, the sound of urgent barking in the distance? Sadly, like many of the best laid plans of dogs and men, this too comes to nothing. Suppliers who tailor their products to fit the ears of border collies prove impossible to locate. How then is Mitzpah going to cope?

I remember looking once more at the maps and making the reluctant decision to abandon visiting Zeilsheim, the site of a major Displaced Persons (DP) camp from 1945–8. It appeared that there was very little left there to see beyond a brief inscription, and the location was too far removed from our route.

The population of the DP camps was made up primarily of Jews who had survived the concentration camps and had nowhere to go and no one to go to after the war. Some had made the difficult and dangerous journey across Europe, on foot, by taking lifts on army trucks, farm carts and overcrowded trains, back to their home towns in the hope of finding at least one other member of the family still alive. Where would they be most likely to go, if not back to the village or town which had once been their home? Coming back to Berehovo, my teacher Hugo Gryn found his mother already there. Seeing her son arrive alone without his father and brother, she realised without the need for any words that they were dead, and simply went and sat on a low chair for one day of formal mourning, as Jewish tradition prescribes for situations when the news of a death is received long after the event has occurred.

But most survivors found no one else alive; at best they met someone who had heard from someone else that an uncle or a sister was still living. They understood at once that they were not welcome in their former homes. Though there were exceptions, often there was a note of dis-appointed surprise in the comment made by non-Jewish acquaintances: 'We didn't think you were going to come back.' Most Jews found their houses occupied and their property taken. Looking through the open doorway, they saw their former neighbours sitting on what had been their chairs, at their family table, eating from their family china. The vast majority then fled for a second time, scouring lists of survivors at railway stations, exchanging whatever information they gleaned with others in a similar plight and pursuing similar hopes. The Red Cross Central Tracing Bureau (the name was changed in 1948 to the International Tracing Service) was active for decades, and had a measure of success in locating relatives across continents and even after many years.

Where should these unwanted people go in an uncertain Europe wrecked by war? Some were fortunate enough eventually to receive a communication from family members inviting them to join them in Britain or Canada. Others went to Palestine, crossing the Alps into Italy guided by agents of Aliyah Bet, the clandestine Jewish organisation intent on bringing the greatest possible number of survivors fleeing their former countries to the shortly to be created Jewish homeland beneath the radar of the patrolling Royal Navy, carrying them across the Mediterranean in swiftly converted onion and banana boats and landing them in secret on the beaches of Caesarea.

But many ended up in DP camps, dispossessed, stateless, often sick, bewildered and in no position to make plans for a new life. Zeilsheim was one such camp, situated in the American Zone on the outskirts of Frankfurt. There are photographs of David Ben-Gurion, soon to be the first Prime Minister of the shortly to be created state but then the chairman of the Jewish Agency, visiting the camp to encourage residents to make *Aliyah*, the 'ascent' to Israel.[1] The camp was the site of many protests against the British policy of severely restricting Jewish immigration: how dare they, by what moral right, after all that had happened?

One of the greatest shocks in preparing for this walk was to learn how little understanding for survivors there initially was among the Allies in 1945. The British and Americans were often only too anxious to return the responsibility for civic administration to the Germans as quickly as possible. The few Jews who struggled home from Theresienstadt and scores of other camps as well as those who were washed ashore from the tides of devastation often found themselves at the end of the queue for the essential calories and minimal shelter for which a bombed-out local population was also competing in large numbers.

This is how Lore Geminder described her return to Frankfurt as a nineteen-year-old survivor of Auschwitz:

We were very cold in the concentration camp, and we are certainly hardened. When we arrived in Auschwitz in the winter of 1944, after languishing for four years in other camps, a rag was thrown at us which was supposed to be a dress. Everything else was taken from us. We had nothing underneath and nothing on top of it, only a pair of wooden clogs. (Why give us more, since we were destined for the gas chambers?) Chance and luck would have it that my mother, my sister and I escaped this fate. My father was shot. Now we are again in Frankfurt and we thought that, for this winter, we shall finally have warm clothing. When we voiced our request in the Economic Department we were told that we had to present a medical certificate that we were ill. Otherwise, no coupon for a winter coat could be issued, not even for concentration-camp prisoners. Take note, not even a coupon, and it is by no means clear that possession of a coupon results in obtaining a winter coat. With coupons for other items, i.e. a vest, one pair of knickers, a slip and two pairs of stockings per person, we had no luck so far.[2]

In June 1945 President Truman created a commission under Earl Harrison to investigate the US Army's treatment of DPs. Its report could scarcely have been more negative:

Generally speaking, three months after VE Day and even longer after the liberation of individual groups, many Jewish displaced persons . . . are living under armed guard behind barbed-wire fences, in camps of several descriptions (built by the Germans for slave labourers and Jews), including some of the most notorious concentration camps, amid crowded, frequently insanitary and generally grim conditions, in complete idleness, with no opportunity, except surreptitiously, to communicate with the outside world, hoping for some word of encouragement and action on their behalf . . . As matters stand now, we seem to be treating Jews as the Nazis treated them, except that we do not exterminate them.[3]

Yet the groups of survivors who found themselves in these camps, sometimes for over two years, demonstrated an extraordinary vitality and creativity. Zeilsheim, where the population had grown to over three and a half thousand by the end of 1946, 'maintained a Jewish theatrical group, a synagogue, a jazz orchestra, a sports club named Chasmonai, and a number of schools, including an ORT school. The camp had a library with approximately 500 books, and circulated two Yiddish newspapers.'[4] A report by the commander of Landsberg DP camp, which lay farther south, particularly caught my attention. Major Irving Heymont noted that:

Never once have I been asked for contraceptives by anyone from the camp, although our German employees frequently ask for them. I discussed this individually with several members of the camp committee. Each told me that the use of contraceptives is highly frowned upon by the camp people. They believe it is everybody's duty to have as many children as possible in order to increase the numbers of the Jewish community . . . [5]

Zeilsheim was eventually closed in November 1948. Ironically, the US army wanted to return the houses to workers from the IG Farben plant in nearby Hechst, but they had to put the date back twice because of the fear of resistance by DPs.

*   *   **

*   *   *

It was already later than I'd intended by the time I met Brian in the hotel vestibule, said a warm goodbye to Isca, promising her that I would take care, and set off. We reached the centre of the city and walked through the railway station where a hundred years ago my grandfather descended from the steam train to set foot for the first time in his beloved Goethe's home town. Yet I couldn't help but sense the presence, as we passed through the long underpass and concourse beneath the lines, of a more sinister journey. Was it to this station that he was brought, under Nazi escort, to be deported to Dachau?

I came across the relevant information by chance. I rediscovered a book on my shelves about which I'd entirely forgotten, *Nach der Kristallnacht (After Kristallnacht)*, given to Isca by the Mayor of Frankfurt, Petra Roth, on her visit there a couple of years earlier. It contained a paper entitled 'From Frankfurt to the Concentration Camp of Dachau' in which it listed the names of all the men deported in that terrible November week.[6] There, among hundreds of other entries, I found my grandfather's details:

> Prisoner number, 25612;
> Date of internment, 14.11.38;
> Name, Salzberger;
> Religion, Israelite;
> Profession, Rabbi.

A footnote referred to an unpublished manuscript by him, entitled 'Erlebenisbericht' ('An Account of My Experiences') held in the archives of the Jewish Museum in Frankfurt. The curator scanned it and sent it to me within a day of receiving my request. A fellow prisoner, who recorded sharing the bunks in Block 20 at Dachau with my grandfather, detailed the mistreatment to which he himself was subjected after his arrest: he was taken together with other internees to the Festhalle, the concert hall, where he was made to roll or crawl up the steps on his stomach. Once in the hall an SS man hit him with his Browning, breaking several of his teeth and ribs. He was then made to stand on his head on piles of nails, which were finally pulled out of his scalp by fellow prisoners once they had reached Dachau. From this hall they were taken to the Südbahnhof, the South Station.[7] So, no, the Central Station was not the place from which my grandfather had been deported.

Another internee described the experience of arriving at Dachau in the following terms:

> When we arrived at the concentration camp we had to go to a house where our hair was shorn and we were photographed, just like criminals. Then we were taken to another house where we had to give personal information and where we were asked how we wanted to die, by hanging or by shooting.[8]

My grandfather always refused to talk about what happened inside Dachau. His deposition ends with the journey there. They were put on a train to Munich; they weren't told their ultimate destination, but one of the SS men sitting opposite him made gestures of hanging; the other quietly got off the train at each station and brought the prisoners glasses of water. 'What subsequently occurred does not form part of my experiences in Frankfurt,' he concluded.[9]

*   *   *

Brian and I found our way to the Main and descended the steep steps down to the gardens by the river, let Mitzpah off the lead and watched his disappearing tail as he raced for several hundred metres down the tree-lined path towards the nearest bridge. It was a glowing, golden morning.

Guy, Anna and Joe were waiting for us with their cameras just before the bridge. Guy reminded me to switch on the radio microphone I was to have attached to me at all times and explained exactly how he wanted us to walk, where we needed to pause and what we had to do once we reached the bridge. We went through this whole process at least twice. I thought irritably of the kilometres we wouldn't be able to cover if we were regularly going to be slowed down in this manner. I fear I even vented my feelings in some choice terms no doubt conveyed via the microphone, to which I had not yet grown accustomed, straight into Guy's attentive ears.

But soon we were free to follow the roads and footpaths along the south bank of the river out of Frankfurt.

❖ It is the most stunning autumn day, cold and bright, my favourite weather and perfect for walking. We follow the Main River towards where it joins the Rhine. It can scarcely be called a tributary being as wide along the stretch we walked as the Thames at Chiswick, and majestic, supporting a constant traffic of the biggest barges Brian and I had ever seen.

The colours of the trees along the riverbank are glorious: red maple, hawthorn with its ruby berries, poplars losing their yellow leaves, dogwood and willows. For a couple of miles our route leaves the water and traverses the forest. Then in the early afternoon, back on the fields by the side of the Main, the sun greets us again and its slanting rays shine towards us as we walk for a while due west.

Guy asks Brian when he meets up with us, 'Why do you love trees?' Brian is a landscape gardener by profession. He isn't able to answer. Some things we love so naturally that our feelings suffer no explanation. When we pray minchah, the afternoon service, for which a *minyan* or group of ten is traditionally required, not, as would no doubt have been more appropriate, standing still, but while we walk, Brian counts ten trees as his quorum of the spirit.

Another beautiful moment in the day comes when we stop at a restaurant for a cup of coffee and I ask for a slice of bread for Mitzpah. The waiter brings a piece of rather modest diameter, which vanishes in a single eager swallow. He goes back for another, then a third and a fourth (walking is a hungry business, especially if you run at least three miles to your owner's every one). Before we leave I ask to pay. 'Bread and water are gifts from God,' he replies. 'They're from Jesus and they're free.' Then he mentions the centennial celebrations of the synagogue in Frankfurt and asks if we were present.

I was surprised to discover on rereading it that I'd omitted from my blog any mention of quite how lost Brian and I got on that first day. It must have been because I didn't want Isca to see it and become worried. Actually, we weren't really lost at all. We knew precisely where we were; what we couldn't fathom was how on earth we were supposed to get out of there and continue along our route. We'd been making excellent progress and had paused in the early afternoon to look through the windows of a tiny, beautiful church. We then chose a small muddy track which ran between the river and a large industrial installation towards the point a few kilometres farther on where we hoped to meet the film crew with their car. We were vaguely aware that the fence to our left was running ever closer to our path, when all of a sudden our route came to a frightening end before a huge deep-water port. The fence was three metres high and topped with tight strands of barbed wire. It took us an hour to retrace our steps and cross the vast refinery in which we then found ourselves. We approached some men next to a digger: 'Follow those lorries,' we were told. The only problem was that the sole exit from the site was straight on to what looked like a major Autobahn. We simply had no choice, and I hustled and encouraged Mitzpah who trotted anxiously at my heals while, hooted at by motorists racing past at over a hundred kilometres an hour, we hurried along the verge in single file. The worst moment came when we reached an intersection with an E-route. I picked Mitzpah up, looked, listened and then raced across the mercifully slim branches of the junction at what I judged to be the narrowest point which still had a reasonable view. After that we all felt we'd had quite enough walking for one day. It was with weary relief that we watched the film crew drive up to our rendezvous. We reached Mainz ten minutes before our engagement at the synagogue, and of those I had only five to feed the dog, pull off my boots, attend to a blister, the only really nasty one I got in all the three weeks of marching,

52

put on a suit and look more like a rabbi. To my shame and regret, I slept through most of the evening's lecture.

❖   What can I say about the new synagogue in Mainz, dedicated only a month earlier, in October 2010? It is perhaps the most original and extraordinary building, certainly the most unique and impressive synagogue, I have ever seen. It cannot be appreciated without some knowledge of the Jewish history of this remarkable town.

It is constructed so that its different sections form the shape of the Hebrew letters of the word *kadosh*, holy. On the door is a tribute to the tenth/eleventh-century scholar Rabbenu Gershom, known as Me'or Hagolah, the Light of the Exile, to whom, among other remarkable rulings, is attributed the ban in Judaism against polygamy. The city has a remarkable mediaeval history. It is one of the triumvirate of towns, together with Speier and Worms, which in Hebrew form the acronym *Shum*; thus their legal and ritual enactments are collectively referred to as *Gezerot Shum* and are of considerable importance in the development of Jewish law. In Hebrew literature Mainz is known as Magenza, hence the choice of the biblical phrase inscribed in several places on the walls of the synagogue, *magen vetsinah*, 'a shield and shelter', which hint in their sound at the town's Jewish name, as well as signifying the community's role as a bastion of learning and teaching. All three of these cities, and not only they but others, including even small Rhineland villages, were seats of profound Jewish scholarship in the Middle Ages. As in Worms and Cologne, the Jewish population of Mainz was slaughtered during the ravages of the First Crusade in 1096. The literature of that period, describing the usually futile, though genuine, efforts of the local bishops to protect their Jews, and the struggles of the Jewish population against the over-whelming arms and cruelty of the Crusaders, details how many families took their own lives in sanctification of God's name rather than allow themselves either to betray their ancient faith or be captured and killed by their foes. Because the community was comparatively small, many of its members are referred to by name and the poems tell in close detail how they addressed their children, how the latter responded to the call for martyrdom, and how they perished. The Holocaust was thus the second time the Jewish population of this beautiful city was utterly destroyed.

The new synagogue is a worthy memorial to this profound history. The actual Beit Knesset, the sanctuary, has, at first sight, a classical simplicity to its design: the Ark is modest, the *bimah*, or platform from which the Torah is read, is in the centre, the gallery forms three sides of a rectangle. But there familiarity ends. The walls are of a matted gold, decorated with what prove on closer examination to be patterns formed by the letters of the Hebrew alphabet. In spaces clear of such ornamentation are inset classical texts, some longer and some shorter. At several points one finds the first and then the final verses of the Torah: 'In the beginning God created the heavens and the earth' and 'Which Moses did in the eyes of all Israel'. As the gaze follows the ceiling upwards as it rises in places to an immense height, but before it reaches the huge, half-hidden windows which nevertheless allow in a great measure of light, one encounters the famous Unetaneh Tokkef prayer:

> On the New Year it is written
> > and on the Day of Atonement it is sealed:
> How many shall pass away,
> > and how many shall be created;
> Who shall live and who shall die;
> Who by fire and who by water,
> Who by the sword and who by wild beasts;
> Who shall be at rest and who tormented,
> Who shall be at peace and who shall be torn apart.
> > But repentance, prayer and charity
> > Have the power to remove the evil of the decree.

According to tradition this chastening meditation was composed by Rabbi Amnon of Mainz in the eleventh century, when, pressured by a local prelate to convert to Christianity, he suffered torture rather than betray his faith. Crawling bleeding to the synagogue, he ordered the Holy Ark to be opened, uttered this prayer and died. Three days later he appeared in a night vision to the rabbi and poet Kalonymus son of Meshullam, to whom he taught the words.

Above the Ark is an amalgam of texts, taken partly from the Song of Songs, and partly from elegies about the First Crusade composed by its most famous poet, Yehudah son of Kalonymus. Thus in contemplation of the holy, the love of God and the terrible price exacted for remaining faithful to it encounter one another.

Very late that night, I studied a poem written in the wake of the Crusades by Rabbenu Baruch ben Shmuel, who had lived in this very city. I had previously translated part of his elegy on the martyrs of Speier, which lies south of here, and of Boppart, which sits farther north on the banks of the Rhine:

> How could it happen
> That we are trodden underfoot
> Together with the books of the Torah?
> Why, God, do you stand far off in times of trouble?
>   Who is like you among the mighty, O Lord?
>
> How the arrogant have risen up in enmity against us!
> The swine of the forest have vexed and devoured us.
> Why are you silent when the wicked swallow up the righteous?
>   Hear Israel, Lord!

The mediaeval Jewish poets knew every word of the Bible; it flowed through their consciousness with the familiarity of their mother tongue. Their works are composed of a mosaic of ancient biblical imagery and phrases, together with allusions to well-known rabbinic interpretations. The subtlety lies in their deployment, which is often disturbing and sometimes subversive. In this instance, the closing line of the first verse is taken from the song of triumph the Children of Israel sang after God had parted the Red Sea (Exodus 15:1–21). But unlike there, when what is stressed is the superiority of the one true God over all the alien deities, here the words are thrown upwards to heaven as a challenge: Aren't you, God, supposed to be mighty? Then why have you done nothing and abandoned us to this fate?

Even more forceful is the close of the second verse. The Shema meditation, 'Hear, O Israel, the Lord our God, the Lord is One', is Judaism's credo and call to faith. It is a statement about God addressed to everyone throughout the ages: listen and know that God is one. But in this instance the direction of the familiar words is reversed and it is God who is called upon to take heed: Down here your people are crying out and dying; have you even noticed up there in heaven? Is this supposed to be your will?

Here faith attains its ultimate strength and reaches its most painful impasse at one and the same moment. These poets testify to how members of their own communities have died in recent generations for their belief, killing their very children by their own hand before slitting their own arteries, rather than allowing themselves and their families to fall into the clutches of the enemy who would only slaughter them with far less mercy. With what other words could they cry out, how else bear witness both to their mortal anguish and to their ultimate trust in God, than with the ancient, familiar formulae of worship? Yet those very words are now stretched and transformed so that they challenge heaven even as they appear to accept its decrees. For it is with the Shema on his or her lips that, according to tradition, the Jew should die.

One is left wondering whether these are words of outrage, despair, or, despite or combined with both, a profound faith that God, so seemingly absent in this terrible moment, is nevertheless the core and source of all things, who, for reasons incomprehensible to us, both hears and knows, and yet permits all this to happen.

Jean Amery's heartfelt cry eight and a half centuries later offers a disturbing comparison. The experience of torture has, he writes, defined him more closely than any creed: 'On my left forearm I bear the Auschwitz number; it reads more briefly than the Pentateuch and the Talmud and yet provides more thorough information. It is also more binding than basic formulas of Jewish existence.' He concludes: ' "Hear, O Israel" is not my concern. Only a "Hear, O world" wants angrily to break out from within me.' There is no one to talk to in heaven; there are only the semi-deaf here on earth.[10]

The poetry of the Crusades heralds an even more terrible literature to come.

Day Two – From Frankfurt to Mainz

From Mitzpah's Blog

Monday 25 October

I thought I was never going to get a proper walk but today I ran at least three times as far as daddy (he's so lazy and slow!). He and his friend Brian kept talking, while I kept on walking. There was lots of beautiful forest and I drank from the Main River. But the best moment was when we went into a café and the owner brought me my very own bread. I've never had my own table service just for me before.

The only part I didn't like was when we got lost and had to walk along a very, very fast and noisy road. I tried to be brave; I only had to be carried twice, just for a few seconds each time. The drivers kept waving at me.

I hope there'll be as much walking tomorrow. I also hope there'll be none of those monuments and other boring stuff which my daddy wastes so much time staring at. I'd better get some rest. It's annoying when he disturbs my sleep so I'm going to climb on to the bed and curl up in the middle, so that there's no space for anyone else. It's his turn to lie on the floor.

Good-night,

Mitzpah

❖ It's almost midnight and the dog has been fast asleep for over an hour when Guy knocks at my door. 'I need to talk to you,' he says. He sits down and begins: 'It was your plan to make a film about this walk, so you wanted it to happen. But you have to give us time. We want to make the best film we can and show you in the best possible light. But if you're not patient and you don't give it proper space and attention every day, all we'll be able to produce is a film about a person in a hurry. We've even got a provisional title, "The Rabbi Who Got Away". You have to give us a chance. After all, it was your idea.' My heart sinks, but I have to recognise that every word he's said is entirely fair. I tell him so. I also admit that it has simply never crossed my mind to consider what making a film might actually entail. 'Think of us as your family during this walk,' he advises. 'We're in this together now,' and that's exactly how it feels from then on.

I go to bed feeling rather ashamed. Sadly it is true; I am constantly in a hurry. My life is a long list of 'have to do's'; my excuse is that it isn't my fault, that as a rabbi I have virtually endless duties and that, whatever I do manage to accomplish, there is always three times as much left undone. How then can I help being in a rush? Furthermore, if I intend to get to those matters which I really want to do for my own reasons, on which a substantial part of my own inner satisfaction depends, then I have to get up early, work hard and keep going, or the day is over before I've even dreamt of them. But there also comes back into my mind my grandfather's words: '*Es ist unedel, keine Zeit zu haben* – It's ignoble to have no time.' There is a certain ugliness to being in a rush, a kind of unintended desecration. Is this the way to carry the light, not just the torch which will be with me for a few weeks now, but God's illumination which burns within each of us and of which we so often fail to take note because we are in a state of constant preoccupation? Is this the way to recognise the light of God's presence in others?

Day Three – From Mainz to Bingen

There is a flame inside my heart.
When I do right it burns before me, lighting me the way;
When I do wrong it sears my spirit and blisters me with shame.

❖   It's another stunning day for walking. Thick mist covers the Rhine valley as we set out by car to the monastery where we plan to start our hike. A pale light illumines the yellow leaves of the nearest trees and the ground is covered by frost. But soon the growing warmth and a perfect blue sky bring a brilliant autumn morning. Our path runs upwards, through the forests high above the Rhine, then down between the vineyards to the village of Rüdesheim and across by ferry to the left bank of the river and the small town of Bingen, where there has been a Jewish community since the middle of the twelfth century. The famous Rheinhöhenweg route is well way-marked, alleviating any fears of getting lost.

Peter, a Protestant minister, had joined me the evening before in Mainz. I had first met him through Catholic friends in the south of Germany who heard him say at a Kristallnacht commemoration that it was time to be in contact not just with gravestones and memorials but with living Jews and their communities. Over the years he invited me several times to speak in small towns and villages in the Stuttgart region. I can't remember what I said on those visits but I do recall some of the questions and comments which followed. On one occasion a lady in her seventies approached me: 'I haven't seen a Jew for many years, not since 1942, when there was an unexpected knocking at our door. I was just a child at the time; I stood behind my father as he answered. A thin, hungry man asked for bread. My father slammed the door in his face. My mother and I have never forgotten the shame of that moment.' She turned away and wept.

Over the years Peter and I developed a strong friendship and when he was promoted to Dekan, a position which sounded like that of a sub-bishop, entailing responsibility for all the regional clergy, he invited me to Crailsheim. 'This was the site of one of the last major battles of the Second World War,' he explained. 'The SS fought the Americans off and they had to retake the town in great force. When the fighting was over there were only three houses left standing.' He brought a group from the town to spend the Sabbath with me in my congregation, a brave visit as they entered not only the unfamiliar world of Jewish life but found themselves also in the disturbing territory of Jewish memory which, inevitably, they entered as Germans. It was an important experience for both visitors and visited.

Our last meeting had been some six years previously, when we spent a day together in Nuremberg. 'Where is the other Israel?' had been one of his first questions to me as we met at the airport; Israel and Palestine had featured ever more prominently in the discussions I had been having with his clergy. I felt hurt and asked him in response what effect 9/11 had had on his world. 'None,' he replied. I remember thinking at that moment that we inhabited different universes.

I was therefore touched by his kindness when we met, and by how deeply he wanted to share a stage of my pilgrimage, especially since his wife Gabriele, who had always welcomed me to their home with great charm, was still recovering from a serious car accident which had left her scarcely able to walk. That Monday night we literally broke bread together and I was moved when, perched on our tall chairs in a busy Spanish restaurant, we blessed and thanked God together for our food.

The next morning Guy, with whom I'd spoken about our last encounter, grilled Peter about Israel.

'Has being a pastor affected your views of Israel?'

'Yes certainly.'

'In what way?'

'I have a responsibility to build bridges, to increase understanding of why Israel reacts in the way it does.' (It was clear that he didn't mean that he necessarily agreed with what Israel did, but that he felt it was his duty to provide insight into what might drive the country to respond as it sometimes did.)

'Where does this sense of responsibility come from?'

'From the centuries of Christian persecution of the Jews, and from being German – these matters commit us to having an ongoing relationship with Israel.'

'What do you hope for?'

'A two-state solution in which Israel can live in peace and with security, but in which the rights of the Palestinian people are also recognised.'

'How old are you?'

'Sixty-eight.'

'Do you think you will live to see it?'

'Yes. We had the Berlin Wall. It came down one day in a revolution without violence. We never thought we would witness such a day. If it can happen here, it could happen again somewhere else.'

As we climbed, we talked about the critical importance of being able to listen to the stories of the other. I remembered the first time I stood in a Palestinian home and looked out through the window on to Jewish Israel; ever since that moment when a different narrative first framed my view, it has never been the same again. No one's truth is ever the whole truth.

We spoke of Paul Tillich, the Protestant theologian who served as field chaplain in the German army at Verdun, where my grandfather was also stationed, and who subsequently taught in Frankfurt, my grandfather's city. Surely the two men must have known each other? Tillich wrote in *The Dynamics of Faith* about the 'broken myth'.[1] This is a 'myth' in that it is a religious or national story, such as the Hebrew Bible or the New Testament, which is of central importance to us in framing and defining our world view and beliefs. But it is 'broken' in that we now realise that it does not constitute an attempt to present the literal truth. Its purpose and value lie in other dimensions. Its meanings and 'truths' are figurative and symbolic; they signify on the moral, psychological and spiritual planes. Alas for those who know, or are in a position to know, that the 'myth' they believe in is 'broken', Tillich wrote, but who still claim that this is not the case and insist on maintaining its literal truth. They end up repressing even basic facts in the effort to prevent their 'story', their world view, from being challenged. They are liable to use power, sometimes even the force of arms, to suppress intellectual openness and integrity. Their attitude stands in opposition to the understanding that we live in a world of multiple narratives and that wisdom and peace can only be achieved by the inclusion of many and differing perspectives.

Mercifully the hills soon proved too steep to leave us much breath for theology. The wonderful views across the Rhine distracted and beguiled us. Two birds of prey rose overhead. Mitzpah barked at horses in a field; they raised their heads and stared at him with obvious irritation. I put him on the lead; he responded by dancing round in circles of delight the moment I released him.

❖ We stop for lunch at a castle set among the vineyards. We've left in such a hurry in the morning that I've forgotten, folly for a diabetic, to buy any proper food. So I go to the restaurant area and ask for some bread. Every table is perfectly laid with a beautiful cloth and crystal glasses; this is the kind of place where you only go for a three-or-more-course meal, and that no doubt only on special occasions. The waiter disappears for several minutes; I assume, wrongly, that I'm not the kind of customer they are used to serving in this kind of establishment and that he isn't going to come back. But return he does, holding out a bag containing three different kinds of rolls together with a bowl of fruit – a peach, a pear, strawberries and blackberries. I make to pay. 'No,' he says, 'this is our gift to you for your journey. Please take it.'

Eventually we came down from the hills to walk alongside the Rhine. It was my first experience of standing next to the great river. Mitzpah was not particularly impressed and kept up his habit of racing ahead, hiding, and then rejoining us as we passed. Eventually he found a shallow bay and paddled a little way out into the water before lying down to cool himself off after the exertions of his day. I was relieved to observe that he never tried to swim where there was a strong current and I was careful not to throw sticks too far out into the water if it looked as if it was flowing fast.

At Rudesheim we took the ferry across to the beautiful small town of Bingen. I discovered afterwards that Guy had conducted a second interview with Peter on the ferry; he had asked him if he thought I was mad. 'He's in no way crazy,' he'd replied. 'On this journey he will discover many things about himself and about the world and make it possible for others to find them too.'

We were met a little later by members of the Arbeitskreis Jüdisches Bingen, who had made it their responsibility to study and preserve what remained of Jewish life and history in the town.

❖ We stop in the street near the site where the synagogue once stood, on a steep cobbled street. The town is set in the hills which climb immediately above the banks of the Rhine, where the tributary Nahe flows into it. At the turn of the nineteenth century a community of some seven hundred Jews lived here, or rather two communities, one orthodox and one liberal. This synagogue had been built by the liberal congregation; inaugurated in 1907 it survived only thirty-one years – until November 1938.

'They set it on fire on the night of the ninth, but the flames were extinguished,' members of the circle explain. 'The next day SA men came from a neighbouring town and utterly destroyed the building,' 'I was a girl of three but I can still remember standing at the corner and seeing the fire,' an elderly lady tells us. 'I was a bit older,' says her husband, who recalls how the SA men smashed off the head of one of the two stone lions carved above the entrance as a symbol of Judah and screamed out as the huge stone fell, '*So soll es sein!* – Thus should it be!' The heads of those lions were later rescued from among the ruins of the synagogue and transported to the Jewish cemetery, where I see them the next day and think of that ghastly triumphant cry. We are standing around a beautiful plywood model, based on the original plans of the synagogue still stored in the town's archives. 'The organ,' says the gentleman, 'was donated by the town as a gift on the occasion of the synagogue's dedication in September 1905. I saw it thrown piece by piece through the windows.'

Outside, we stand in the street for a long time around a group of three *Stolpersteine*, or 'stumbling stones', set in the cobbled pavement. I squat down to read the inscriptions. 'That's exactly what the artist intended,' observes my host Beate Goetz. 'The idea is that they should attract the attention of passers-by, who then pause to read and bend down to look more carefully.' Here had lived a family of three; the stones record their names, their dates of birth, and the year when they were deported. They were all taken to Lublin in 1942. At the bottom of the stones, each in size no more than five or six inches square, is a row of three question marks: where had this family finally perished? That, presumably, would never be known. Beate explains that there are already some fifty of these stones around Bingen, always set outside the houses where the individuals or families had actually lived, not those 'Jews houses' to which they were often forced to move prior to deportation. 'It's always a local decision to place such *Stolpersteine*,' she says, and tells me how in Bingen even schoolchildren have held cake sales to fund them. Others were paid for by grandchildren, the descendants of friends, those who remembered . . .

Stolpersteine are the creation of the German artist Gunter Demnig. 'Ein Mensch ist erst vergessen, wenn sein Name vergessen ist,' he wrote. 'A person is only forgotten if his name has been forgotten.' He cannot have known when he fashioned and set the first such stone that they would become the world's largest memorial, with over two hundred thousand located in several countries across Europe. They record not only the names of Jews who perished or fled but also those of the Sinti and Romani people, homosexuals, Jehovah's Witnesses, black people, Christians opposed to the Nazis, members of the Communist Party, fighters in the resistance, and the physically and mentally disabled who were killed in clinics by lethal injection or gassed in mobile vans.

❖ Mitzpah, tired after running sixty kilometres to my more sedate twenty, has curled up for a rest next to the stones. I recall as I look

at him how the Nazis required all Jewish families to surrender their
pets, along with their radios and other possessions which might offer
the opportunity of keeping in touch with the outside world or provide
a measure of companionship and solace. One account I read
described how the animals resisted. They intuitively knew that they
were being taken on their final outing; this was a walk on which they
were instinctively unwilling to set forth. I well believe it.

It was many months before I had the opportunity to study the book
about the history of the Jewish community of Bingen which the society
had given me. Strangely, it was late on the night before the dedication
of my own community's new synagogue when I finally read it. It was
titled *Zur Geschichte der Juden in Bingen am Rhein – Festschrift zur
Einweihung der neuen Synagoge in Bingen*, 'Towards the history of the
Jews in Bingen on the Rhine – A Special Publication to Mark the
Dedication of the New Synagogue in Bingen'. Dated 21 September
1905, it was written by Dr Richard Gruenfeld, the district rabbi. Next to
it on my desk lay our own publication. I turned the pages to find the
order of service and was struck that we had included some of the very
same prayers. We would be saying a prayer for the country in which we
live; they had said a *Gebet für Kaiser und Grossherzog*, a prayer for King
and Duke. I leafed through to the final pages of the *Festschrift* and noted
the postscript, to which my hosts had referred during my visit: 'Since
the preparation of this booklet for publication, we have been informed
that the Council of the Town of Bingen has most generously offered the
Israelite Religious Community a celebratory gift of 6,000 marks on the
occasion of the dedication of the synagogue, to be used to meet the
costs of the organ.' Had the good rabbi been told that scarcely more
than three decades later that organ would be hacked into pieces, thrown
out of the windows and burnt by agents of the national government, he
would surely not have believed it.

I tried to imagine how it must have been on the day of the great
dedication – the decorous joy of the community rejoicing in its achievement, the sense of responsibility at being successful *Deutsche Bürger
jüdischen Glaubens*, German citizens of the Jewish faith, the civic pride

65

in hosting the dignitaries who no doubt attended with genuine pleasure and not a little awareness of their indebtedness to certain well-to-do Jewish residents, the music both Jewish and patriotic. In 1905 my grandfather would have been in his fourth year of rabbinical school. It is most unlikely that he would have attended the ceremony, but it was the sort of occasion I imagine he would have enjoyed.

*   *   *

I was taken to see the museum in honour of the great Christian mystic Hildegard of Bingen (1098–1179). She established her own convent in the town after the Pope had recognised her mystical gifts and effectively declared her a modern-day prophet. She possessed remarkable talents in several fields and remains famous for her visions, writings and music. My hosts had made special arrangements with the curator to keep the museum open until late and I was given a personal tour.

❖   I ask the director about Hildegard's music. 'But you're listening to it even as we speak,' he replies. In the background is a gentle, beautiful and melodious singing.

According to tradition, though it is unlikely that the evidence bears this out, Hildegard undertook either three or four journeys, preaching and teaching through the Rhineland, in the towns along the Moselle and even farther afield. Apparently it is almost inconceivable that a woman could have travelled and lectured in this way at that time.

Hildegard's visions are very detailed and complex in their use of motifs, colours and scriptural references. I am shown a number of illustrations; they strike me as being rather like a series of inter-pretative *Midrashim* turned into pictorial art. The director points out to me her depiction of the old and blind synagogue next to the young, all-seeing church, a familiar image from the period. Hildegard had had dealings with Jews. 'It's a mistake,' says the director, 'to project the idea of the ghetto backwards across the mediaeval period. That came later, in Frankfurt with the Judengasse, then in Venice. The Jews often lived in the centre of the town. They may officially have been the property of the bishop but they enjoyed considerable

communal and legal autonomy. Courts would often sign the judg-
ments of their Jewish counterparts without understanding a single
word of the Hebrew documents.'

The picture the curator shows me is very striking, especially as the
touch screen display is so brilliantly organised that one can highlight
any part of it. I listen to Hildegard's own description of what it means
from her *Liber Scivias*. The blind synagogue carries Moses in her arms;
below in her lap is Abraham with a knife, perhaps representing
the definitive Jewish practice of circumcision. Beneath him are the
prophets, twelve figures in all. 'Her arms are crossed in defiance,' the
director explains. 'She is portrayed as refusing to accept the truths of
Christianity. Her feet are red with the blood of the killing of Jesus, the
evidence of deicide.'

Hildegard will inevitably have seen this figure as the non-compliant
other; to me it represents my people, it is me. Only a person with
expert knowledge would be able to discern whether Hildegard has
redeployed the familiar motifs of her time in such a way as to make
the figure less, or to render it more, sympathetic. But I find her far
from unappealing. She holds Moses warmly in her arms; though the
figures wear Jews' hats, their faces are pleasing. Here is a culture
expressed as close and self-affirming, a company of scholars, prophets
and teachers who do not seem to me to invite scorn but rather
respect. At least so I choose to interpret it.

That night I had dinner with members of the Arbeitskreis. Throughout
my visit they showed me the utmost generosity and courtesy; they had
even paid my hotel bill in advance. I understood that none of them was
either Jewish or of Jewish descent. So what made them do this work?
The reasons, it emerged, were multiple: a feeling for history; a sense that
Jews had been an important part of the home town which they loved;
because they still had personal memories; because their families had
had good relations with Bingen's Jews; because they were good and
dedicated people who genuinely cared.

'There's not a week when there aren't at least three emails from
descendants of Bingen Jews,' explained Beate. She would often meet

them on their visits to the town and take them to the cemetery. One man had promised his dying father that whenever he was in Europe he would come to Bingen to visit his grandfather's grave. He had faithfully kept his word.

Eventually the group decided to host a reunion of former Bingen Jews. 'The responses to our invitation were reserved,' they acknowledged. In their replies some of those invited wrote frankly about their fears at the thought of returning to Germany. 'But you should compare them to the letters of appreciation we received afterwards. The ice was soon broken.' A convivial relationship was quickly established with those who chose to accept. 'One lady phones me regularly from Israel,' Beate said. 'And there's a man who calls from time to time from Namibia.' Namibia? Yes – Jews from Bingen live in the United States, South Africa, South America, Israel, England, Sweden, South Africa, even Namibia.

From Mitzpah's Blog

Tuesday, 26 October

I swam in the Rhine today. It was the biggest river I'd ever seen so I only stayed in the water for one minute. I did it just to get my fur all wet and then climb out and shake myself all over my daddy's friend.

This afternoon we stopped to look at some stones in the pavement with names on them. I could feel that everyone was talking about something sad. Then they told me that dogs were taken away by the Nazis too. If that ever happened to me my heart would feel so sore with love for my family and I'd be so frightened that I wouldn't want to live any more.

Daddy was a little upset this morning for a quite different reason. He thinks mummy told him that she and the children miss me more than they miss him. I bet it's true. After all, what good does he do around the house? But I lick up all the crumbs and keep the place tidy. Then I go and lie on everyone's bed and make sure no one's feeling lonely.

Good-night,

Mitzpah

PS Though I'm taken down to breakfast here every morning, it isn't quite the same because I miss the children giving me pieces of their toast.

❖ Mitzpah wakes me at three a.m. He is growling quietly at something in the room which disturbs him. I quickly realise that it is the light of the torch, our portable *Ner Tamid*, which is shining against the opposite wall with a powerful nocturnal brightness, like a miniature local moon. I shift the beam out of his sight and he sleeps soundly until he hears me brush against his food bag soon after dawn.

Day Four – From Bingen to Bacharach, and back to Frankfurt

'And the place thereof shall know them no more.'

The next morning we met at the cemetery:

❖   High above the village, on steeply sloping ground now overgrown
with tall trees, the old Jewish graveyard overlooks the Rhine; it is one
of the most beautiful sites for a cemetery I have ever seen. The oldest
tombstones date from the seventeenth century; the newest, with the
settlement of Jews from Russia in this area, are from the current
decade. It must have been a hard journey in former years for the
horses if they had to pull the hearse up the steep lanes, or maybe the
dead were carried slowly and patiently on foot by their faithful
community to their final place of rest.

In 1870, when the congregation divided, an orthodox section was
created, separated off by a high wall. Only the lowest part of the
structure remains today, and of what significance should one regard
such barriers in the light of subsequent history? One grave I see has
a lengthy inscription in Hebrew, a proper eulogy, on one side, while
there is a detailed German text on the other: the two sides of the
German Jew perhaps, as Rabbi Samson Raphael Hirsch (1808–88)
saw it in the second half of the nineteenth century, the *Yisroel-
Mensch*, participating fully in the cultural, intellectual, scientific and
civic life of the state, without surrendering anything of his, or her,
orthodox commitment, living, and dying, in both worlds. How many
Jews, Muslims, people of complex and manifold identity live in two
or more worlds like that today? Only for most of us the texts are not
so discreetly separated, the first on one side and the second on the
other, but intermingled, sometimes inextricably.

Another grave has a small marble plaque at its foot in commemoration of a woman who sought refuge from the Nazis in France. She gained French citizenship but was subsequently betrayed as a former German Jew; at one point the French authorities differentiated sharply between long-standing citizens of their own country and immigrant Jews. Brought to Drancy, she was due to be deported to Auschwitz but was murdered before she ever got there. Her family has created this remembrance for her here, gathered her unto her ancestors in an incomparably more tranquil place than where she actually died.

Not far away is the grave of a student of medicine marked with the international insignia of the Army Medical Corps. He was killed in 1915, fighting for his fatherland on the eastern front. Strange, these contradictory destinies, now recorded so peacefully side by side.

On one grave I notice withered flowers, chrysanthemums, gladioli, late-summer blooms betokening a recent visit. Who has come and placed them there? My hosts cannot tell me.

I put on my *tallit* and *tefillin*, prayer shawl and phylacteries, in a small walled-off area just above the cemetery where the *ohel*, the chapel, had once stood. I was going to wander among the graves while I said the morning prayers, counting them as my quorum, respecting the silent communion of this congregation long gone. But I stop suddenly, remembering a passage from the Talmud: Rabbi Yonatan was walking through a cemetery with his *tzitzit*, the ritual fringes of his garment, dangling down and trailing over the graves. 'Draw them up,' his colleague admonished him, 'lest the dead say: "Today the living mock us, yet tomorrow they come to join us" ' (Talmud Berachot 18a). As the Talmud explains, one does not mock the poor, and the dead are regarded as poor because they can no longer praise God and perform the commandments in the way the living are privileged to do. I step swiftly back and say my prayers alone.

Before leaving the town I went to the Post Office to send off some parcels. It would be my daughter Libbi's fifteenth birthday in three days' time and I was rather taken with some chocolate witches I had seen for sale in the café on the ground floor of the guest house where we

71

were staying. I'd originally hoped that Libbi might join me for a couple of days and take the opportunity to practise her German, but understandably she preferred to spend her birthday at home. The lady at the counter was charming; she directed me towards birthday cards, wrapping paper, envelopes; she even leant me scissors and tape. So I posted off one package especially for Libbi and another, from Mitzpah, for the rest of the family. To my joy I found out later that they had arrived at the perfect moment, just as she was about to set off for the synagogue on the Shabbat morning of her birthday. In future parcels I included small gifts for the rabbits and guinea pigs too, though I doubt there can have been enough to share between all twenty-nine of the latter.

I'm often asked, 'Does it feel strange to be in Germany?' Perhaps the most puzzling thing is that overall my answer is no; on the contrary, I experience moments in which everything seems so familiar that this itself feels disturbing. How can I be so at home in a country where I was never at home and which would, had they not escaped in the final months before the war, have murdered my entire family? A friend asked me a more astute, and more insidious, question, 'Did you ever find yourself somehow feeling German?' No, I don't think I did, especially as I'm not sure I would know what 'feeling German' might mean today. But I've certainly caught myself feeling comfortable, or what I prefer to call 'continental'; these cafés in Frankfurt and Cologne seem so familiar with their menus of *Mohnkuchen*, *Sachertorte* and *Schlagsahne* (whipped cream). When we were growing up my grandparents lived only round the corner; on our at least thrice weekly walks there my brother and I used to guess the number of paving stones – was it seven hundred and seven or seven hundred and ten? – between our house and theirs and assiduously count them. Our grandparents' friends were almost all fellow refugees and the lingua franca was a combination of German and English, often mixed up in the very same sentence. Their world was more Germany than London. As a child I just assumed that this was how one grew up. It was only far later, when, as a guest of the church in the Stuttgart region, I was welcomed into circles of friendly, generally not so young men and women busily talking about their everyday life and sharing memories while all the time passing round elegant plates of pastries, that I realised that what I had received was not a British but a refugee childhood in a small island of continental Europe set in North West London. Even when the conversation moved on to the Bible I still felt at home, until questions arose about Jews.

My grandparents' lives in Britain reminded me of the saying about the Exodus, applied to those recalcitrant moments when the former slaves wanted to exchange the unknown perils of their journey through the desert for the familiar routine of bondage: 'You can take the Israelites out of Egypt, but you can't take Egypt out of the Israelites.' So they were taken at the last moment out of Germany, but one couldn't take the Germany out of them. Nor would they have wanted it to be removed from them, with its high culture and decades of rich artistic, communal and family memories. That's the fate of many refugees, even some of those who truly suffered in their homeland. They miss the skies and mountains, the food and gatherings, the conviviality and comradeship they experienced in the very countries which persecuted them. However, for those relatively few survivors of the camps who came afterwards to Britain, matters were very different.

Thus the world I had encountered as a child made me feel strangely at home in countries I had never previously entered.

After my father's sisters died in Jerusalem I sat with my one and only cousin Michal and went through the letters and photographs we found in old boxes inside suitcases unopened for decades. The contents of an unpromising off-white linen bag were to engage, fascinate and trouble me for years. In it were somehow gathered letters between my great-grandmother and her six children. The correspondence began in 1938, by which time three of them, Alfred, Walli and my grandmother Ella, had emigrated to Palestine. Ernst was to flee to England after being interned for several weeks in Sachsenhausen following Kristallnacht and then travel on to America during the war. The two remaining sisters, Sophie and Trude, were to perish with their families in Europe. Most of the letters were addressed to my great-grandmother, but some dated from after the war, long after she had been gassed and burnt in Auschwitz. How the correspondence got into that small bag and why it ended up in a suitcase in that flat in Rechavia, I will probably never be able to discover.

Their terrible end is not presaged in Trude and Sophie's letters from the summer of 1938, not unless there is some deliberate defiance in their contents, a determination to assert the continued ordinariness of life in spite of the seeping terror. But such an application of hindsight might be cruel; what the letters seem to show is just how everyday and normal much of their life remained. Trude, who lived in Posen, now Poznan, where her husband was a leading doctor at the Jewish Hospital, chided her family for almost forgetting her birthday:

My Dear Ones – This time I waited before writing as it was my birthday on Wednesday and I wanted to be in touch when it was over. Incidentally, I've received no congratulations from any of you and letters from Ella, Walli and Ernst with a card from the dear Redlichs [Trude's sister and her husband] and your sweet letter arrived only yesterday. As I'd been invited out so often during the past year I took my revenge and asked everybody over for coffee and cakes in the *Logengarten* on the 9th June. For after the meal I arranged a visit to the garden, with the possible added extra of a few midge bites. The veranda was laid for 38 persons. Frau Linder decorated all the tables with yellow pansies and Marta baked excellent cakes. There were two nut cakes, one Madeira cake, one *Blechkuchen*, one *Königskuchen*, *Vanillenkipfeln*, *Bisquitroullade* and shortbread. Coffee, made from half a pound of very fine beans, and five bowls of whipped cream, were contributed by Frau Chone . . .

She then proceeds to list her various presents.

I put aside the dictionary and abandoned the effort to find the exact English translation for all the various kinds of cake. I resorted to memory instead. Were not *Vanillenkipfeln* those rich, moon-shaped biscuits my grandmother loved and which we had on special occasions in Hodford Road but that I didn't like because they were too full of ground nuts, although they were considered expensive and laid out only on the very best plates? Isn't *Blechkuchen* that delicious pastry, full of butter and eggs, which can be used as a base for apple and plum flans, making them almost as good as chocolate cake? Yes, I felt at home in the cafés of Germany.

Day Four – From Bingen to Bacharach, and back to Frankfurt

Just a day earlier, on 11 June, Sophie, Trude's elder sister, had written from Holleschau in Czechoslovakia, as it was then, where she lived with her husband Josef and (mercifully, in view of what happened to them) no children. Sophie is in some ways my favourite; I never of course met her, but she looks both beautiful and kind in the pictures I have seen:

> I've got a great deal of washing this week. It'll have rained itself out by Wednesday, so we'll be able to dry it in the garden. It's a bad year here for preserving fruit . . . On the other hand, I've put away 10 kilos of blackcurrant compotte and 5 of blueberries. I've still got so much jam from last year that I'm going to leave it until the raspberries come before starting again.

Her letter reminds me of my father. Every year we would bottle many pounds of gooseberries and blackcurrants, until freezing them became the simpler method. I can still see him explaining how the jars had first to be heated in the oven so that they didn't crack when the boiling fruit was ladled in, then sealed before they cooled down so that the contracting syrup would create the vacuum by which the fruit would be preserved. Nicky and I grow raspberries and redcurrants, gooseberries, even damsons, though they are nothing like the continental *Mirellen* which my great-aunt Sophie had no doubt been bottling. Her life, it seems, was not unlike ours, that is, in its peaceful years. I feel a strange continuity with her, with them, my father's family before the war, especially as they too were rabbis or the children of rabbis, as well as gardeners and the sort of people who appreciated a decent slice of cake.

Neither Sophie nor Trude were to survive. Both were murdered with their families. Sophie was deported to Theresienstadt on 18 January 1943 together with her mother. Relatives told me that they believe she was shot with her husband Josef, who was very wealthy, so that the Nazis could seize their possessions. This does not strike me as an adequate explanation since the Germans had plenty of other ways of robbing them of their home and fortune without actually killing them for that specific purpose. I recently found in the archives of Yad Vashem in Jerusalem the documents testifying to the fact that they were only in

Theresienstadt for a few days before they were sent on to Auschwitz and gassed on arrival. A letter from a local lawyer, Dr Pokorny, sent to their brother Ernst in America in response to his enquiries after the war states that: 'Sadly till this very day nothing more is known of her [Sophie's] subsequent fate; it is probable that she perished in a Polish concentration camp.' A later communication from the notary office in Holleschau states that Sophie's husband Josef died on 1 February 1943. We know that my great-grandmother was sent east to Auschwitz where she was murdered at the end of 1943. Her close companion Recha offered to go in her place. My great-grandmother would not hear of it. 'You,' she said, 'are young. I have lived my life.' She knew what was coming and was not afraid. Recha survived Theresienstadt and joined Ernst and his family in New York after the war.

The same lawyer's letter details the fate of part of Sophie and Josef's estate. A remarkable document testifies to how a neighbour handed the jewellery and household silver entrusted to her by Sophie to a local solicitor after the war. The hearing, it carefully records, began at 14.00 hours on 26 September 1946 and took place in the home of Helena Vodickowa who informed the notary that 'some time during the year of 1942, without prior announcement or invitation, Sophie Redlich brought her, Helena Vodickowa, some family jewellery and silver table-ware for safe-keeping'. But Sophie had neither provided an inventory nor left any guidance as to what should be done with the items in the event of her and her husband's deaths. A long list of valuables follows, including necklaces, brooches, rings, sets of twelve fish and meat forks and knives, cake forks, twelve coffee spoons, one wedding ring and 'one metal bowl for ritual uses with a Hebrew inscription'. The hearing closed at 16.00 hours. The lawyer took the objects away for valuation.

I keep thinking about that phrase 'without prior announcement'. In what spirits had Sophie arrived at that door? What had depositing those family treasures with her neighbour meant to her? Was it simply a precaution 'just in case', or did she know what lay in store for her husband and herself? What person can believe that he or she is going to be murdered?

I wished I knew how to find out what happened to all those precious objects; I would dearly like to have just one of them as a reminder of my great-aunt Sophie.

A letter from Trude dated 31 October 1941 described how her life had changed; it was sent from the Polish town of Ostrow Lubelski, to which the Nazis had deported the family from Posen soon after their bloody conquest of the country. Alex, her husband, had been very ill:

> It was a combination of a bad flu and total exhaustion. He's become thinner and is now being looked after very carefully so that he regains his strength. Hopefully he will soon be able to practise again because there are lots of people waiting for him. It's also a critical question of survival, because I long ago sold off our old bits and pieces. One hasn't got much anyway and life has to continue and there are five of us after all. Arnold [her son] helps around the house and in the practice, wherever it's needed. He also helps me with the washing. I wash alone and as the river is near we go out together so long as it is still warm enough to wash in the water.

The best time of the day, she writes, is in the evening, when, if there is enough fuel for the flickering petroleum lamp, she can lie down and read.

Matters were to get far worse. In a letter dated 6 August 1946, the president of the city of Poznan informed Trude's brother Ernst, in a reply to his urgent enquiry from New York, that Trude had remained in Ostrow Lubelski until 9 October 1943, when she, her husband and her only son were deported to Lubartov, and from there to Treblinka 'where they probably perished together with the other Jews'. The date is puzzling, as Treblinka ceased functioning as a death camp after the uprising and breakout of 2 August of that year, though a labour camp of the same name continued to exist a few miles away. The final paragraph of the short letter requested the payment of an administrative fee of 200 zloty, to be sent to the city office marked with the reference number X/1–4909/46, in return for the courtesy of having been supplied with the above information.

How could I be so brazen as to feel at home, even for a few stray minutes, even momentarily, in Germany? And yet a part of me almost did.

My mother's mother would sometimes get confused in her later years and muddle the local Golders Hill Park, where she still loved to be driven on fine days and would compare the dogs out on their walks to Prinz, the beloved greyhound of her childhood, with the Palmengarten in Frankfurt where she would take her three beautifully dressed young girls for their promenade and no doubt be accosted by many admiring members of the congregation. It seemed to me sometimes as if the view backwards over her life were like a landscape composed of two soft hills, but between them, not always visible from the distance, was a chasm, a fierce, steep and unfathomable gorge, from the terrible roar of the murderous torrent at the bottom of which she had somehow extricated and preserved herself and her family. One couldn't get far enough away for any length of time for the sound of those waters to become inaudible, but it was possible to look back across the view and ignore for a few moments that great and shattering discontinuity.

Yet this in itself was frightening. If what had seemed so safe then, if what, to my father's aunts, had failed to reveal its true murderousness even in 1938, was indeed so seemingly similar to what was now – this world of cakes, gardens, fruit-picking and kitchen stoves – then perhaps the world I was living in today was no more secure than their world had been. Perhaps that gorge would cut across our journey once again farther on, somewhere maybe only just out of sight? If what had felt so safe hadn't proved safe at all, what could safety really be?

*   *   *

❖   Mitzpah and I have a wonderful day's walking, the first for just the two of us on our own together. When the *Jewish Chronicle* calls me on my mobile for a protracted interview, the poor dog becomes resentful; he keeps bringing me sticks and, nudging my hand, implores me to throw them for him. 'You promised me this was just for the two of us,' he seems to be saying.

I pause by a sign just above a small sandy beach on the left bank of the Rhine. Mitzpah stares at it for a moment then runs down into the water. His German is mercifully inadequate: the sign says, 'Dogs must be kept on leads on the beach.' Mitzpah races merrily along, spins round in a swift dance and goes flying off behind some bushes. Soon afterwards we pass a number of beautifully planted allotments.

A lady is working in her vegetable garden and her small dog greets Mitzpah in friendly fashion at the gate. The lady and I exchange a few cheerful words and for some inexplicable reason I add that we're headed for London. Meanwhile I notice to my horror that Mitzpah is busy weeing over her herbs. '*Das macht nichts,*' the lady says kindly. 'It doesn't matter.' But I feel an apology is due.

I sit on the veranda of a small restaurant where I've stopped for a coffee and Mitzpah is offered his very own dinner: it looks like raw chopped pork. I feel awkward, hesitate for a moment, but see no reason why I should be obliged to refuse. It goes straight from the waitresses bowl into the dog's mouth, making no physical contact with his Jewish owner. Anyway, who says dogs can only eat kosher meat? Their main culinary problem occurs on Passover, when even dogs may be given no leaven because their owners are forbidden to possess it.

Trains pass by every two or three minutes; the path Mitzpah and I are following runs between the railway lines and the river. I cannot help but think . . . Both in *If This is a Man* and in *The Truce*, Primo Levi poignantly describes how those who have some view between the planks of the cattle trucks in which they are being transported to Auschwitz name to the others the stations, the mountain passes and the countries left behind . . . A universe later, the few individuals to survive out of thousands finally greet with an unspeakable mixture of pain, joy and sheer numbness the first Italian railway stations through which they travel on their way home.

Yet at the same time I have the warmest personal associations with trains, with those night journeys through France to Switzerland when my parents took us on holiday to the mountains and the snow. The trains now passing are beautiful, with the sort of carriages in which one would like to sit and stare at the mountains while drinking a good cup of coffee.

I wonder if any sight or perception ever signifies only one thing.

High up on the opposite bank of the Rhine I can see people working in the vineyards. Yesterday Peter and I came upon a cross beneath which was written the quotation from the Gospels: 'I am the vine stock and you are the branches.' Peter pointed out to me the difference between the thick rootstock and the thin branches. Farther on we saw a group of men pruning them, leaving just a couple of short shoots on each plant. 'They're Polish Gastarbeiter,' Peter explained. 'There'll be more of them with the new EU regulations.' I know that Peter's community has worked hard for the wellbeing of such groups. It struck me how the parable teaches precisely that we are all, Poles, Germans, Jews, branches on the same vine, all dependent for our very life on the sap from the same roots. And, of course, I thought about the poem sung so many times on the Day of Atonement, *Ki Anu Amecha*, 'For we are your people', with its many pastoral images of the bond between ourselves and God, including the verse, 'For we are your vineyard, and you are our keeper.'

*   *   *

I'm once again sitting in a café, this time in Bacharach, near the end of this day's walking. My thoughts are complicated; for a while as I've been approaching this village I've been thinking about Heinrich Heine, Jew, German, genius, lyric poet, sardonic satirist, convert to Christianity who never really meant it, regretted it one minute later and repented of it truly in the many years during which he lay in Paris, where he had fled from the Prussian censor, paralysed on what he described as his 'mattress grave'.

Heine's *Rabbi of Bacharach* is a gripping but incoherent work set in the late Middle Ages. After completing the first section he abandoned the project and only returned to it many years later, so it is in reality two distinct works strangely and unsatisfactorily welded together. The story begins on Passover night when the rabbi suddenly becomes aware that strangers have deposited the body of a Christian child beneath the festive table at which he and his wife are reciting the *Haggadah*, the traditional account of the Exodus from Egypt. During the pause which normally marks the arrival of the meal, the rabbi beckons to his wife, the beautiful Sarah, and bids her follow him out into the night:

Hastily the Rabbi grasped her hand and quickly drew her away through the dark alleys of Bacharach, quickly through the town gate, out on to the highway leading along the Rhine, towards Bingen . . . [1]

They flee. They sail down the Rhine and into the Main to seek refuge in Frankfurt's Judengasse: Heine's description of their desperate journey is unforgettable:

It was one of those nights in spring which, though soft enough and starry, raises strange shivers in the soul. The fragrance of the flowers was deathly. The birds chirped as if glad to vex someone and yet vexed themselves. The moon cast malicious yellow stripes of light over the darkly murmuring river. The tall, bulky rocks of the cliffs looked like menacingly wagging giants' heads . . . [2]

That afternoon and early the next morning I explored the alleyways of the town. A beautiful wood-framed house caught my attention; written in large letters was the date it had been built, 1364. Useless photographer as I am, I took several pictures until one of them clearly showed those numerals. That house would have been standing there not only when Heine visited here in the early nineteenth century but even when the fleeing rabbi and his beautiful wife made their hurried escape to the flowing Rhine. I climbed the steep steps up to the imposing ruins of the Wernerkapelle, build over a period of almost one hundred and fifty years from 1287 to 1430 to mark the site where the body of a murdered Christian child was supposedly found. According to the legend, the corpse lay, unharmed by wild animals and smelling of violets, illuminated by a bright circle of sunlight. The murder was blamed on the Jews who, it was alleged following the classic formula of the blood libel, required Christian blood for ritual purposes. Tragically and almost incredibly, such charges of ritual murder, particularly numerous in Germany, are not unknown today. A plaque now stands outside the church providing the visitor with the history of such libels and making it absolutely clear that they are precisely that – lies.

I was glad when Guy and I left the place to resume our ascent through the vineyards.

I spent that night back in Frankfurt, studying Torah with the Liberal community in the Bet Midrash, the house or room dedicated to study of the Torah, above the main sanctuary of the Westend-Synagoge. I was glad to return there; I was slowly developing a relationship of my own with this city my grandparents had so much loved, with its avenues and cafés and with the beautiful synagogue itself. But I was always chasing memories, listening for echoes, pursuing the same questions: How was it then? How did it all happen? On my first visit to the town I had wandered for hours through its streets after dark, past the Börneplatz where the great synagogue had stood, dedicated in 1882 and burnt to the ground on Kristallnacht, and where the walls of the old cemetery have themselves been made into a memorial, then down to the Mainz-quai and by the Römer.

I also went past the new buildings of the municipal library. It was in this institution though, of course, in other premises that my father's great uncle Professor Aron Freimann served as librarian and curator of Jewish books for thirty-five years. When he was offered the position in 1897 the collection numbered 11,118 volumes; by the time he left it comprised over forty thousand works, making it the most significant Jewish library in mainland Europe. A deep love of his vocation, a profound knowledge of Jewish history, a vast expertise revealed in the extensive list of his publications, and a winning manner with people enabled him to make significant additions to the collection and gain important bequests. In 1899 he was able to acquire the library of his teacher Abraham Berliner, consisting of 4,880 titles. In 1901 the widow of Willhelm Carl von Rothschild, the last of the Frankfurt Rothschilds, offered Freimann the opportunity of choosing a selection from among his rare books. In this manner 3,754 volumes, including incunabula and unique editions, came to the library. In 1902 Freimann prepared an exhibition of the Judaica collection and put together a special catalogue for a conference of orthodox rabbis in the city. In 1903 he acquired the personal library of the Munich banker Abraham Merzbacher, which included some 6,000 books and over 100 Hebrew manuscripts, among them an illustrated code of Maimonides from the thirteenth century and 43 incunabula. There were also many first editions, such as *Bomberg's Talmud*, printed in Venice between 1519 and 1522.

In August 1931, to mark his sixtieth birthday, Freimann received a telegram from the Mayor of Frankfurt, Oberbürgermeister Ludwig Landmann:

> To the most highly respected Professor Freimann! I beg you to accept my heartfelt congratulations on your sixtieth birthday. May you be granted many more years of successful work at our municipal library and in the fields of knowledge you have chosen to cultivate. With the highest respect, Yours . . . [3]

An article in the *Frankfurter Zeitung* for 6 August was devoted to his achievements.

Yet scarcely more than a year and a half later, on 30 March 1933, he was '*beurlaubt*', placed on long-term involuntary leave. On 4 April of the same year he was obliged to return the keys to the library and on 1 January 1934 he was permanently 'retired', following an order of the Prussian Minister of the Interior made on 21 September 1933. He had already been forbidden all access to the institution to which he had devoted by far the greater part of his working life.

Since 1927 the head of the Frankfurt municipal library had been Richard Oehler, one of the few librarians active in the Nazi Party. When the Nazis came to power, he placed a ban on all Marxist writings and ordered that any other categories of literature which should, according to Nazi ideology, not be available on loan were to be marked as *gesperrt*, barriered, and only given out upon the approval of a special application. Following a complaint that Jews were still persisting in making use of the facility, access to the library was banned to those few non-Aryan readers who had continued to frequent it.

The books, however, were to remain in Frankfurt. Salman Schocken, who founded his own publishing company and later built the Schocken Library in Jerusalem, offered to buy the collection in 1934, but his overtures were rejected. A further, and very different, attempt to purchase the books was made in 1936 by Dr Wilhelm Grau in Munich. He had been appointed head of the department for research of the 'Jewish question' in the newly created Reichsinstitut für Geschichte des neuen Deutschlands (National Institute for the History of the New

Germany), and was convinced of the unique importance of the library for his work. He was however unable to persuade the then mayor of Frankfurt, Friedrich Krebs, to part with the collection. He argued in the first instance that such a sale would attract negative international attention, and, further, that it was

> especially to a city like Frankfurt, which had in the course of the centuries been forced to suffer more under Jewish influence than almost any other town in Germany, that the sources for [such] research should richly flow. Since, as leader of the community, I have the legal obligation to manage the resources entrusted to me carefully, conscientiously and efficiently, it is sadly not possible for me to authorise [the sale].[4]

It also emerges that the collection was considered by the mayor to have profound intrinsic value; this lay not, however, in the rich Jewish civilisation embodied within it, but in what it might have to offer students of other disciplines, such as Semitic languages and New Testament Studies, as well, chiefly, as the rich mine of materials it proffered to researchers of Aryanism and its relationship to the vexed question of the Jews. In the event, Krebs's decision proved well justified. The new institute foundered in Munich and was transferred to Frankfurt, where the collection of Jewish books was massively increased by loot from the Jewish libraries, synagogues and homes of Eastern Europe. Some three hundred thousand volumes were crated up and shipped to Frankfurt.

The library was destroyed in the Allied bombing raids of 20/21 December 1943 and January and March 1944. However many of the most valuable books survived; they had been removed to safe locations outside the city together with other civic treasures.

Professor Freimann fled with his wife and only daughter to America, where he died in New York on 6 June 1948, just one month after his nephew and soulmate Alfred had been burnt alive in an Arab attack on the ill-fated convoy of scholars to the campus of the Hebrew University on Mount Scopus during Israel's War of Independence. The inscription on his grave reads:

> Here lies buried the outstanding scholar, our teacher Aron,
> Son of our teacher Israel Meir Freimann,
> Grandson of the author of *Aruch LaNer*,
> Who died on the 18th of Av, 5631,
> The last president of the holy community of Frankfurt-am-Main,
> The greatest historian and bibliographer of his age,
> Beloved of God and beloved of creation.[5]

Blessed are dogs, who are not subject to being haunted by history.

At the close of the evening I said farewell to the by now familiar Westend-Synagoge. I wasn't planning to return during this particular journey. I was struck by how vibrant it had once again become with Jewish learning and prayer, from Liberal to Orthodox, a pluralism of which the creators of the concept of the *Einheitsgemeinde* would have been proud.

Within months of the last deportations from Frankfurt, which continued to take place even as the Third Reich was collapsing, Jewish life, palely and beset with horrors, was beginning once again. I came across the following eye-witness report from the *Frankfurt Rundschau* for 12 September 1945:

> This was the most moving hour since the arrival of the Americans. In the burnt-out, hastily repaired synagogue in the Freiherr-von-Stein-Strasse gathered what remained of the large and famous Jewish community of Frankfurt, this community that was known the world over for its high culture, scholarship and hundreds of charitable foundations. Now the remainder of this community sat in the last Jewish house of God in this city that had not been totally devastated by animal-like hatred. In a room that no longer had an organ or the old seating but was lit comfortingly by candles sat the last ones remaining of 35,000 people, the survivors of extermination camps, those who had been saved from the gas chambers, a heart-stoppingly low number. They sat between many American soldiers from Frankfurt and the surrounding region. It was difficult not to shed tears in this hour.[6]

From Mitzpah's Blog

I'm having the most wonderful time walking and running. But I sense that my daddy is sad some of the time. I don't understand it: I'm with him, so what else can he want? He's fine when we're in the countryside, but it's those old places which upset him. I'd like to help. Is there anything I can do?

By the way, he thinks I can't read German. But he's wrong. I know that sign by the side of the path said: 'Dogs must be kept on leads on the beach.' But did you think that was going to stop me? The very next thing I did was to have a little dance on the sand. It's important to make a clear statement about unnecessary rules.

It's my belief that the world should be shared without any discrimination between one kind of creature and another. After all, who do those humans think they are and why do they imagine they're so much better than us?

Love,

Mitzpah

Day Five –From Bacharach to St Goar

I was glad to have one more morning in my grandfather's city; I could hear his voice speaking inside my head, reminding me of all the stories I had loved. He had relished teaching, extending his regular rabbinic work with weekly lessons in many of Frankfurt's high schools. Once, his class of eighteen-year-old girls had behaved so badly that he felt obliged to inform them that, were they ever to conduct themselves in such uncouth fashion again, he would have to forgo the familiar *Du* and address them with the formal *Sie*. They all wept and never did it again. How things have changed!

I also wanted to spend more time in the city where Franz Rosenzweig had lived and taught. Rosenzweig grew up in what Gershom Scholem later described as 'the desolate Jewish wasteland in Germany, of which the word *assimilation* gives only the slightest hint'.[1] Disillusioned with the post-Hegelian philosophical tradition of German idealism, he became convinced that God was to be sought not in theories of history but in religion with revelation at its heart and with its emphasis not on an all-encompassing philosophy but on each and every specific human action.

In October 1913 he was on the verge of embracing Christianity, as had so many of his contemporaries, convinced in lengthy discussions with his cousin Eugen Rosenstock that this was the only spiritually and intellectually viable option. But he wanted, he said, to accept Christianity specifically as a Jew and therefore made a point of attending services over the High Holydays. He spent the Day of Atonement in the small orthodox synagogue in the Heiderreute-Strasse in Berlin, where my great-grandfather would serve as rabbi a decade and a half later, and emerged a different person. He probably went there because apparently his mother, horrified to learn of his plans, remonstrated that if he dared attempt to attend Yom Kippur services in his native Kassel she would tell the authorities at the synagogue not to let him in. Looking back several years later, he described the experience of that Yom Kippur and the discovery of the spiritual wealth which lay within his own tradition in a letter to the teacher whom he had so much admired at Freiburg, and who had specially created a university position for him, Friedrich Meineke. Rosenzweig felt obliged to explain why he had decided to reject the academic path in favour of accepting the leadership of the Freies Jüdisches Lehrhaus, the Open Jewish Study House in Frankfurt:

> It was then (one can only speak of such matters in metaphors) that I descended into the vaults of my being, to a place whither talents could not follow me; that I approached the ancient treasure chest whose existence I had never wholly forgotten . . . But now this cursory inspection no longer satisfied me; my hands dug in and turned over layer after layer, hoping to reach the bottom of the chest. They never did. They dug out whatever they could and I went away with armfuls of stuff – forgetting, in my excitement, that it was the vaults of myself I was plundering![2]

Rosenzweig recognised that it was not just within himself that these treasures had been hidden, but that his experience was symptomatic of a Judaism which, since the Enlightenment, had become progressively more alienated from itself and denuded of its native content, while attempting to hide its nakedness in borrowed clothes. Catchwords like 'humanity' or 'democracy' were no substitute for a rigorous engagement with Jewish tradition, he argued in his address on the opening of the Freies Jüdisches Lehrhaus in 1920, the same year as he wrote the letter to Meineke. It would not do to pass them off as noble concepts which were somehow Jewish in essence by backing them up with loosely fitting quotations from the Torah matched by parallel sentiments from Goethe or the other German classics. Jews had to engage with the Hebrew language, the classical Hebrew texts and serious Jewish practice, no part of which he was prepared to consider abrogated. It was time to return to the core of Jewish identity:

> All of us to whom Judaism, to whom being a Jew, has again become

the pivot of our lives – and I know that in saying this here I am not speaking for myself alone – we all know that in being Jews we must not give up anything, not renounce anything, but lead everything back to Judaism. From the periphery back to the centre; from the outside, in.[3]

Rosenzweig was deeply sceptical of the love of German culture which had, in his view, rendered the Judaism of his generation so anaemic. In a letter to his friend Joseph Prager, written on 22 January 1922, after the sudden death of the charismatic orthodox rabbi and brilliant orator Dr Nehemia Nobel who had drawn him to Frankfurt and with whom he had studied daily, he observed how much better the latter's sermons were than his lectures: 'Only there did he believe himself able to manage without loans from the Christian and pagan cultural spheres, and even *there* one was never sure one wouldn't be handed a quotation from "the master" . . . '[4] The *Meister* was, of course, my grandfather's beloved Goethe.

The nature of Rosenzweig's commitment to a traditional Judaism of both study and observance is clarified in a famous exchange of letters with Martin Buber during the summer of 1924. Buber lived in Heppenheim, not far from Frankfurt, and Rosenzweig had succeeded in engaging him to teach at the Lehrhaus. Buber was in this respect more of an antinomian; for him, to treat religion as a legal system was to create an impenetrable barrier against the immediate experience of God:

> I do not believe that *revelation* is ever a formulation of law . . . I cannot admit the law transformed by man into the realm of my will, if I am to hold myself ready as well for the unmediated word of God directed to a specific hour of life.

In his reply Rosenzweig conceded that the specific formulation of the law was indeed the work of human beings. (He argued that revelation ended with the words 'And God spoke'; the ascription of specific content to what God said was inevitably an act of interpretation.) But he insisted that God indeed commands:

> For me too, God is not a Law-giver. But He commands. It is only by

the manner of his observance that man in his inertia changes the commandments into Law, a legal system with paragraphs, without the realisation that 'I am the Lord', without 'fear and trembling', without the awareness that the man stands under God's commandment.[5]

In a later letter to teachers at the Lehrhaus, he adds:

I should not venture to dub 'human' any commandment whatsoever, just because it has not yet been vouchsafed me to say over it: 'Blessed art *Thou*.'[6]

When asked whether he put on *tefillin*, phylacteries, in the morning, he is famously said to have answered 'not yet'.

The fascinating future of that 'not yet' was cut short by Rosenzweig's early death, just as the Jewish revival of which he was a pre-eminent leader was thwarted by the rise of Nazism and strangled by the destruction of German Jewry.

One of Rosenzweig's greatest undertakings was the translation of the Bible into German in collaboration with Martin Buber. The Bible had already been rendered into German approximately a century and a half earlier by Moses Mendelssohn, partly in order to enable Jews to gain access to the vernacular of the state in which they were seeking the full rights of citizenship. (Unlike others, he maintained that such rights should be granted by the state unconditionally and not as a quid-pro-quo in return for Jews 'proving' themselves worthy by some prior process of civic self-betterment.) Jews knew Hebrew and spoke Yiddish, but German was largely a foreign language to them. In the 1920s Buber and Rosenzweig embarked on a similar project with the opposite intention, so that Jews, by now often totally alienated from the language of their own culture, could savour the rhythms, syntax and literary structures of the original Hebrew, in so far as it was possible to convey them in even the best of translations. Jews, for whom doorways into the wider culture had been created slowly and with great difficulty during the late eighteenth and the nineteenth centuries, had in the meantime availed themselves of them to such a degree that by this time all that was often left them of their own faith was ignorance and alienation. At least while the Judengasse still stood, said Rosenzweig in his inaugural speech for the Lehrhaus in 1920, the traveller still came home at dusk. Now he no longer did.

Rosenzweig did not live to see the completion of this massive work of translation. Illness struck him from nowhere; one day in late 1921 he began to stumble. His symptoms were diagnosed as the beginnings of a sweeping paralysis which soon confined him to the single room, where, tended by his wife, he continued to work and teach until his death in 1929. Many years later Gershom Scholem recalled: 'Whoever once was in that room in Frankfurt and heard his questions answered and heard the eloquence of that mute saint, surely he knows what a miracle happened to us here.'[7]

Rosenzweig died in 1929; he remains the herald of rediscovery, of a process of exploration and re-entry into Judaism for thousands of late twentieth and early twenty-first century Jews, who, having made their home in secular Western culture, have been drawn back like him to those half-remembered vaults to rediscover the lost and hidden treasures of their own selves.

*   *   *

Guy and I took the train from Frankfurt's Hauptbahnhof and, changing at Bingen, quickly found ourselves back in Bacharach. Mitzpah too enjoyed the ride. He has always preferred to have a place of his own rather than having to lie on the floor, a predilection which I'm happy to tolerate so long as I've remembered to bring a towel to spread over the seat in question so that subsequent passengers don't have to sit down on tell-tale traces of his fur. On this occasion he was cheerfully ensconced at my feet until, having gone to the toilet, I returned to find my place occupied.

It was another beautiful day for walking. This time I didn't take the easy route along the cycle-path by the edge of the river but the steep way-marked path which climbed among the vines and past the castles high on the Rhine's left bank. A coffee, a croissant (shared by Mitzpah, who is always allowed into these restaurants, unlike in animal-loving England) and we were ready to be off.

❖   Thankfully the blister situation has settled down rather well by this time. I clocked one a day for each of the first two days, but since then mercifully none. I blame them on my own bad choice of outer socks; the inner socks selected for me by Nicky were absolutely brilliant. Equally excellent are the blister-pads I was given; since applying them I have scarcely felt any pain. I don't think I've taken a single step which made me wince. Those blister plasters are also a gift; they came in the post from Canon Nicholas Sagovsky and his wife, the kindest of people, after we had shared a Shabbat dinner together. I thank them from the soles of my feet.

Our path leads through vineyards and woodlands. In one place the route is so steep that a metal ladder has been placed between the terraces with a thick wire to hold on to for balance. We marvel at the workers dressing the vines: how can they possibly keep upright on these impossible slopes? At some points the space between the walls dividing the plantations is so small that I think of the biblical prophet Balaam on his donkey, where the angel sent to stop him from going to curse the Children of Israel stood in a pass between the vineyards so narrow that 'there was no room to turn aside either to the right or to the left'. To avoid God's angel, which she could see but her master had failed to notice, the poor animal had no choice but to lie down, and be beaten for her pains. Unlike that recalcitrant but wise and perceptive donkey, I don't think Mitzpah lay down once. He had a wonderful time – and so, to be truthful, did I on that beautiful autumn day. I only wished I could have shared it not just with the dog but with all my family.

I prefer the woodland to the vineyards. The former are composed of oaks, birch and hazelnut – I even saw a walnut tree. I'd been hoping to find a few wild apple trees here and there with over-ripe fruit, the sort of thing Keats must have been referring to in his ode 'To Autumn', that 'season of mists and mellow fruitfulness'. It would have been rather nice to eat one or two on the way, exactly as the Torah prescribes for the traveller passing through someone else's fields and orchards: 'You may pick, but not put any into your bag.' The woodlands were glorious and rich, but I found no apples.

The vineyards feel very different. Perhaps this is the inevitable price of cultivation. But I notice that wherever one finds an empty field where the vines have been uprooted, presumably prior to being replaced with younger stock or a different variety, the earth is all but barren. Where is the glorious wealth of weeds and wildflowers? Admittedly it's late October, but no withered riches are in sight, only always the same single species of groundcover. Once or twice we pass strongly smelling fertilisers; the intense odour of drying piles of pips and crushed grapes isn't pleasant either.

We look down from hundreds of feet above the water at the vast and powerful Rhine. Here are beauty and industry together. On either side of the river rise forested hills and ancient terraces devoted to viticulture. But along the banks are busy railway tracks and restless roads, while barges pass by constantly on the current.

The Rhine is considered the European river most tampered with by humans. Its very course was altered substantially for the greater ease of shipping. Shallows were deepened, treacherous rocks removed or circumvented, floodplains put to other uses, woodlands bordering it largely cut down, while manufacturing along its thousand-kilometre reach increased, with the discharge of so many chemicals that it became one of the world's dirtiest rivers. It once supported many tens of species of fish; by the 1940s there were found in parts of its waters and some of its tributaries only three. It was shocking to learn how the river was mistreated and what a utilitarian and anthropocentric philosophy lay behind this abuse:

> Widespread among European engineers was the perception that the perfect or 'ideal' river was really a canal: straight, predictable, easily controlled, specifically designed for navigation, not prone to flooding, easily contained within a single channel, and not so sluggish as to breed disease . . . Of the nearly seven hundred treaties, agreements, blueprints, and disputes that came under the purview of the Rhine Commission between 1816 and 1916 not a single one concerned itself with water quality, the floodplain or biodiversity.[8]

It was only with cross-European cooperation after the Second World War that matters began to improve. By 1990 there were once again some forty species of fish in the Rhine's waters. Presumably this figure has since increased. The river's worst polluted tributaries, such as the Wupper, which were still then considered to have some of the lowest grades of water quality, have become steadily cleaner. We may even have returned to an appreciation of the Rhine close to that of Hölderlin, my mother's best loved poet:

> But where is the man
> Who can remain free
> His whole life long, alone
> Doing his heart's desire,
> Like the Rhine, so fortunate
> To have been born from
> Propitious heights and sacred womb?[9]

*   *   *

❖   Walking through the village of Oberhausen I suddenly see a large stone monument with a *Magen David* held in a cleft in its centre. It is a memorial to the town's former Jews, both those who fled and those who perished. I read the list, surnames familiar to me since my childhood in our refugee family: Kahn, Seligman . . . It is a totally unexpected moment. I silently recite the Kaddish, the sanctification of God which is the traditional response to the memory of the dead.

After a short break for lunch, Mitzpah and I set out towards the rock of the Lorelei. It is a grey and louring afternoon, a fit sky under which to approach this looming, sinister landmark. My grandparents would speak of it often; the fate of Heine's poem on the subject heralded and epitomised their own. Börne and Heine were two of their heroes, both Jews from the Rhineland, both harbingers of liberty. Börne was born in 1786 as Loeb Baruch, son of a fiscal agent, in the Judengasse, the Frankfurt ghetto. This institution, the entrance of which is now the site of a museum, stood from 1462 until the requirement for Jews to reside within it was finally abolished in 1811 as part of a swathe of civil rights granted in the wake of Napoleon's victories, most of which would be withdrawn in the years of Prussian oppression after his defeat. Börne belonged to one of the first generations of Jews able to access a higher secular education. He abandoned plans to study medicine in favour of a civil service career which eventually led him to the political journalism through which he became famous. Like Heine, he converted to Christianity as a formality, purely out of professional convenience and with no conviction, and like Heine he was forced to flee the Prussian censorship and reside in Paris. By the time of his death his outspoken struggle for liberty had made him 'a moral icon for generations of German patriots, democrats and political exiles'.[10] In this his Judaism, even though he had formally renounced it, had clearly played a decisive role:

> Yes, because I was born a servant I love freedom more than you. Yes, because I tasted slavery, I understand freedom better than you. Yes, because I had no fatherland at birth, I wish for a fatherland more ardently than you, and because my birthplace wasn't bigger than the Judengasse and because the ghetto gate marked for me the beginning of a foreign country, a single city is no longer enough for me as a fatherland, nor is a territory or a province. Only the entire, magnificent fatherland will satisfy me, as far as its language is spoken. [11]

I ponder this passage with admiration, and ambivalence. He captures exactly that Jewish sensitivity to marginality informed by generations of uneasy living at the dangerous intersection of persecution and often grudging, conditional toleration. Yet his song to liberty ends in notes which have an uncomfortable after-echo; I hear them again in my grandfather's ardent patriotism of 1914, and in his impassioned speech at the dedication of a war cemetery near Verdun where he was called upon to give an address in the presence of the Kaiser's son:

> Comrades! Thus do the dead greet us! Be steadfast; be loyal! Our loyalty to Kaiser and country, to people and fatherland, has been sealed with our deaths. We have died so that you may live . . . [12]

Does freedom always have to ring with nationalist tones? Was not this perilously related to that nationalism which would render my grandfather himself an outcast, despite his Iron Cross, less than a score of years later?

However, reflecting again on Börne's words, it strikes me that he may offer a clue to this strangely ardent patriotism at the heart of so much of late nineteenth- and early twentieth-century German Jewry, a sentiment which has elicited puzzlement, if not scorn, from many who have since been able to evaluate it with the bitter benefit of hindsight. 'Because I had no fatherland at birth, I wish for a fatherland more ardently than you' – is this the psychological secret behind that deep love affair between Jews and Germany (a one-way affair, its critics, probably justly, called it)? At last, after two thousand years we have a homeland! If so, it was, as the Zionists were increasingly going to point out in the early decades of the twentieth century, a misapplied affection. Or would it be fairer to describe Jewish devotion to the fatherland as the desire to prove themselves worthy in the eyes of the Gentiles of the equality so slowly proffered them, as if it could at any moment be withdrawn, as indeed it so violently was?

But it was Heine whom my grandparents truly loved. Born in 1797 in Düsseldorf, his career partly paralleled that of Börne. Though close while a student in Berlin to the circle of scholars who created the discipline of *Wissenschaft des Judentums*, the scientific study of Judaism, he too followed the path of assimilation, formally converting to Christianity for the sake of the professional opportunities it purportedly offered him and which, he wryly noted, never materialised. 'I am now hated by Christian and Jew. I deeply repent my baptism; so far I can't see at all that I've been better off since – on the contrary, I've since had nothing but bad luck,' he observed in a letter to his friend Moses Moser, in January 1826. Years later he wrote, with that brilliant and laconic humour which characterised his political writing: 'That I became a Christian is all the fault of those Saxons who settled all of a sudden in Leipzig, or of Napoleon, who had no need to invade Russia, or of his teachers who instructed him in geography at Brienne but failed to inform him that Moscow winters are extremely cold.'[13] He would, in other words, never have converted, were it not for the fact that equal opportunities were denied him as a Jew.

Like Börne, he dipped his brilliant, acerbic pen in the ink of freedom, and when the Prussian censors came too close in following its trail, fled to Paris where he lived for thirty years before dying there, a Jew by deep conviction. His ashes, he ordered, were never to be returned to Germany. Indeed they were not; instead the Germans, as he had warned the French a century before, came after them, smashing and obliterating every trace of his grave in the Montparnasse cemetery in March 1941 during the Nazi occupation of Paris.

My grandparents had a beautiful edition of Heine's *Buch der Lieder*, a masterpiece which he wrote when he was only thirty and which placed him among Germany's greatest lyric poets. In my memory I hold the book in my hands and stare at the exquisite paper-cuts of lovers, children and animals with which the poems are illustrated.

My grandmother used to talk about Heine's return to Judaism. It happened during the long years of his illness, when that great bon-viveur and admirer of beauty lay helpless on his bed in Paris, tended by his mistress Mathilde whom he promptly and properly made his wife upon learning of the incurable nature of his infirmity:

> I owe my conversion simply to the reading of a book. A book? Yes, it is an old, homely-looking book, modest as nature and as unaffected; a book that has a workaday and unassuming look, like the sun that warms us, like the bread that nourishes us; a book that seems to us as familiar and as full of kindly blessing as the old grandmother who reads in it with dear, trembling lips, with spectacles on her nose. And this book is called – quite briefly – 'the Book', the Bible.[14]

I have often pondered Heine's description of how he rediscovered his faith. The God he finds is the traditional deity of his ancestors, the personal God, the God who is all-powerful over history, the God who hears our prayers and answers them with actions, the God who has arms to save:

> Yes, I have returned to God like the prodigal son after I had long kept swine among the Hegelians . . . On my way I found the God of the Pantheists, but I had no use for him. That poor creature of dreams is interwoven and overgrown with the world, really incarcerated in it,

and stares at you without will and without power. To have a will one must be a person; and to manifest it, one must have his elbows free. If one desires a God who is able to help – and that after all is the chief thing – one must accept his personality, his transcendence, and his holy attributes, his goodness, his omniscience, his justice, and the like. The immortality of the soul, our persistence after death, is then thrown into the bargain just as the butcher throws some good marrow-bones into the shopper's basket gratis if he is pleased with his customer.[15]

Why it is so important that God be both personal and powerful is movingly explained by his heart-rending description of the final walk his body allowed him to take:

> ... It was in May 1848, on the day when I went out for the last time, that I took farewell of my dear idols to which I prayed in the days of my happiness. I was hard put to it to crawl as far as the Louvre, and I almost broke down when I entered the great hall, where the blessed Goddess of Beauty, Our Dear Lady of Milo, stands on her pediment. At her feet I lay a long time and wept so as to move a stone to pity. And the Goddess looked down on me so compassionately and yet so desolately as though she would say: 'Seest thou not that I have no arms and therefore cannot help thee?'[16]

Would Heine's God still have arms to save ninety years later, when the Nazis came to destroy his grave? With what self-mocking witticism would he have defied them then, when only his tombstone was within reach of their harm?

❖ I called Isca on my mobile phone shortly before I reached the rock of the Lorelei. My grandparents would speak of it often. There is an ancient legend that a siren dwells on top of the massive crag, luring mariners to their deaths with her beautiful singing. It was still apparent from the sharpness of the river's curve and from the speed and obvious strength of the current that navigation of this stretch of water was dangerous even today and required a great degree of skill.

Heine's poem about the legend is arguably his best known work:

Ich weiss nicht was soll es bedeuten,
Dass ich so traurig bin;
Ein Märchen aus uralten Zeiten,
Das kommt mir nicht aus dem Sinn.

I don't know what it's supposed to mean
That I should feel so sad;
There's a legend from ancient times
Which will not depart from my mind.

I find this far more sinister than the sombre rock itself. It reminds me of the Pharaoh in the Book of Exodus who 'knew not Joseph' (Exodus 1:8). The Talmud asks whether he has really never heard about the achievements of the famous Hebrew vice-regent of Egypt, or whether he is merely pretending not to know.[17] It is chilling to consider what follows – the branding of Joseph's descendants as an alien threat, their marginalisation and enslavement and soon afterwards the murder of their children, first in semi-secret, but then openly and brazenly. Matters were to pursue a similar course in the Third Reich.

Denial of a people's achievements is frequently a prelude to further forms of degradation and repression. This is scarcely unknown in our own societies. All too often those in search of asylum are branded as good-for-nothings; talk to some of them and you soon discover that they have degrees, are doctors or teachers, and desire one thing above all: the opportunity to belong and to make a contribution to society.

As I look at the rock, my grandparents' faces appear before me. The *Lorelei* was doubly a part of their lives. Heine was at the peak of the German Jewish culture they so much loved. The fate of his *Lorelei* represented the stripping away from them too of all dignity and respect, to the point where my grandfather was made to perform humiliating exercises in a hall in Frankfurt, prior to being interned in Dachau. Had it not been for the tenacious love of his family, he too would have been left in a nameless unmarked grave.

Heine, who was a sardonic political commentator with an extremely sharp wit as well as a lyric poet of unsurpassed genius, is widely considered to have predicted the rise of German fascism. He warned the

French, who had been the rulers of Düsseldorf at the time of his birth, not to abandon the Rhine, not to disarm and not to trust Germany. Christianity may have tamed the Nordic spirit, but the cross was breaking:

> the day will come when it will pitifully crumble into dust. The old stone gods will then arise from the forgotten ruins and wipe from their eyes the dust of centuries, and Thor with his giant hammer will arise again, and he will shatter the Gothic cathedrals . . . There will be played in Germany a drama compared to which the French Revolution will seem but an innocent idyll.[18]

I remember ringing my brother in tears after passing the sombre rock. Even now I can't fully explain why it affected me so deeply; maybe it's because the fate of Heine's *Lorelei* somehow epitomised that of our own family and history, decades of achievements treated as if they were less than nothing, offensive stains on the pristine page of a *judenrein* fatherland.

*   *   *

The day's walking was far from over; my map told me that the village of St Goar was only a few kilometres away and I was determined not to miss it. I called Mitzpah to my side and hurried on; I'd been thinking about this place since I first came across it while researching my route. The kilometres fell swiftly behind us and soon we were sitting on the steps of the church in the tiny village square. Here in the fourteenth century the *Sefer Hamaharil* was composed, a key text of Jewish law and tradition; at any event its author described himself as 'Rabbi Zalman of Sant-Goar'. I am moved that there should have existed in the late Middle Ages such profound Jewish learning in such a small place. It testifies to something characteristic of Jewish life in the Diaspora, that Jews carried with them the culture of Torah, in manuscripts, but even more profoundly in memory, in traditions heard, absorbed and lived, and that wherever they found themselves they unfolded it around them, immersed themselves in it, and through their particular customs, interpretations and responses to new realities, preserved its vitality and carried it into the future.

The *Sefer Hamaharil* describes the religious rulings and practices of

Rabbi Yaakov Moellin (1365–1427). Through a chain of teachers and pupils it came to have a profound influence on Rabbi Moshe Isserles (c.1520–72), who used it as a key source in composing the *Mappah* with which he supplemented the *Shulchan Aruch*, the great code of law compiled by the Sephardic rabbi, legalist and mystic Joseph Caro, through the edition of glosses describing Ashkenazi, that is, central European, practices.

Referring to his own abilities with self-deprecating modesty, the author describes himself as *cherpat adam uvazui, mechuneh Zalman Misutigvera* – 'scorned of men and contemptible, known as Zalman of St Goar'. He writes that it had not been his intention to undertake the task of compiling this testament to his master and teacher, but many had pressed him to do so. They even took materials from him and copied them, thus forcing him to write this book. What truly qualifies him for the task, though, is his intimate knowledge of the great Rabbi Yaakov Moellin's teachings, especially the laws of the festivals, which he personally heard him rehearse in three seminal sermons each year.

❖ I've brought with me the short section from the *Sefer Hamaharil* on the laws of Chanukkah, the chapter which treats most obviously of the subject of light. On each of the eight evenings of this Festival of Light one further candle is lit on the Chanukkiah until on the last night there are eight in all. This recalls the Talmudic account of the miracle of the oil when the Maccabees rededicated the Temple after recapturing it from the Seleucid Greeks in the middle of the second century BCE. They found only sufficient oil in a state of ritual purity to burn on the Menorah for one single day but it miraculously lasted for eight. The Chanukkah lights are always kindled with a *shammash*, a servant candle, which isn't itself counted among the number for that particular night. One might have thought that this servant candle would then simply be blown out. But on the contrary, explains the *Sefer Maharil*, it is placed higher than the other candles because it has served them, and it is God's wish that 'the lowly should be set on high'.

I ponder this for a few moments at the close of my day's walking. Do we 'set the lowly on high'? Or do we effectively treat whole groups of people as merely there to work for us, forgetting that even in the smallest interactions they are to be honoured, their thoughts, feelings and labour respected and appreciated? I had never before bothered to think about what this elevation of the servant candle might mean.

I stare across the Rhine, fast moving, vast in the overcast late afternoon. Here, then, in some room lit by just such a modest flame Rabbi Zalman will have picked up his quill and written down those words, striving to remember exactly how his teacher had expressed them and upon which texts and precedents he had based them. Here in this tiny Rhine-side village Jewish culture was perpetuated with love and devotion, down to those minute details of rituals we still follow faithfully to this very day.

Later, we drive the short distance into Koblenz. The city is twinned with Petach Tikvah in central Israel. As it happens, pupils from the Israeli high school are visiting and Mitzpah and I are invited to join a delightful celebration for the staff and sixth formers of both institutions at a local college.

From Mitzpah's Blog

Daddy took me to a school and carried me on his shoulder to show me off to everyone. (Actually he told a big lie. He said that he and I had been walking together. It isn't true. I run ten times as far and as fast as he does.) There were school children there from both Israel and Germany and they were all really kind and friendly to each other and to me. For at least half an hour three of them tickled my tummy at the same time. I want to come back here very soon.

Daddy put a raisin bun down on the table. But I've been watching very carefully and I know he's been eating too much sugar, so I quickly gobbled it up. After all, I'm responsible for his health on this journey.

Speaking of health, each night he puts some horrible cream on my paws. I know he does it to make them feel better, but the taste is disgusting when I lick the stuff off, and I'm going to do so every time. So someone please tell him to stop.

PS Tomorrow is the eve of the Sabbath: do you think they have that delicious special bread we have at home here in Germany too?

Love, Mitzpah

Day Six – From Koblenz to Saffig

I lie on the earth,
I kneel
In the ring of my horizons,
And stretch my hands
With an entreaty
To the west, when the sun sets,
To the east, when it rises there,
To each spark
To show me the light
And give light to my eyes,
To each worm that glows in the darkness at night,
That it shall bring its wonder before my heart
And redeem the darkness that is enclosed in me.

Kadya Molodovsky: 'Prayers'[1]

The June following my walk I'm invited back to Germany, to a Church conference, the biennial Evangelische Kirchentag, which takes place this year in Dresden. Through the window of the hotel room I can see the night skyline of the city's famous domes and spires. How strange and haunting a beauty! Every one of these beautiful buildings was destroyed, and rebuilt after the war. The latest to be reopened is the remarkable Frauenkirche. A picture from the 1960s still shows cows grazing in front of the ruins; now the domed church is surrounded once again by busy alleyways and crowds queue up for guided tours. A poster invites the visitor to participate in a dawn contemplation in a room at the top of one of the towers at 6.30 in the morning. I'd like to attend. I've often found that the prayers of different faiths have a special power to awaken the heart with their unknown yet resonant liturgies.

I'm stirred by being in Germany again; I feel that I'm back on my journey. I look round involuntarily for Mitzpah, expecting him to be lying there asleep on the hitherto impeccably white duvet, just as he was every night while I walked home from Frankfurt. I'm sorry that on this occasion I haven't been able to bring him with me. There is a need for exploration which will not leave me alone; it has become part of my life's journey, not just through the different countries in which my family came to reside, but also across time, between the generations, my grandparents, parents and children. I realise that the purpose of my life is partly to span the gap between them. The light I aspire to carry will come to rest, more than anywhere else, in my children's hearts. The depth of this responsibility disturbs me and I pray that nothing I ever do may cause them hurt and that I may be given the grace to transmit the flame as wisdom and love.

*　　*　　*

❖　Mitzpah and I spend the night in Koblenz, the beautiful city where the Rhine and Mosel Rivers meet. I learn later that the name of the city is derived from the Latin for confluence, this having been an ancient Roman settlement. The next morning we set out early for the village of Saffig which has the smallest synagogue in Germany which still functions as a living community. My friend John is due to join me at some point during the day and I am looking forward to the moment when he calls me to say, 'I'm here; tell me exactly what path you're on so that I can meet up with you.' I'm only sorry that he isn't able to bring his own dog Pippin with him, a fellow border collie and a good friend of Mitzpah. But I find out later that he's left her with Nicky and the children who are delighted to have this replacement canine company. 'She trips along very daintily,' says Nicky over the phone, when, out walking with Pippin, she catches John and me strolling along with Mitzpah.

Meanwhile Saffig is at least twenty kilometres from Koblenz, assuming I don't get lost and choose reasonably direct paths, and I'm due there by one in the afternoon. I manage a prompt start and am soon walking along the banks of the Mosel, looking for the lane which should lead me to the first village on my route. But I soon become confused between the many turnings.

I go into a baker's shop to ask the way. 'I think that's the road you have to take;' just to make sure, the kind lady calls her friend over who helpfully observes: '*Ich denke, er soll in der anderen Richtung gehen* – I think he ought to go in the opposite direction.' I discover that it isn't necessarily wise to ask which way to go. In fact, it reminds me of what usually happens when you enquire, before starting prayers at a *Shivah* in a house of mourning, 'Which direction is east?' Almost without fail fingers are pointed towards at least three of the four points of the compass. By and large I manage to find my way today, and it's a complicated way at that, via four different villages, on paths and small country roads, to Saffig.

But the walk doesn't start well. The bridge I have to take across the Mosel proves much farther away than I had imagined. When it comes into view I realise that it is not a beautiful ancient footbridge but a major road link; Mitzpah and I walk along the edge of the traffic lane eager only to reach the far side as quickly and safely as possible and resume our riverside wanderings.

I get lost again in the many tiny streets of an extensive village and am grateful that Guy, Joe and Anna are driving alongside with their cameras and rescue me with their sat-nav. Incidentally, Mitzpah finds it strange that a car with friends in it should stop periodically next to him and keeps wanting to jump in. I suggest they hang a string of sausages out of the window, rather than a camera, and see what happens then.

The best incident, and one which Mitzpah, who is not especially observant as dogs go, totally failed to notice, occurred yesterday as we were walking through a small town. A cat was sitting in a shop window and took offence at the notion of a dog passing by outside. She jumped hissing towards the glass, showing off her teeth and claws. Out of all possible feline attire she might have worn, she was adorned with a cross on a chain around her neck. It was too good a moment not to record on film. 'Let's try walking past again and see if the cat does it a second time,' suggested Guy. The animal duly obliged. This constitutes the sole moment of overt hostility I have so far encountered in Germany.

Outside the village the road narrows to a track which eventually becomes a footpath. We pass through orchards, fully grown and newly planted apple trees, cherries, pears and plums. One field is full of pumpkins and gourds; the greenery has been killed off by an October frost leaving the fruits lying on the ground where they have grown, red, yellow, amber and green. Another area is planted with rows of gooseberries and blackberries; a pity, I comment to Mitzpah, that we're travelling this way so late in the season.

A warm greeting awaits us outside the small synagogue in Saffig. The sound of running water soothes our tired bodies; Mitzpah puts his head down and drinks. We'd walked almost five hours with only two brief pauses. Dr Ries, the leader of the community, introduces me to the mayor and the Catholic priest.

Above the door of the synagogue are written the words from the Psalms: 'This is the gateway to the Lord, let the righteous enter in.' Next to the Hebrew the same text is inscribed in German. To one side and also in German is a translation of the Shema, 'Hear, O Israel, the Lord our God, the Lord is one.' This is followed by a memorial dedicated in the name of all the people of the village to its Jewish inhabitants who fled or perished during the Nazi years. Here had lived a community of some thirty or more families, over eighty individuals. Most managed to escape; seven are known to have been killed. The synagogue, scarcely bigger than a large room, though greater in height and beautiful in proportion, had been damaged on Kristallnacht but not destroyed.

As we stood by the synagogue door the priest drew me to one side. 'We need Jewish–Christian dialogue in this country,' he said. 'We miss it and we badly need it. I mean real theological discussion. What goes on today is all about Israel and politics and isn't helpful. That's not what I have in mind; we require genuine Jewish–Christian theological debate.' I was otherwise preoccupied and it didn't occur to me at the time to question him more deeply about what he meant. With one part of myself I may half have thought, 'They expelled most of the Jews from here and killed all the rest; and now people miss the conversation.' But that would have been unfair. We want engagement here, the priest was saying, and it's of serious importance to us both.

*   *   *

The *Evangelischer Kirchentag* in Dresden offers me the chance of participating in just such a theological conversation. It is exactly the kind of context which my grandfather so much valued, and in which my teacher of Jewish history and theology Rabbi Dr Albert Friedlander took such a leading role. It allows me to deepen my inner engagement with the history of my family and with the German–Jewish encounter overall. Here was a relationship torn apart and abandoned, and its wounds were calling to me to come back and examine them. It was an unfinished relationship, for not only among the dead but in countless living memories lay knowledge which had to be brought to light and from which we needed to learn. Job's cry was reaching me: '*Eretz al techasi dami* – earth do not conceal my blood,' words which had been scratched and daubed on to the walls of the torture cells of Europe with stones, nails and blood. That blood was still pleading with us to listen to it today.

*   *   *

❖   We enter the small synagogue. The vault of the high ceiling, the simple design of the walls and windows, moves me at once. The place where the Ark, destroyed in the November pogrom, had stood is left empty; a menorah has been placed there as a memorial. The new Ark is set to one side. The *Ner Tamid* is a small simple lamp of metal and glass; it is absolutely beautiful.

We've only been in the synagogue for a few minutes when the door opens and there stands John. He is as delighted to see me as I am him and instantly takes Mitzpah in his arms, lifts him up and spins round with him in great affection. I'm relieved to the point of tears. I cannot explain why; maybe I've been feeling more alone inside than I've allowed myself to realise, but I know that with John's trusted companionship I will be safe. I don't mean 'safe' in any physical sense; I've encountered only respect and friendliness in Germany so far. I mean 'safe' in a moral sense, safe in exploring this encounter with an unthinkable past in a manner which is neither unreflectively vindictive nor inadequately critical and over-readily accepting. I feel now that I will neither betray the present through a punitive unwillingness to allow the past to be gone, nor that same past through a heartless unpreparedness to listen to its echoes and read the signs of the terrors which it wrought.

I know very few people whose moral judgment I so deeply and implicitly trust. John grew up in South Africa in a Jewish family of Lithuanian origin. He was imprisoned under the Apartheid regime for his friendship with black poets. He was tortured and did not imagine he would escape with his life; every dawn fellow prisoners were led out for execution. After several months he was taken to the airport and told never to return. Since then he has become a therapist of international renown. Much of his life is devoted to supporting victims of torture and to fighting for the right, enshrined in the United Nations convention on refugees, of those fleeing persecution to remain in an often cold and heartless Britain.

Dr Ries stands at the *bimah* and sings. This melody to the 23rd Psalm is unfamiliar; I listen carefully to every syllable. He will sing it again on Sunday at the rededication of a small country synagogue halfway between Koblenz and Trier. Friends of his, from what I understand not Jewish, have worked on its restoration for many years, re-glazing the windows, recreating the interior in patient and enduring acts of reparation and devotion. Unfortunately it is too far out of my way and sadly I won't be able to attend.

Dr Ries now shows us a facsimile of one of the most famous of all Jewish prayer books, the *Worms Machzor*. The colophon tells us that it was 'Written by Simchah bar Yehudah for my uncle Baruch bar Yitzhak'. The work, or at least part of it, wasn't in fact undertaken in Worms but in Wurzburg, in 1272. We look together at texts deeply familiar to Dr Ries, a scholar of Hebrew calligraphy, epigraphy and music – poems for Shabbat Shekalim, one of the special Sabbaths in the weeks preceding Passover, and *Tefillat Tal*, the prayer for dew, recited on the first day of that festival, sections of the liturgy often neglected today, together with all the history they contain. The volume is exquisitely beautiful. He has brought it here specially to show it to us, a unique and precious treasure redeemed from the past.

He tells us the story of the *Machzor*. I may have misunderstood him, but this is how I recall what he said. Sometime before Kristall-nacht, when the synagogue in Worms was destroyed, the *Machzor*, one of the most precious Jewish manuscripts in existence, was seized by the Gestapo and taken from the city to Darmstadt. It was smuggled out of the cellars by Dr Friedrich Illert, the curator of the Municipal Museum of Worms, who had been sent there to work on the classification of confiscated documents. At the risk of his life he brought the two heavy volumes back to Worms. Here, a minister in the Cathedral, the *Domprobst*, hid them in one of the towers until the eventual arrival of the American army, when Dr Illert returned them to the accompanying Jewish chaplain.

In the car Dr Ries tells us about the experiences of his own family under the Nazis (his father was Jewish and his mother Catholic): flight, hiding, uncertainty, separations. It was only after the war that it became important to his father that he and his son engage with Judaism. Dr Ries's own attachment to the faith deepened as a result of his love of music. John relayed to me afterwards how he had told him over dinner that sitting alone in the Cathedral playing the organ he had come to feel that his spiritual home lay in Judaism, and he had made himself fully a member of the Jewish people. I am moved by his humanity, scholarship and dedication.

About a month after my return from Germany I found myself sitting at a Chanukkah celebration next to Professor Marc Sapperstein, Principal of the Leo Baeck College for the training of rabbis in London. 'I thought I heard you mention the Worms *Machzor* when you spoke about your walk,' he said. I nodded. The professor then proceeded to tell me how his father, Rabbi Harold Sapperstein, had been a chaplain with the American Forces during the war and was briefly stationed in Worms. One of his first concerns on entering the city was the fate of the synagogue and the graveyard. The former lay in ruins; it had been burnt on Kristallnacht and then dynamited for three successive days.

But the graveyard had escaped desecration. Shortly before the Germans left the town in the spring of 1945, when the Allies were already across the Rhine, the order had been received to destroy it. But the local commander courageously claimed that he had superior instructions directly from Himmler not to damage this ancient historical site. As a result the graveyard survived the war intact.

Professor Sapperstein continued that his father's next question concerned the fate of the famous *Machzor*. It was pointless asking; it had surely been burnt. Nevertheless he made enquiries. They soon led him to Dr Illert who at once informed him that the *Machzor* had been saved. Later he wrote an account of his momentous discovery.

> Dr Illert explained that he had a 'premonition' that a 'spontaneous' attack would be made upon the synagogue, so he removed the *Machzor* and placed it in safe-keeping. Then he brought us down into the darkened basement of the Municipal Hall where the town archives were kept, and he placed in our hands the two heavy volumes that make up the priceless work.
>
> That night we could not sleep. Since electric power in the town had been knocked out, we sat studying them till morning by the light of candles, really more fitting anyway. The writing was still in excellent condition, the coloured illumination still clear and beautiful. The pages were stained with age, and perhaps even with blood. As we turned them, we thought of the generations of scholars who must [also] have turned the pages of this *Machzor*.[2]

This then was the other half of the story I had first heard in that tiny synagogue in Saffig where Dr Ries had shown John and me the facsimile. It seems to me, though I may have misremembered what I was told, that the two accounts of how Dr Illert saved the *Machzor* don't entirely tally, but I'm as much interested in and moved by how the event is recalled as in what precisely occurred.[3]

Listening to Professor Sapperstein, there came into my mind the image of a modest brown parcel I had received from Catholic friends in Germany many years earlier. It contained a series of very small silver cups engraved with the design of a tiny house or hut which could even have been a Succah, a booth with a roof of leaves and branches made for the Feast of Tabernacles. Accompanying them was a note; its content, as I remember, went something like this:

> My father served on the Eastern Front. One day he developed tooth-ache; the army dentist told him to find some silver or gold and he would cap the tooth. He bought these cups in the market in Kiev. In the event they were never used; he had the dental work done during a furlough back home in Germany. Later, he wanted to have the cups melted down to re-use the silver, but they are very beautiful and the entire family objected. My father is no longer alive now and I think it's time these goblets are returned to the people to whom they belong.

For weeks I debated in my mind whether or not it was right to use them to make Kiddush, the blessings over wine with which the Sabbath and festivals are sanctified. Where had they come from? Were they in fact Jewish ritual objects at all? What about the owners from whom they had been stolen, and who had almost certainly been murdered? Then I recalled the deeper meaning of the Hebrew word *lekaddesh*, to sanctify God both in life and through and beyond death. On the following Friday night I filled the cups with wine and said the blessings.

John and I had dinner with Dr Kahn and his wife, the head of the Jewish community of Koblenz, and with Dr and Mrs Ries. Over the course of the long, slow meal Dr Khan kindly told me his story. His wife, who had survived Theresienstadt together with her parents, leant over from time to time to say that he should 'let the man eat his dinner'. But I was completely engaged in listening. I couldn't follow all the details of the numerous adventures, swift decisions, fortuitous circum-stances and deft adaptations which Dr Kahn described. But I shall never forget how in between relating these appalling memories he would periodically lean back and chuckle and look at me with a huge smile. He was a man who had understood the art of survival or, at least, whatever art there could be which might contribute favourably to the improbable chance of emerging from the death camps alive. He recounted numerous split-second choices – not to join a group, to board a train through this particular door, not to take a certain route. Then he would turn to me with that laughing smile before continuing with the next twist in his extraordinary story. 'Did you come across Primo Levi at Auschwitz?' John asked him, prompted by a reference to Italians at the camp. 'Of course I knew him,' Dr Kahn replied. 'He was my friend,'

I felt completely bewildered; I was quite unable to connect Dr Kahn's manner in the recounting of his story with the content of what he was recalling; it was almost as if it had all happened to someone else. How was it possible to share such terrible memories, and pause in the middle and smile as he had done?

Afterwards John and I wandered along the banks of the Rhine for a long time.

❖   Mitzpah evidently did receive some challah that Friday night, or at least the nearest equivalent I could find, because he reports no complaints. In fact his blog for this date records nothing whatsoever. Bless him, he must be a more scrupulous hound than I had previously credited him with being, since he refused to commit the dire trespass of writing on the holy day of rest. The Torah only mentions that your ox and ass should have repose on the Sabbath, but had it envisaged the close companionship which would come to evolve between dogs and humans it would surely have included them in its directives.

Shabbat in Koblenz

❖   The next morning I manage to get us thoroughly lost, even with a map in my hand, although I'd walked along these same streets the previous day and found my way perfectly well. When we finally reach the Mosel I say to John that it's still a long walk along its banks to the synagogue, then look up and see a Star of David on top of the building right next to us. The Lord must have guided our footsteps; we've ended up exactly in front of synagogue. 'What, so late?' says the *shammes*, the sexton, whom I'd met previously at an earlier event in the city. 'We got lost,' I explain and resolve to have more sympathy for latecomers to religious services in my own community in the future.

A man gets up and explains in German and Russian how moved he is by the Torah scroll used here for the first time this morning. If I understand correctly, it had been hidden at great risk in the Soviet Union and then brought with much difficulty back to Germany. John and I are equally stirred by this love of Torah, this courage and determination.

The Ark is opened for Anim Zemirot and I comment to John that this mystical hymn was composed in Germany, probably not far from where we now are. I am suddenly gripped by an unexpected feeling of being deeply rooted in this place. Only this morning over breakfast I had read further in the *Sefer Hamaharil*; the notes referred repeatedly to Minhag HaRhinus, the religious custom in the Rhine lands. This is a region of ancient and long-standing Jewish learning and devotion. There have been over a thousand years of Jewish history and creativity here. It passed through my mind that the same could scarcely be said about London. I had not expected to experience such an intense feeling of Jewish depth and connection in Germany, of all places.

In the evening just before the close of Shabbat I step out of the hotel and discover two *Stolpersteine* beneath the autumn leaves. I squat down and study the inscriptions:

Born 1889; deported 1942 to Ishbiza; murdered, Sobibor.

These *Steine* are a permanent invitation to memory, as Markus Roentgen so powerfully writes: 'They are names, people, irreplaceable – the amorphous stone waits to be inhabited by an observer who will so thoroughly recall into memory a human being, a member of the Jewish community of 1933–41, that he or she can no longer fall back into the abyss of namelessness or be finally and utterly destroyed.'[1]

It seems as if the very building in which we've been staying belonged to the Jewish family memorialised here. Some seventy years after they'd been taken from their apartment, the home in which they had in all likelihood felt safe against the world for many years, John and I have, for all we know, made Kiddush and sung the Kabbalat Shabbat service in their living-room.

*   *   *

Seven months later I stand in a memorial gathering before the opening of the Kirchentag in Dresden. One hundred and twenty thousand people will be coming to the city over the following days to participate in an immense range of lectures, discussions, prayer meetings, encounters and musical events. Two or three thousand of them are assembled in the large open space of the Altmarkt to share in this commemoration. The theme is stones; we are each asked to pick up a stone and take it with us as we process in silence through the town to the synagogue, rebuilt on the same site on which it had formerly stood. A large screen carries the text of a plaque installed in the Kreuzkirche, the oldest church in Dresden, in 1988:

> We were silent when their Houses of God were burnt;
> when the Jews were stripped of their rights, murdered
> > and driven out.
> We failed to recognise in them our own brothers and sisters.
> We ask for pardon and for shalom, for peace.

There follows a meditation on the nature of stones, hearts turned to stone, memorial stones, stones which offer testimony, the weight of stones of guilt. 'Who will remove the stones from my soul?' a young girl reads. I move away, seeking a private corner, shaken by the whole event. As I make my way to the side of the crowd I catch the words of another speaker, telling in brief the history of the Jews of the town: 'In 1349 Jews were burnt here in the Altmarkt; they were blamed for the Black Death.' Turning aside, I notice the inscription on the low concrete wall now in front of me: 'This is a place of admonishment, memory and reflection. Here were burnt the bodies of thousands of victims of the air raids of the 13th and 14th of February 1945. On those days the horrors of war, taken forth by Germany across the entire world, came back to our own town.'

I recall the words my grandfather overheard as he walked through the crowds in the Börneplatz after Kristallnacht, '*Das wird sich rächen* – This will be avenged.' Later I read in a history of the Dresden synagogue, burnt down almost a century to the day after it was first dedicated, its ruins dynamited and its stones used to make roads so that within a month of its destruction there was scarcely a sign that it had ever existed, that a man standing in the crowds watching on the following morning of 10 November said: 'This fire will return. It will travel in a great circle and make its way back to us.'[2]

My thoughts go to the pictures I've seen of Dresden after the Allied bombings, of the smoke rising from the piles of corpses brought to the very spot where I am now standing. Although Goebbels promptly added a nought to the figures for propaganda purposes and the numbers remained in dispute for many years, it is now widely agreed that the death toll on those terrible February nights amounted to approximately twenty-five thousand people. Town officials apparently arranged for personnel experienced in the incineration of large masses of bodies to be brought from Auschwitz-Birkenau. Victor Klemperer and his wife tried with thousands of others to escape from the burning ruins of the city:

The dead were strewn across their path: often just a pitiful bundle of clothes. The skull of one corpse had been ripped away and the top of the head was a red bowl. A severed arm with a fine, pale hand lay on the ground. It reminded Klemperer of a wax model from a barber's window.[3]

'We didn't recognise in them our own brothers and sisters': the words remain with me. No, it's not the same; contrary to the claim of the far right neo-fascists who gather in Dresden every February, this wasn't the 'Allied Holocaust', nor was there any such thing. But how many of us, in how many countries across the face of the earth, should inscribe those words on our hearts, 'We didn't recognise our own brothers and sisters'?

Later that night thousands of people gather on either side of the Elbe. Young people stand on the bridges offering the cheerful columns filing by – school friends, youth groups, musicians, food vendors – tall white candles. '*Hast du schon eine Kerze?* Have you got your candle yet?' One girl with a sweet face insists on a hug from everyone who passes by; she is justified in feeling safe here.

Darkness comes and thousands line the walkways on either bank of the river; for hundreds of metres, on the bridges, on the terraces of museums and restaurants, down to the water's muddy edge itself, are the quiet flames of burning candles. Then, as a choir sings from downriver, thousands more lights pass floating by on the water, red and white, like souls in a long procession, neither fast nor slow, borne gently on the current. Is the idea that there should be one candle for every human being who perished here in the Holocaust and in the terrifying raids of February 1945? On those nights, recalled Victor Klemperer, ragged and bewildered crowds moved silently by on either side of the Elbe, some pushing carts with the meagre remains of their possessions. Is this commemoration? Is it atonement? It seems as if the entire city is standing in quiet, humble vigil.

Prayers are led over loudspeakers. 'We have met one another and found pleasure in our encounter. Now darkness has fallen. Let us close with the words of the 121st Psalm: God bless the inhabitants of this town and all its guests. God guard your heart and your soul. God protect your coming in and your setting forth, from this time onwards and for evermore. Amen. Good-night.'

I have never participated in anything quite like this in all my life and doubt I ever again shall.

* * *

After the close of Shabbat, John, Mitzpah and I are given a lift by my long-standing friend Gudrun Hörner to the monastery of Maria Laach.

Pater Viktor speaks perfect English with an Oxford accent. He greets me with the utmost friendliness and leads me along corridors and through doorways, past crosses and pictures of the Virgin Mary, till I think that I'll never find my way out again. 'Would you like me to show you the way back?' he asks, perceiving my bewilderment. 'Yes please!' Pater Viktor, one of the monks responsible for the care of visitors and pilgrims, is an old hand at this art of hospitality. Mitzpah follows cheerfully enough, though he feels a bit restless later. Grateful that the welcome extends to quadrupeds, I comment that in former days pilgrims must have arrived with their donkeys and horses, maybe even with dogs as well. The monastery must presumably have been equipped accordingly. Pater Viktor nods; I have visions of donkeys being led to stables and horses stalled with straw and oats.

John and I and my friend Mrs Hörner are given the most cordial welcome. Her generosity once again overwhelms me: there are three carrier bags in the corner of the room filled with food for the film crew and me, and another entirely full of dog food because it's the holiday of Alle Heiligen in Germany on Monday and for the next two days all the shops will be closed.

The chambers to which I'm shown scarcely fit my preconceptions of the monastic cell. I'd imagined a simple room with a table, a chair, a bed, a jug of water and a Bible. I guess the rigours of monastic discipline aren't applied to guests like me. Instead I'm shown to a huge suite of rooms: an ante-chamber leads into a vast sitting-room with sofa, writing desk, library, easy chairs, all made of beautiful woods and spaciously arranged, while next door is a bedroom (the bed soon sampled by Mitzpah) with its own selection of religious books and German classics. There are crosses on the wall before me and to the side, while a large cross is positioned above the bed.

I cannot but confront the issue of what this means to me, and I discuss it over dinner with the Prior.

What does the cross signify to a Jew like me? I cannot resolve this matter easily and the question stays with me, but not with the same intensity as at this moment, where I see it all around me. I feel at once grateful for the hospitality extended to me, and uneasy. I'm glad of Mitzpah's company; without it I might not be able to sleep. It is, as I explain to the Prior over bread, cheese and salad, deeply important to me to come here. The lamps of our own different faiths will only bring a limited illumination to the world if they are darkened by a lack of understanding, warmth and active cooperation between our religions.

But still – I am a Jew who loves his Judaism. So what of the cross? My first thought is that it is a Roman instrument of torture. I recall my grandfather explaining how the streets of ancient Israel were at times lined with people punished in this shocking and appalling way, many Jews besides Jesus the Jew. But there can be no evasion of the fact that the cross is the pre-eminent symbol of Christianity. I explain to the Prior that I cannot, as no Jew can, see in it the suffering of the divine son of God. But it is not difficult to translate the image into that of suffering humanity and to appreciate that wherever God's creatures suffer, there God must be suffering too. John, who has worked so long with the victims of persecution and violence, observes as we pass these many crosses that he is puzzled as to how one can find the godly in such a picture of torture. But what we can all see in it is the image of intense sorrow and pain.

The theoretical concerns of theology are one matter, but the stark historical reality is quite another. The cross has often brought misery and death to the Jews, in the Crusades, at the Inquisition, in the blood libels and accusations of poisoning wells, tormenting the host and causing the Black Death, in the complex and entangled relationship between the Church, in many periods of its history and in numerous places, and anti-Semitism, up to and including the Holocaust.

But, I remind myself, the cross has also at times brought life. Jews were sometimes hidden in monasteries and convents; there were priests who saved lives; Jewish parents, despairing of any hope for the survival of their children, deposited them with nuns and monks. I recall my grandfather's friend, the minister and writer Albrecht Goes, and his stirring essays on what must be learnt from Judaism, and I think of many friendships of my own.

*   *   *

I sit in Dresden and reread these words with complicated feelings. Yesterday I was part of a three-hour symposium on the theme of *Versöhnung*, reconciliation. It was followed by an almost equally lengthy debate on the history of Jewish–Christian relations in Germany since the Holocaust. Free from the worry during the latter discussion of how to make my own contributions in clear and unhesitating German, I listened intently to every word:

> It began with a few courageous individuals, Jewish leaders who emerged among the survivors, members of the Confessing Church returning from labour camps, political refugees come back home after the end of the war. It grew out of the personal relationships forged between them; they needed each other in the ever hostile environment of those postwar years when former Nazis retained their posts in the judiciary, academia, schools. The issues had to be faced: a thousand years of anti-Semitic teaching by the Church, of marginalisation, exile, persecution and the burning of Jews had now led to the worst mass murders in history. What was needed was a completely new Christian theology. The classic Christian under-standing that the covenant between God and the Jews was broken for ever and that God had established a new and enduring bond with the Church, a view visible across Europe in the iconography of the *Ecclesia* as the young bride and the *Synagoga* as the bent, blind and abandoned old woman, had to be refuted. The eternity of the unbroken relationship between God and Israel had to be affirmed. The Church had to cease teaching that the Jews killed Jesus; the death-sentence was passed by a Roman tribunal. Whoever henceforth claimed that the Old Testament existed only to pre-figure the New, or who supported the mission to convert the Jews, was preaching a pre-Auschwitz theology. The real breakthrough came with the reform of the school books . . .

The enormity of these issues overwhelmed me. And I'd been sitting there as if it should have been taken for granted that at a major Church event Jews would be invited to engage in free, open, unprejudiced, equal dialogue. Well of course they should be, but it could scarcely be taken as a given that such an opportunity would be created here in Germany. I was moved by the depth and courage of this achievement.

I could not help but return to the subject of the cross, so often and over so many centuries the symbol of scorn and contempt for the Jews. To me and many others it has come to represent the death not of one Jew, but of millions. Yet could it not at the same time mean something entirely different: our shared, universal horror before cruelty, our abhorrence at causing other human beings pain, our pity and anguish in the presence of suffering?

What, then, of *Versöhnung*, atonement, reconciliation? During my turn on the platform I was asked if it was right to connect it, as is so often done, with *Vergessen und Vergeben*, forgiving and forgetting. No, I argued; forgetting is precisely the opposite of reconciliation, which must be founded on repentance and which must therefore begin with remembering, with the honest recognition of what we have done. The value of reconciliation lies not in piecing relationships back together into some false whole, but rather in learning from the past and using that learning for the sake of the future.

During the discussion I acquired two new German words: *Versöhnungsromantik* and *Versöhnungskitsch*, roughly translatable as 'sentimentality about reconciliation' and 'junk about reconciliation'. I have encountered both phenomena and found them deeply upsetting and annoying. I remember some years ago bridling in public at the seemingly well-intentioned question, 'Isn't it time that you forgave the Holocaust?' with the unspoken implication that in such matters as forgiveness Christianity had a superior ethic to that stubborn old Judaism with its God of justice and revenge. I was glad to be provided with a vocabulary with which to describe such insensitive and ignorant naivety. A person who spoke in that manner was not further advanced but rather well behind on the road to understanding and needed to be helped to see the signposts marking the beginning of the long and challenging path toward reconciliation.

Still on the platform, I continued: 'However, one cannot vicariously grant forgiveness to those who hurt not oneself but someone else; only those who have suffered the offence can be party to any kind of reconciliation or atonement for it.'

(On reflection I find myself partially disagreeing with what I said then. It is true of forgiveness but not necessarily of reconciliation. The latter can be effected by later generations; we can come together one, two or even more generations after terrible events to learn from the past. Whether we are children of survivors or children of perpetrators, it is precisely by neither blaming nor being afraid of each other that we can, with the gifts of courage, honestly and humility, listen to one another and, specifically because of what our ancestors did or went through, use what we learn to work in an especially compelling and committed way towards a deeper and more universal humanity. In general I find the whole question of forgiveness less important than the key issue of what understanding we can gain from the past so as to behave differently in the future. The former mainly concerns the bad conscience of the perpetrators; the latter will determine the future of humanity.)

I added that just as present generations cannot grant pardon for sins commit by past generations, so they cannot hold those guilty who were not alive at the time. That too would be a form of oppression. 'I don't entirely agree,' argued one of my Christian interlocutors. 'To be the descendant of perpetrators is clearly not the same as to commit the offence oneself, but it doesn't leave one free of responsibility either. It's like moving into a house in which grievous wrongs have been committed. When one becomes the owner of the house, one cannot consider oneself disassociated from the actions which were executed there.' I ponder this comment for many days. Is there such a thing as inherited responsibility? Can we be born into an inter-generational bad debt of conscience? Or are we only ever responsible for what we ourselves do, or allow to be done in our name, while what we inherit is the tortured, complex and self-concealing reality in which we have to live? Or does it depend partly on us: the more of an individualist we are, the less we experience the burden of the past, whereas the more deeply we identify with our people, the more we feel implicated in what they have done? Or maybe even asking the question provides its own answer: we are never free from the burdens, and blessings, of history.

*   *   *

121

❖ 'How will you sleep tonight?' Guy asks me. 'What do you think you'll dream about?' There is a large cross above the bed where, mercifully, Mitzpah is happily curled up on the blankets.

I don't answer Guy's question. But I'm glad to be here; it matters to me to be here. I have been given an exceptionally kind welcome, and with a film crew (by now I simply think of them as friends who are sharing the adventure) on my tail, I'm scarcely an unobtrusive guest. I'm here because of our shared humanity, our shared search for good, our need to understand and support one another on this path, which is after all, however we may articulate it differently in the various languages of our particular symbols, the same journey towards the discovery of our true humanity and of God.

Over supper the Prior speaks of new Christian understandings of the Hebrew Bible, of reading it within its own autonomy, as part of its own tradition, not as a precursor to Christianity. The conversation is convivial and good-humoured. Mitzpah sleeps – until Guy asks me to ask the Prior what he thinks the company of the dog will add to my journey. (You can't ask that, I tell Guy, without translating my own comments into German.) But the Prior's reply is spot-on: 'It reminds us of what our religion has too often forgotten by placing man at the centre of the universe. All of nature and the whole of the world belong to God.'

From Mitzpah's Blog

Today I found a bun in the street and ate it in one mouthful while no one was looking. This morning we went to shul. I had to wait as usual but the service was a lot shorter than it is at home. I think that's a good idea. I expect God finds long prayers boring too.

Tonight we're sleeping in a monastery. I've never been in one before. The monks wear long black cloaks with hoods and are very friendly. Daddy says that we have to eat in silence and that I mustn't bark during mealtimes. I'll try to do what I'm told.

I've been looking around our bedroom. We don't have pictures like those on the walls of our house back in London. At home we don't have any of those statues either. Most of them have got this man in them and they're doing something to him which looks very painful. I don't think dogs would ever treat another dog like that.

There's a nice rug next to the bed and I had thought I'd sleep there, but daddy seems to need me to curl up on the bed, so I'd better do as expected.

Mitzpah

Day Eight – From Maria Laach to Remagen

In March of the following year, when we were finally able to establish the date on which we could move into our new building without any serious risk of further delays due to late snow, unexpected electrical problems or general snagging, I wrote to the Prior and Pater Victor to invite them to attend the ceremony of the lighting of our new *Ner Tamid*. A few days later I received a charming postcard with a regretful apology and the following greeting:

> We would like to conclude with the lines of an enthralling aria from the famous oratorio *Judas Maccabaeus* by Handel, with its libretto by Thomas Morell:
>
> > Father of Heaven! From thy eternal throne
> > Look with an eye of blessing down,
> > While we prepare with holy rites
> > To solemnise the Feast of Lights.
> > And thus our grateful hearts employ;
> > And in thy praise
> > This altar raise
> > With carols of triumphant joy.
>
> May this blessing and joy flow for ever from the Eternal Lamp which Jewish tradition is to mankind.
> With warm greetings, yours cordially,
>
> > Pater Petrus, Prior, and Pater Viktor

The picture on the card is of one of the stained-glass windows of St Stefan's Church in Mainz, created by Marc Chagall in the closing years of his life: an angel reading a book is flying over a candelabrum below which sits a man in studious contemplation of a religious text. The work is an illustration of the words from Psalm 119, one of my favourite verses: 'A lamp unto my foot is thy word, a light upon my path.'

I'm touched and humbled by the sensitivity and generosity of spirit of this gift.

*　　*　　*

❖ I wake up and see the torch of the *Ner Tamid* shining where I had left it in front of me the night before; I turn round and look at the cross on the wall behind me. Mitzpah is curled up on the blanket by my feet.

We go outside together; it's just after seven and people are coming to pray. Rain falls heavily for the first time since I set out; maybe it'll clear by later in the morning, but if not, *kadimah*, onwards, anyway. I have three quarters of an hour before Pater Viktor comes to take me to breakfast and a meeting with some of the monks, so I go back inside and for the first time use his towel to rub Mitzpah dry. He loves this ritual and even agrees to lift his paws so that I can clean off the mud. I then carefully spread the towel out on the bed and the dog duly makes himself comfortable.

Pater Viktor comes to collect me. He tells me that the monastery kitchen has already phoned him asking, 'What does your rabbit eat in the mornings?' I reassure him that it's not the first time a misused spellcheck or unfortunate error has given me long ears. Unable to contain their curiosity the kitchen staff had further enquired if 'he's like they are in Anatevka?' That, I'm afraid, I cannot answer. As we walk down the long corridors we discuss how to continue and develop the connection between us.

I shall be sorry to leave here without more time to listen and talk. I value genuine inter-faith meetings, especially when coupled with humour, conviviality and heartfelt engagement. They teach me three things: I learn about the other person and what matters to him or her; I learn about myself, because there is nothing like the encounter with those whose religion is different to make one realise what is truly important in one's own tradition; and I gain a clearer focus on the essential values we hold in common. These invariably go straight to the heart: standing before God, struggling to be humane, kind and honest, and loving and respecting life in all its forms.

John, Mitzpah and I walk on together; a rainy dawn turns into a radiant autumn day. John points out the hornbeam trees, among his favourites. The wood, he observes, is so hard that it's used to make the small parts of pianos. If I could, I would have taken a fallen branch home for my son Mossy who's become an expert at wood turning. The colours of the leaves are stunning. The monastery of Maria Laach sits next to a high mountain lake which fills the crater of a former volcano. A ring of autumn gold surrounds a circle of bright blue.

We continue our conversation about the cross. John comments that one of the ways to think about it is as an expression of humility. The monks we met, their welcome towards us as open and professing Jews, their interest in engaging in discussion, represent an openness and humility which offers the possibility of developing new trust after all that has passed. When Rabbi David Lazar joins us later in the afternoon, having travelled specially from Sweden, he asks me whether I would expect Christians visiting the synagogue to conceal their crosses. 'No,' I answer. 'Just as I wouldn't anticipate having to hide my skullcap in a church.' He agrees. He experiences a beauty in being able to express and honour differences.

Our route takes us over hills and through villages to a final escarpment from where we have a view back down to the Rhine. Our path then narrows to descend sharply through the forest into the small town of Bad Breisig. Mitzpah runs merrily ahead, free from the fear of traffic and the constraints of his lead. He's loving every moment. Only later, as we walk swiftly along the Rhine through the dusk, he suddenly vanishes. I'm used to his disappearances: he's up ahead investigating, turning circles round an imaginary flock of sheep or hiding behind a tree, only to jump out a moment before we pass. But he always comes back within a minute or two of my calling. Not this time however. Mercifully he has quite a lot of white in his fur, not to mention the tip of his tail, so he's never entirely invisible in the dark. We call and call, but no Mitzpah appears. I begin to feel anxious. John agrees that we need to go back to look for him. But he has a train to catch at the next town of Sinzig so he proceeds apace while David and I turn round and begin our search. By now I'm seriously worried. But within seconds John hails us; there is Mitzpah, eager as ever, trying to explain that curiosity had got the better of him and all that he had done was to run half a mile ahead.

Once again I realise that, as much as I look after the dog, the dog also looks after me.

Darkness overtakes us on the path by the Rhine; we cannot find the road which leads into the town of Sinzig and the station where John has to catch his train back to the airport in Cologne. We walk ever faster, led by an intuition which fortunately guides us in the right direction. Eventually a long bridge takes us over the motorway and the railway lines, which we follow until we reach the station. Guy, Joe and Anna are waiting for us; they want to film John leaving. 'You stay with Anna while we go up to the platform,' says Guy to David; there are a couple of gangs hanging around the car park and underpass, and the place feels angry and unsafe.

I'm sad to watch John go; our partnership over the last three days is a testament to over twenty-five years of friendship, a bond sealed by the sharing of many of our deepest preoccupations – how the Holocaust has affected our families, the concern for human dignity and the struggle against cruelty, what the soul is and how to deepen our spiritual life. I feel more vulnerable without him.

The second he has gone a huge freight train hurtles screaming past the platform. I grab Mitzpah by the collar and hold him tight; something sinister and violent haunts the darkness round this station. I see in the dim light haggard figures of Jews with battered bags, a fleck of brightness, the yellow star, below the shoulder of their tattered coats, watching, waiting, on this same platform. I need to go.

We drive to Remagen. Tonight there are no meetings (almost the only such evening on this walk) so the five of us go out for dinner. I had asked David to bring rabbinic texts about light so that we could study them together. He speaks about the compelling nature of light, why it is that we are drawn to candles and find them romantic and appealing, why we love the dawn and the dusk. He opens with the verse from

Proverbs (20:27): 'A candle of the Lord is the human soul, searching all the inner chambers of the body,' then follows with this Midrashic amplification:

> Bar Kappara opened his discourse: 'For you shall illumine my lamp.'
> The Holy Blessed One said to Adam: 'Your lamp is in my
> hands and my lamp is in your hands.'
> 'Your lamp is in my hands' (as it is written). 'The lamp of the
> Lord is the human soul.'
> 'My lamp is in your hands' (as it is written). 'To cause an
> eternal light to ascend.'
> The Holy Blessed One said: 'If you have lit my lamp, then
> I shall light your lamp.'[1]

We debate whether this theology of mutuality, that we need God, but that God also needs us, might lead to arrogance, as if we were equals. I argue that it doesn't, for what is the meaning of God's light being in my hands? – Only the awareness that in this material world the responsibility for carrying out God's will lies within my power. How else is justice to be done and compassion shown, if not through human action? The realisation of God's dreams lies with us. This chastening thought requires us to cleanse ourselves so that we don't obscure God's light.

I call home that night, as I do at least twice each day. I also speak to Isca and my brother: our aunt, Isca's sister, has just had a major stroke. I wonder if I should come back home, but they tell me not to abandon my walk. She's in hospital and hasn't regained consciousness; even if I did come back to London there would be nothing I could do. So I phone frequently and think about my aunt's life as I walk through the land of her birth.

Her name is Ruth but we all call her Dodel; it's what we've always called her since I can first remember. We say it's a name she chose for herself, but of late I'm no longer sure. When she was four and a half she contracted polio; one day she woke up and couldn't move her leg. She was cured thanks to the excellent medical supervision of Professor Caro, head of the Jewish Hospital in Posen and her beloved grandfather. But afterwards, or perhaps that was always her manner anyway, she was slow, and her father, who wrote witty poems for all family occasions, composed the couplet:

Immer langsam, immer langsam, immer langsam voran,
Damit die Dodel, die Dodel auch mitkommen kann.

Go slowly, go slowly, go ever so slowly,
So that Dodel, even Dodel, can keep up with us too.

'It isn't very nice, is it?' Dodel said to me recently; especially as she felt she owed the aches which came back to trouble her in her late eighties to a return of some of the symptoms of her childhood affliction. Since that conversation I've wondered whether she really did choose her nickname or whether it simply stuck and she too got used to it; it became her. It was true; she was slow, pedantic, a perfectionist, a lover of everything in its proper place, just so. When she was a child her homework, and when she was older her home had to be exactly right, harmonious; each stroke of the pen, each book precisely where she wanted it. She was the middle child; the three sisters were labelled by their parents 'the clever one' – that was Lore, my mother; 'the good one' – that was Dodel; 'the pretty one' – that was Isca, who became my second mother. Coming in between two such illustrious sisters really did frame my aunt's life.

It was only six weeks earlier that Nicky and I had driven up to Manchester, helped the removal company pack Dodel's life away into brown cardboard boxes, put her beloved cat Tovah, Princess Tovah as my aunt referred to her adoringly, into a cat box, in which she was duly miserable, assisted Dodel into our car and brought her down to London. It was four days after her ninetieth birthday. The Manchester years had been happy and creative; she had lectured widely in her fields of anthropology and psychology, seen patients, many of whom had become devoted friends, enjoyed the cultured company of fellow refugees from Europe, painted, sung, listened to and composed music and appreciated the wide views over the Cheshire meadows, trees and sky. Here at last, it seemed, after Frankfurt, Surrey, London, Edinburgh, Oxford, London again and Cambridge, she seemed settled, at one with her life. Here she calmly and carefully nursed her mother, a time of healing for them both; she died peacefully in Dodel's bed.

But these last few months had been hard; there were many phone messages, 'I'm lonely, when are you coming?'; 'I'm desperate!' and, as her health and memory waned, 'What are you doing to help me? I can't go on like this.'

Sorting through her things was a wretched affair. Here were nine decades of living, painstakingly packaged and ordered. Even the plastic yoghurt pots were cleaned and stacked in order of size. Now, while Dodel sat in the other room with Tovah, bewildered by the pace of what was going on around her, Nicky and I went through her cupboards. It felt as if we were throwing half her years into black plastic bags. I cut myself badly on a protruding hinge during my tenth trip down to the bins; I felt I had received my just reward for thus rummaging through her life.

My aunt was twelve when the Nazis came to power and just eighteen on Kristallnacht. 'They smashed all the windows of the Jewish youth club in the street below,' she recalled, 'it was absolutely terrifying.' Isca remembered how calm Dodel had remained. 'We must do something,' she had said; 'we'll sew, we'll darn socks.' It was Dodel too who suggested, during the interminable wait for their transit visas, that they write once again to the British authorities just in case their papers had been lost. She was correct; they had to apply all over again and their waiting resumed for further anxious weeks. They left Germany on 9 April 1939 with all that mattered – their lives. Not once did I hear any of them complain about anything they had lost in Germany. Only the love letters my grandparents wrote to each other every day for the entire duration of the First World War; of these I heard them say with deep regret, 'The Nazis destroyed them all.'

Dodel went to Stoatley Rough near Haslemere in Surrey. It was a school for refugee Jewish children. There she, who was soon afterwards to become a gifted teacher in the Montessori method, was not employed as a tutor or a classroom assistant. Instead, she and other older refugee children were made to dig a swimming pool. When Yom Kippur came round and she requested the day free so that she could fast, it was suggested that the only reason she could possibly be wanting to do so was in order to claim an extra large meal at the close of the day. Things never fell out easily for my aunt.

This was as true of the end of her life as it was of her childhood; she had been scarcely six weeks in her new surroundings in London and might have enjoyed a fresh lease of life amid the company of fellow refugees, when she had her stroke. For twelve weeks she struggled from infection to infection, sometimes restless, sometimes fearful, sometimes, mercifully, calm. She never regained her powers of speech; the most she could manage in any manner that we could comprehend was 'yes' or 'no', and even then we weren't always sure she meant what she said. I often thought of the commentary to the Talmud which allows that where there is no more hope, one may pray for a person's release from suffering. Finally, on a Friday morning in January, she passed quietly away. Her face when I saw her soon after her death was peaceful, composed, beautiful, as she was in the best of her life, and as she would have wished to be for always.

'How long after you arrived in this country were you all separated?' I asked Isca as we walked slowly back along the path towards the chapel after laying Dodel's coffin in the earth. I felt deeply sorry for Isca. Everyone was there at that cemetery now. Her elder sister Lore had arrived here first, dying in 1962, then her father in 1975, followed thirteen hard years later by her mother. Her husband, my father, had joined them on Israel's Independence Day in 2007, and now the younger of her two older sisters would rest here for ever also. Out of all that generation no one was left but her.

'About two or three weeks,' she replied. So within less than a score of days after arriving penniless in a strange country, these sisters, used to a warm, vibrant and artistic family life, were parted from their parents and from each other. Lore was the most fortunate: she went to Glasgow to continue her studies. Isca was sent to rural Yorkshire to learn nursery nursing at a home where the mice ran up and down the curtains during the night and she was forbidden to pick up a baby if it cried. Dodel went south to Surrey. Their parents stayed in London, receiving clearance to remain in the capital, when they found themselves categorised as 'enemy aliens' upon the outbreak of war, because of my grandfather's work as a rabbi, which was presumably taken to mean that he posed no threat to national security.

Yet each of the sisters created a successful life. Dodel left teaching to pursue her studies at Edinburgh University, much to the sorrow of St Christopher's School where she was loved by the children. She followed with a doctorate at Oxford, research in Cambridge and then a variety of teaching positions coupled with work as a therapist in Manchester. But what I loved most during my visits in the last years of her life was to hear Dodel reminisce about Germany. It was not only that she had a wonderful memory for all the numerous members of our family, to hear about whom was a revelation for me who had grown up in a tiny refugee circle round a small table at which, when every single one of us was present, we had to lay just seven places. Thus there were Onkel Bruno and Tante Fienchen, whose daughter Evchen Dodel had adored, and whose other daughter Lottel had gone to Moscow with her committed communist husband and died there of hunger after childbirth. There was Onkel Max, whose family descended on Frankfurt for every festival and filled the home with poetry, music and drama, and who fled to Montevideo. I still remember his telegram when my grandfather died: '*Tief betroffen, werde schreiben* – Deeply affected, will write.' Dodel was somehow at home while she shared these memories, truly at home, as if she had returned to a world prior to being a refugee, as if, in some mental geography untouched by Fascism and war, its borders were still intact and its population unravaged.

There wasn't room for all Dodel's effects in her small sheltered flat in London, so several boxes of her papers remained in our house, stored safely in the attic. On the night before her funeral I spent some hours looking through bundles of letters; almost all of them were from Dodel to her parents, who had kept them safely until, perhaps after their deaths, she was able to reclaim them. The earliest were dated in the nineteen-forties; there were cards and envelopes from Cambridge, from Israel, from holidays in Britain and Europe, from Manchester. Almost always the address began 'The Ark'; this was what my aunt had always called her home, to which carefully arranged wooden animals, and in later years Tovah the cat, would welcome the visitor. Until that moment

I had always thought about this name from the inside – an ark full of all living things, carefully cared for by Dodel/Noah. But it struck me that I had also to look from the outside in and see these treasures as a collection of vital artefacts saved from ruin and adrift upon the desolate waters. 'Yes,' said a man I scarcely knew after I mentioned this at the funeral, 'it's a fitting image for the life of the refugee. They call it the silent Shoah, this scattering of people across the earth, each with his or her lonely memories in a place which never really knows them.'

*   *   *

That night I was so tired that I looked at the torch shining in the net pocket of my rucksack and thought for a moment, before I came back to myself, 'What on earth am I doing with that lamp left on? I must switch it off at once.'

From Mitzpah's Blog

We went in a boat this morning. Daddy was rowing on a lake and I wanted to jump into the water to catch the splashes coming off the oars. But I wasn't allowed; humans always stop us having fun.

I upset my daddy today. I really didn't mean to. It was dark and we were walking along the Rhine when I heard these really interesting noises up ahead so I ran on to see what they were (people are so slow anyway and there are so many interesting things they don't seem to be able to hear). But I hadn't realised quite how far I'd run and when I came back I found that they all thought I was lost. They'd been calling and calling and looking everywhere. I didn't mean to make them worried.

Sometimes my daddy seems frightened. I didn't think humans were scared of anything but now I realise that this isn't true. Sometimes I can smell when he's afraid and sometimes I see it in his face. He looks as if he's staring at things which aren't there. I try to scare them away for him by barking a lot, but he doesn't seem to like that either.

I can only do my best. I'll try to remember to stay near him.

Love,

Mitzpah

Day Nine – From Remagen to Bonn

We have reached the town of Remagen. From now on the route will pass less through countryside and more through industrial zones and cities. Ahead lie Bonn, Cologne, Düsseldorf and Duisburg which all but merge into one vast conurbation. By the time I've passed them I'll be near the Dutch border and most of the walk will be over.

The town of Remagen became famous as the location of the only bridge across the Rhine to be captured intact by the Allied armies in 1945. There are different accounts of how this was achieved. According to all opinions it was largely due to the sheer speed of the American advance. The simplest supplementary explanation is that the Germans had no time to blow the bridge up. But according to other views that isn't the whole story: Polish engineers forced to work with the Wehrmacht sabotaged the mines and, though there was an explosion, it wasn't sufficiently powerful to destroy the heavy bridge. Reinhard Schilling, who kindly accompanied us for the day in Koblenz, tells me something different again over the phone: the German officer in charge realised that it was important for the Americans to get across the river as speedily as possible in order to advance east and prevent the Russians from occupying the whole of Germany. Even in those terrible times there were, he says, officers who saw sense, like, apparently, the German commander of Paris who, against Hitler's orders, surrendered the city rather than allow it to be destroyed to no purpose.

The bridge did not survive the war; only ten days after its capture, on 17 March, it collapsed under the weight of crossing American armour, with the death of thirty soldiers. After the war it was never repaired. Instead, the towers at either end were turned into a memorial museum to peace. David and I walked down the Rhine to see them; a thick mist covered the river and a fine drizzle was falling. The towers loomed through the grey morning; as the sun strengthened we could just make out the ruins on the other side. It was a fitting fate which had befallen them. The bridge never had any value as a civilian crossing point. It was built on the orders of General Ludendorff to enable German troops to cross to the Western Front in the First World War. They used it again in 1918 in the retreat which preceded their defeat. Now its broken remains stood there like a haunted reminder of the futility of violence.

Earlier I had studied the guide to the museum: 'Every day let us work for peace with our mind and heart,' it read. 'May each person begin with himself.'

There is, surprisingly, a Jewish aspect to the history of the Remagen Bridge. Gunther Plaut, later to edit an excellent compilation of commentaries on the Torah, was serving as a chaplain with the American forces in the spring of 1945 and recalled the sequence of events in his memoirs. It was the night of Passover:

> We began the Seder but did not get past the first few songs. The news spread quickly: 'Everyone back to his station! We're on the move!' The Rhine had been crossed at Remagen by the Ninth Armored Division of the First Army. I threw the boxes of matzos into the jeep and off we went towards Remagen. There, at that lovely bridge which afforded the Allied troops their first crossing *en masse*, I stood with Joe on top of our jeep crying, 'Matzos, matzos!' Heads emerged from tanks, troops came by on trucks. 'Seder tonight,' we yelled. 'Pesach, matzos! Celebrate the liberation!' Within half an hour all our boxes were gone – it was the most exhilarating time I could remember.[1]

*   *   *

❖ After David leaves I walk all day on my own, except for Mitzpah, who races happily up the steep forest hills. Actually, he's been unusually restless this morning. Maybe it's because of the late start; maybe he feels insecure at this constant travelling, at this nightly change of place. But he barks a lot and once even, tearing his lead free from the chair where I'd tied it, runs out into the road after a car. This cannot be tolerated; it frightens me and I discipline him smartly. But once we're on the move he's happy, especially as I throw him lots of sticks. I take care to feed him plenty of extra rations as well, to compensate for all those miles of running. We even share my cheese sandwich.

The scenery has changed. The vineyards are mainly behind us to the south. The earth is muddy and slippery now, grey clay. The forests are more extensive, serious, tall. The going is far from easy, the climbs are steep and long; I emerge at length into a grove of walnut trees.

I've never seen anything like this; though all the other trees in the forest still have their leaves and present a panoply of colour, these tall brown branches rise bare into the cold air. They speak of the lean glory of winter. I search the ground; at first I find only the blackened remains of casings, but at length I find the broken shell of a nut. Yes, this definitely is a grove of walnut trees. It's beautiful. On the path in the distance a row of horses watches. The cold deepens as darkness draws the trees closer about us; families go home with their bags of gathered booty. Mitzpah races back and forth. I wish Nicky was here; this is a place we might talk about in twenty years' time: 'Do you remember when we stood beneath those walnut trees, when the winter first greeted us among their freezing branches?'

As I walk my mind reverts to a question Guy asked me last week as we sat on the steps of the church in St Goar, talking about the laws of Chanukkah in *Sefer Hamaharil*: 'Who do you think you are, a candle or a *shammash*, a servant?' 'We're all both,' I answered, an evasive and unhelpful response. Afterwards I think more deeply about what the difference between them might be.

My mind goes back to the verse with which David began his teaching last night: 'A lamp of the Lord is the human soul, searching all the chambers of the womb.' I recall the blessing with which one refers to a living scholar: *Nero Ya'ir*, 'May his or her light shine forth.' The candle burns in us all; the question is only how well we enable it to do so. I often think, as Chanukkah approaches, of the Maccabbees' dilemma (forgetting for a moment that the story of the oil which should have lasted only one day but burnt for eight is just a legend. Or maybe it's precisely because it's a legend that it's so important.) If you know you've only enough oil for your flame to burn for a single day, do you light it or do you refrain from lighting? Do you 'go for it', or do you wait for a more propitious hour, for a time when the reserves are more plentiful, the outlook better? Are you impetuous, or over-cautious?

But the reality is that we always have a limited supply of oil and the art is to have the faith to let it burn. True illumination, genuine inspiration, always creates a flame which lasts many times longer than it should according to any solely logical analysis. It reaches down to discover inner resources hitherto unknown; it draws forth the light in others. When its own flame finally wanes and gutters, other fires are already burning. One has to light one's candle.

What then is the *shammash*? The *shammash* is the candle which enables others to find their own light. There are people, often quiet and modest, who have exactly that ability to encourage others, who sense what they are capable of doing and who, by their support, help them to find the courage to do it. I admire those who create opportunities for other people, who are enablers, who dedicate themselves to assisting others in growing and finding fulfilment, whose steady, sometimes even chastening 'I believe in you' guides and fosters those around them. They create light; they more than deserve their place set slightly higher on the Chanukkiah.

We reached Bonn on the night of Alle Heiligen and the centre of the city was quiet. Guy set me down outside the tall black iron gates to the university where I was due to meet with a professor of theology and his students. I remember sitting in the darkness drinking coffee and staring at the street, wondering how I was to recognise him, or whether anyone would turn up at all. But he arrived punctually and led me into a church of fine inner simplicity, where we sat in the front row and talked. Though I can't recall the content of our discussion I remember thinking about my grandfather once again as I left, of how he enjoyed such collegial encounters between Christians and Jews. I believe that for him anti-Semitism remained the exception until the 1930s, despite the sharp rise of the political right during the economically challenging 1920s and the numerous racist factions which threatened the precarious stability of the Weimar Republic. He recorded in his memoirs how in the First World War at the front he and his Catholic and Protestant colleagues could be seen daily making their way to the officers' mess engrossed in friendly debate.

This led to another question which had long been troubling me: In Remagen there was a small, not especially aesthetic, memorial to the former Jewish community. The inscription referred to the 'Deutsche Juden' who once lived there. David wondered whether the word 'Deutsche' was used to distinguish them from Polish or other Ostjuden, Jews from the East (who were sometimes less than graciously received by their co-religionists). I thought this unlikely; in my view the purpose was probably to emphasise that these people were Germans, precisely in order to acknowledge what was denied with such violence during the Third Reich – that they were in every sense citizens of the country and that they regarded Germany as their *Vaterland*, their true and only homeland.

But were they not deluding themselves?

The question raises issues which go not only to the core of the German–Jewish dilemma, of the much pondered meaning of the complex cultural symbiosis between Jews and Germany, but to the very heart of what is meant by identity.

It was Reinhard Schilling who, as he walked with us through Koblenz, referred to President Bush's alleged challenge after 9/11: 'You're either with us or against us.' One can understand such a response in the hour of terror, but it is, to my mind, a limited way to approach the general question of identity. This paring down, this need for a clear and simple assertion, 'you're either this or you're that', is precisely what disturbs me. Are we not rather complex and composite beings? Are we not formed of many sources, the air and water, scents and winds of different places, the intonations and accents of different countries and regions? Is a person solely and purely a Jew one hundred per cent through and through; does that completely and exclusively define everything about him or her? Or did we listen to *Winnie the Pooh* and *Paddington Bear* as well as the Shema meditation when we went to bed as children? Just this receptivity to the plurality of the cultures which form us is what the purists, the idealogues of so many cults and religions, both political and spiritual, want to suppress.

I've never forgotten the day I went to a certain *Yeshivah*, a college for the intensive study of Torah, in Jerusalem and met the man who was to be my spiritual advisor. 'When we get to know each other better,' he said to me in our first conversation, 'I'll share with you the secret of how even Shakespeare is based on Jewish sources.' That was enough; I never returned for a subsequent visit. I'm always suspicious of the pressure towards absolute ideological conformity. It reminds me of the story of Procrustes' bed (in the parallel Hebrew legend, *Mittat Sedom*, the bed of Sodom) in which they used to test out every stranger. If he was too tall for the bed, they cut off his legs; if he was too short they stretched him out as on a rack. What he was never granted, unless he happened precisely to match the length of the bed, was to remain exactly as he was. Those who, often unconsciously, behave with such intolerance and demand such conformity from others always end up at odds with reality, which is invariably complex and refuses to be reduced to simple, totalitarian formulae. I'm not such a purist that I would argue against any form of obedience to custom; it's only reasonable to dress, speak, employ manners and in general conduct oneself in accordance with the prevailing civilised norms unless there is good reason not to do so. But when it comes to the truth of who we are, our culture, ideas, innermost feelings and associations, I have a fear of the absolutist simplifications of those who demand of others that they must prove to us that they are but one simple, consistent thing.

Why this issue is of such importance is because it is precisely through embracing the plurality of who we are that we become able to develop a more embracing empathy. As Jews, we can understand the Hindu family who aspire to send their children to a good school, and who at the same time want them to learn the language, music and rituals of their ancestors, or the Muslim family who live in Britain and worry about their grandparents in Pakistan. We share the reality of struggling with different ways of life in a constantly evolving synthesis and are therefore well placed to help to create a tolerant British, or German, or indeed European, culture, while nurturing our Jewish, Muslim, Hindu or Sikh traditions and commitments. Such is my ideal. We need both to make a blessing of our differences and to foster our shared European culture, together embracing its democratic values and rejoicing in and protecting its freedoms.

My grandparents were German Jews. They were German in the sense that they loved this Germany, its woodlands and rivers, its language, poetry and theatre, its towns and castles. My grandfather was thrilled to be called to serve the Jewish community of Frankfurt because it was a wonderful congregation, but also because this was the great Goethe's *Geburtsstadt*, the birthplace of his beloved poet, and an outstandingly beautiful city rich in European culture. He was proud of being German and was even one of those many German Jews who won the Iron Cross in the field of battle, little good that it was to do him later. (He was a member of the German War Graves Commission and would often be invited to speak at memorial gatherings. But even before Hitler came to power matters had come to such a pass that he needed police protection.)

Were they all then fools, those German Jews? Should they never have engaged in what has been dubbed a 'one-sided love affair' with a land which didn't want them? Or are such thoughts not only a cruel misuse of hindsight but a confession of hypocrisy, considering who we ourselves are?

Yet the much quoted phrase with which many German Jews described themselves, *Deutsche Bürger jüdischen Glaubens*, 'German citizens of the Jewish faith', troubles me. In such a hyphenated identity I would definitely place 'Jewish' first. For 'Jewish' will accompany me every-where, wherever I may end up living and in whatever land I should be when I die. This aspect of my identity is not contingent; it is the core of me, wherever I may be driven or choose to go. Perhaps this above all is what I have learnt from the Holocaust, and what I now teach my children and my pupils: British, German, American – these connections and allegiances are very important, and I too love many aspects of my secular identity. But Jewish is who I ultimately am; it is the heart of me and I shall carry my Judaism with me and strive to be true to it in whatever land my days may be spent.

*   *   *

I don't know if the city has a memorial to its best known Jewish poet Ephraim ben Yaakov, usually known as Ephraim of Bonn, who was born here in 1133 to a family of scholars. The Second Crusade passed through the region in 1146, as he recorded in his memorial chronicle: 'I, the young man who writes these words, was thirteen years old, and I was in the fortress of Walkenburg with my relatives, mostly from my mother's family, may her soul rest in paradise.' He witnessed further persecutions towards the end of his life in 1197: 'But blessed be the God of Israel who saved me from trials and contempt, for three days before the disaster I came to Colonia. Yet I lost a great part of my possessions, may my maker replenish my lack.' He had been living in the great communities of the Rhineland, re-established after the destruction of the First Crusade scarcely half a century earlier, studying and teaching alongside the other scholars of his generation.

His is one of the few accounts in Hebrew sources of the fate of the Jews in mediaeval England. He recorded the massacre in Clifford's Tower, where, faced with the choice of death or forced baptism most of the community preferred to die by their own hands. In the event those Jews who opted for the latter were also slaughtered. In this their destiny was no different from that of the Jews of Mainz, Worms and Cologne, of whom Ephraim was no doubt also thinking:

Afterwards, in the year 4551 [1190 CE], the Wanderers came upon the people of the Lord in the city of Evoric [York] in England, on the Great Sabbath [before Passover], and the season of the miracle was changed to disaster and punishment. All fled to the house of prayer. Here Rabbi Yom-Tov stood and slaughtered sixty souls, and others also slaughtered. Some there were who commanded that they should slaughter their only sons, whose foot could not tread upon the ground from their delicacy and tender breeding. Some, moreover, were burned for the Unity of their Creator. The number of those slain and burned was one hundred and fifty souls, men and women, all holy bodies. Their houses moreover they destroyed, and they despoiled their gold and silver and the splendid books which they had written in great number, precious as gold and as much fine gold, there being none like them for their beauty and splendour. These they brought to Cologne and to other places, where they sold them to the Jews.[2]

However Rabbi Ephraim's best known work is probably his poetic account of the *Akedah*, the binding of Isaac. The Torah describes how in this, his tenth and ultimate trial, Abraham is told to take 'your son, your only son, whom you love' and offer him up as a burnt offering in the place which God will show him (Genesis 22:2). Recognising the intended place from afar, father and son leave their servants behind with the donkey and proceed on foot to the site destined for the altar.

Isaac turns to his father: 'My father.'

'Here am I.'

'Behold the fire and the wood, but where is the lamb for the sacrifice?'

'God will provide the lamb for the sacrifice my son.'

The two of them walked on together.

Abraham answers Isaac using exactly the same word with which he had previously responded to God: '*Hinneni*, here am I.' But for which of the two of them is he actually there? His reply to Isaac contains a subtle but devastating ambiguity: does one place a comma between the words 'sacrifice' and 'my son', as plain sense would suggest, so that Abraham is understood at once to be reassuring Isaac and prophesying the ultimate outcome in which he would sacrifice, if not a lamb, then a ram? Or is the comma to be placed after the word 'lamb', leaving the rest of the sentence to read 'for the sacrifice my son', a pained and indirect avowal of what Abraham cannot bring himself to say overtly? At any event, Abraham builds the altar, binds his son and is about to slaughter him when the angel of the Lord intervenes, calling, 'Abraham, Abraham . . . set not your hand upon the lad, nor do him any harm.' To many modern interpreters the meaning of the story lies precisely in this moment: the customary practice of sacrificing one's child, believed to have been so prevalent in other cultures of the period and indeed expected of the chosen hero of the deity, is abhorrent to the one true God.

But this is not at all what the event signifies to Ephraim of Bonn or to his co-religionists during the Crusades, or to those who preceded him

142

during the Greek and Roman persecutions, on whose interpretations
his poem is based:

> Then did the father and the son embrace,
>   Mercy and Truth met and kissed each other.
> Oh, my father, fill your mouth with praise,
>   'For He doth bless the sacrifice . . . '

> He made haste, he pinned him down with his knees,
>   He made his two arms strong.
> With steady hands he slaughtered according to the rite,
>   'Full right was the slaughter.'

> Down upon [Isaac] fell the resurrecting dew, and he revived.
>   [The father] seized him]then] to slaughter him once more.
> Scripture, bear witness! Well-grounded is the fact:
>   'And the Lord called Abraham, even a second time from heaven.'

In other words, not only did Abraham actually kill Isaac but he even
tried to repeat the deed when his son was miraculously resurrected. It is
only at this point that the ministering angels intervene and 'Overpower
God with a flood of tears'.[3]

When Ephraim of Bonn wrote his poem the narrative of the binding
of Isaac had already been central to Jewish self-understanding for more
than a millennium. The ancient liturgy for the New Year describes how
when the Children of Israel blow the *shofar* on that holy day it is
accounted unto them in heaven 'as if' they have sacrificed themselves
for God's sake. The *shofar*, traditionally a ram's horn, reminds us – and
God – of Abraham and Isaac. But, just as the animal replaces the child
in the story, so there is hopefully always an 'as if': what God cares about
is the intention, our readiness to give absolutely everything for our faith,
not the literal deed. Yet in this prayer we remind God that generation
after generation we have proved ourselves more than true; time and
again through the centuries Jews have been forced to die for their
beliefs. If this is what we have done for the sake of our relationship with
you, we argue, then surely you in turn should do all you can for the sake
of your relationship with us.

But in Rabbi Ephraim's poem the 'as if' has gone; the father has actually slaughtered his son, just as so many parents did during the Crusades in the towns he knew so well along the Rhine. As his fellow Hebrew poets often noted, Abraham did not have to go through with the terrible deed, yet God still called him 'beloved' and rescued him from every misfortune. What then about us, they cry, for whom there was no merciful reprieve at the last minute and who have been compelled to perform the awful act not once but many times? How great must be our reward! God, will you not look down at long last upon those who have given everything, including their lives and the lives of their beloved children, for your name's sake, and vindicate them in the sight of their cruel and mocking enemies?

The poem and others similar to it also pose a challenge to Christianity. In effect the authors are saying to their Christian contemporaries: you consider yourselves more pious and faithful than us; you took the story of the binding of Isaac and understood it to prefigure the crucifixion of Jesus, in which your God actually dies. However, among us it is not just one human being who has had to perish, but many, as generation after generation we lose our lives at your hands for the sake of the sole true God.

The following extract from the *Encyclopaedia Judaica* about the history of the Jews of Bonn makes chastening reading. Their fate was not untypical of that of Jews of other towns in the region. The many centuries of almost uninterrupted Jewish presence in Frankfurt are the exception rather than the rule in the history of the Jews of Germany:

During the First Crusade in 1096 the Jews in Bonn were martyred. A Jewish community again existed there in the twelfth century which, following a murder accusation, had to pay the emperor and the bishop a fine of 400 marks. A Platea Judaeorum [a Jewish street] is recorded in Bonn before 1244. The Jews engaged in moneylending and many became wealthy. In an outbreak of violence on June 8, 1288, 104 Jews were killed. During the Black Death (1348–49) the community was attacked and annihilated; the archbishop took over its property and pardoned the burghers for the crimes they had committed. Subsequently, there is no record of Jewish residence in Bonn until 1381. During 1421–22 there were 11 Jewish families who paid the archbishop of Cologne an annual tax of 82 gulden. The Jews were expelled in the fifteenth century, but later returned. In 1578 the Jewish quarter was looted and many Jews were taken captive by a Protestant army besieging Bonn; they were later ransomed. During the seventeenth century the Jews in Bonn, who lived under the protection of the elector, mainly engaged in cattle-dealing and money lending. They were attacked in 1665 by students from nearby Deutz. The Jewish street was destroyed during a siege in 1689, but a new Jewish quarter with 17 houses and a synagogue was built in 1715. It was closed at night by guarded gates.[4]

From Mitzpah's Blog

Daddy and I got cross with each other this morning and he really told me off. All I did was pull my lead loose and run out into the road to chase a car. He came after me and told me never ever to do that again. Why does he always side with the cars and not with me? Those cars are so dirty (though I do like to travel in them). I hate most of all the ones which come up from behind and frighten me.

The Bible says, 'God leads me in the paths of quietness.' That means that if they are noisy and full of traffic they must be the wrong ones. What don't humans understand about this obvious truth?

But we had a lovely day afterwards and I ran and played a lot. I think we're still friends.

In the evening we sat in a huge church. I wanted to test out the echo. As there was hardly anyone in there with us I barked, only two or three times. The sound was wonderful but I was told to shut up. Why are people allowed to listen all day to their own voices when I'm always told to be quiet?

Love,

Mitzpah

Day Ten – From Bonn to Cologne

❖ It's half past six in the morning; Mitzpah and I have just been out for him to do what a dog has to do and for me to search for a place open at this early hour where I can get a cup of tea. I return with the booty and a croissant and share the latter with Mitzpah. He isn't satisfied with his portion and pulls the empty bag back out of the waste-paper basket to lick out all the crumbs.

I haven't been able to sleep. Maybe it's because the hotel backs directly on to the railway station and trains rush past all the time. I find the book of stories written by my mother. (Actually, 'stories' is an inadequate translation; the German genre of Maerchen lacks an exact English equivalent.) One of my last memories of my mother is of her sitting on my bed correcting the proofs when I was five and had the measles. It must have been not long after that that she went into hospital and never came back. The book is called *Himmel und Erde*, Heaven and Earth, and I brought it with me because of one particular story entitled *Der Zauberwald*, The Magic Forest.

It concerns a young boy called Joseph who's afraid of the dark. One night his parents go out, forgetting to leave his door open and the light on in their room. Joseph is both terrified of the darkness and fascinated by it. He is drawn towards the window and the huge forest outside: 'Was there a wish hidden behind his fear, the wish to conquer his inner self?' He climbs down into the night and hurries along the garden path, through the gate and out into the forest. At once the familiar fear overcomes him and he turns around to go back. But the house is gone. All around him is only the forest, alive with movement, with rustling, scuffling noises and the sound of the wind. Panic-stricken, he runs headlong through the dark; hands reach out after him, eyes stare at him, voices whisper to him. Breathless he stops, his shirt torn, his body scratched, his fingers sore. For a while he slowly feels his way forward from tree trunk to

146

tree trunk until at length he reaches the forest's edge. There he pauses. The moon sails through the sky before hiding briefly behind passing clouds. The wind blows. The trees breathe in through all their many branches:

> The night was not a stranger; it was quiet. It held no hidden ghosts, only a great and hitherto unknown life.
>
> Joseph shut his eyes. All at once the world shone from within, its golden light piercing the darkness. Suddenly the realisation overcame him: beyond the forest is light.

I wonder if this was my mother's experience in her final weeks of life when she lay weak and sick in the Glasgow Royal Infirmary. Or was she, did she remain, afraid of the final darkness? 'Am I dying?' she asked a family friend on the day before her life ended. So she knew.

I wasn't taken to visit her, not even once. It was the strange and to me incomprehensible wisdom of the day that such contact would be bad for both parent and child. Thirty years after her death, when visiting Glasgow for other reasons, I went to the hospital and asked if they still possessed her medical records. I was five years too late. The pastor on duty, who stayed behind specially to help me with my enquiry, informed me that patients' notes were kept for a quarter of a century; after that they were destroyed.

Though lovingly brought up by Isca, my second mother, I guess I am one of very many people who have a part of themselves which is always listening, always unconsciously trying to reconstruct out of insufficient memories, family legends many times revised and the clues offered by chance references and occasional encounters ('I was friendly with your mother') who their mother was.

> I always knew it; it's true [says the little boy in the story]. I stand here unafraid and full of joy. Beyond the forest is light.[1]

The torch on my desk shines against the wall.

*   *   *

❖ The walking is easy and after a couple of hours Mitzpah and I stop for what I tell myself is a well-earned coffee break. We've covered ten kilometres and it's only half past eleven. It's a little bit of a route march today, from Bonn to Cologne, straight along the left bank of the Rhine. The map says that the distance is twenty-three kilometres, a comfortable walk. But the signposts on the cycle path say thirty-five, which is a little too far since I have to be there by three-thirty. Mitzpah adds somewhat to the length of the day's exertions by suddenly chasing off, deaf to the world, in the opposite direction. He's gone at least half a kilometre before I catch up with him. He evidently prefers Bonn to Cologne. It is indeed reputed to be a rather more up-market city.

But Mitzpah has had a good day so far. Joe, Anna and I throw sticks into the water and he dives and plunges for them. The current runs fast, so we're careful not to tempt him out of his depth. Afterwards we come upon a huge gathering of ducks and swans. I keep Mitzpah on his lead; he's liable to challenge swans (at least here they're not the property of the Queen, though a yacht called *Britannia* has just sailed past). But the thing about swans is that they challenge back, and I have no desire to see the peaceful convocation of water fowl disturbed by our passage.

Someone has pinned prayers to the trees which line the waterside path. Yesterday, high in the hills, I passed a shrine to Mary: *Maria, bitte für uns*, 'Mary, plead for us.' I translate this image of a woman, a young mother, beautiful, loving, whom we ask to intercede for us, into Jewish terms as Rachel with whom Jacob falls in love at first sight, Rachel who dies in childbirth. I remember the poignant verse from Jeremiah we sing at the New Year: 'A voice is heard in Ramah, bitter weeping; it is Rachel, weeping for her children' (Jeremiah 31:15). The midnight prayers recited by pious mystics are known as *Tikkun Leah* and *Tikkun Rachel* – but they do not portray these women as divine or as the mother of the divine. It is the very human within Rachel which cuts into the heart, the mother dead so young, the mother tormented by the fate of her children whom the prophet envisions being led by their Babylonian masters past the site of her grave, past her weeping presence, and off into far distant exile. This face of maternal compassion and suffering – we know it too as Jews. Rachel stays in my mind for a long time after I pass that prayer on its wooden board at the threshold of the forest. I find it easy to understand why Christians pray with such emotion to Mary.

Yesterday was Alle Heiligen and I'm told by students I meet later that it's the custom among Catholics to light a candle on each of the family graves: 'Go to the cemetery in the evening and you'll see; there'll scarcely be a grave without its candle.' I learn that it's the practice to take the flame from the Easter candle lit earlier that day in church. I'm asked if one has to light the *Yahrzeit* candle, the memorial light which Jews kindle each year on the Hebrew anniversary of the death of a family member, from any particular source. 'Not to my knowledge,' I reply, and we talk about the relationship between candles and the soul.

I meet up again with Guy, Joe and Anna a couple of kilometres further on. My mind is still on the issue of the correlatives in Judaism for Christian symbols and whether looking for such parallels is in itself a worthwhile approach. But Guy asks me what I'm thinking about as we begin to walk through the big cities in which the Nazi horrors were perpetrated. How uneasy do I feel? Do places have memory; do they retrain traces of what once happened there?

I do believe that the residue of what has been done remains to haunt the sites where it was enacted, both for good and for bad. But what does this actually mean? What ontological status does the past retain? Is it still floating here behind the veil of the present? Is it restored by memory only, when someone visits there who knew, or who has learnt, what once transpired in that street, inside that house? I'm not sure.

Thoughts of the past come over me unpredictably, not all of the time, yet they haunt me all the same. An old man passes me without a smile; his wrinkled face bespeaks an age of eighty-five or older. Then the classic question, familiar to every Jew who has visited Germany or Austria since the war, courses through me in an instant, 'What were you doing back then?'

One never knows, supposing the other person does recognise one in that moment of passing as Jewish, if one serves as a reminder of shame, or of hate, or of self-righteousness, or of nothing at all. A couple of German friends have told me that they have reached the political opinions they now hold, or have moved to the town or country where they now live, to distance themselves absolutely from their parents who remain unrepentant Nazis.

Guy repeats his question. My mind goes back to the moment in Sinzig railway station when I said goodbye to John. The thought had overwhelmed me then that perhaps this very platform was the place where the town's Jews had said farewell to their homes for ever. Thence the journey would have been eastward, perhaps to Riga or Izbica; then, if they were still alive months later, onward to Sobibor or Auschwitz.

The synagogue in the town still stands.

There are also moments when I walk along a village street, especially where the houses are made of the dark basalt which characterises parts of this region, when I imagine it patrolled by the SA and some sense of danger and horror still drips into me from a seventy-years-distant past. But one can't even begin to imagine what it was like if one wasn't there at the time. I recall my grandparents describing a scene in the street – it could have occurred any time after 1933. They passed one of the many propaganda posters with the inscription *Die Juden sind unser Unglück*, 'The Jews are our misfortune', a slogan invented not by Goebbels or by Julius Streicher of *Der Stürmer*, as I had thought, but by the historian Heinrich von Treitschke many decades earlier, heralding the rise of political anti-Semitism in the late nineteenth century. My grandmother is about to make some comment when my grandfather discreetly nudges her, 'Don't say a word;' two men in Nazi uniform are watching them closely.

I think too of the account my grandfather once gave me of the birthday party of a non-Jewish friend, an opponent of Nazism. It was a small gathering of trusted companions and words were spoken openly. Within days the man was arrested. After his release he courageously invited the very same group of friends back to his home and asked them: 'Which of you was it who betrayed me?' Silence. Then the door opened and his son entered: 'I did it, father. They told us in the Nazi Youth to report on our parents if they were traitors.'

I enjoy the next stage of my walk somewhat less and feel inexplicably tired. The footpath keeps going, with light woodland on the left. But to the right the Rhine is now some tens of metres distant; instead of the brightly flowing water the fence of a vast industrial complex borders the route. Mitzpah bounces along unaffected. But to me the atmosphere smells different; the fresh, clear tang of hillside air is gone and in its place is the dirty-sweet smell of chemicals. For a moment I even think I must be walking past a sewage-treatment plant. I'm glad when I've passed the last of the pipes and containers and grass flanks me on either side once again. I'm reminded of the feeling when one goes on holiday to the country and opens the door of the car or train for the first time: how rich and fragrant is the air! And when one comes back to London and exits the train in Euston station, how very different it smells.

On the previous Shabbat afternoon, John and I, in the kind company of Reinhard Schilling, had been given a personal tour of the Museum of the Rhine in Koblenz. The exhibits are fascinating: there are boats which would have been pulled by horses straining along the towpath (which is probably more or less where I now walk). If you had no horses you hired men, ten or twenty to haul your cargo up-river, our guide explains. There are tugs with vast steam engines: it takes hundreds of horsepower to pull one of today's huge fully laden barges up the Rhine against the powerful current. There are pleasure boats, one of which had apparently belonged to the Bishop of Koblenz, who'd been obliged to sell it when he went bankrupt. There's a picture of the engineer Tulla who did so much to straighten the course of the river and make it incomparably more amenable to shipping, but who, in so doing, caused it to lose so many of its flood plains and such quantities of the cleansing water reeds and sands which filtered and purified its waters that it became one of the most polluted rivers in Europe. There are specimens of some of the many kinds of fish once to be found in the Rhine, and which, thanks to thorough environmental measures instituted over recent decades, can again be discovered there today. There are salmon in the river once more, but, we are told, they don't make it back to their spawning grounds near Lake Constance because the Dutch fish them all out. (I must enquire about this after I've crossed the border into Holland.) There is a huge pike; I remember my father talking about one of his mother's best Shabbat dishes: pike stuffed with gefilte fish.

But the grim days for the river's eco-system are by no means over. The water temperature is not as cold as it should be; waters used for cooling atomic power plants are taken from and later flushed back into the Rhine, warming all their surroundings with their temperature of twenty-five degrees centigrade.

At the end of our tour we are shown a map of the great waterways of central Europe.

John asks, and our guide explains, why there should have been Jewish settlements all along the river. The answer is probably because there was work with the ships and in the wine and grain trades. The river was a massive employer. He also explains why there are so many castles: each one controlled its particular stretch of water and the increasingly impoverished traveller had to pay the toll and offer his wares at every stage. You could be taxed well over twenty times if you journeyed right upriver and when you finally got to your destination you might well find yourself with nothing very attractive left to sell.

*   *   *

One of my objectives on this journey had been to meet with members of the Muslim community in Germany. So I was very grateful when friends created introductions in two of the main centres, Cologne and Duisburg (though the latter was sadly not to materialise.) I became engaged in Jewish–Muslim dialogue after 9/11; to my shame, I had failed to realise beforehand how important such relationships were. Since then I have been on Al-Mustakillah television many times (though not recently), have taught at the Muslim College in London, have been invited to serve on numerous panels, have participated in a regular dialogue group of imams and rabbis and have formed a few close friendships.

Some of these experiences have been very moving. Once a Muslim journalist came to our house and sat down and wept. 'Why can I cry and feel safe here?' he asked. The answer we discovered together was that we had a shared understanding of what it meant to have a complex identity, to belong and yet not to belong, to feel at home and yet a stranger, to love our faith and yet be critical of it, all at the same time. 'My father says our real home is in Islamabad. But I look at him and see that even he couldn't return there, let alone me. Britain is my home now; I believe in democracy, freedom of speech, the equality of women. And I'm a committed, practising Muslim.' We understand each other implicitly.

But other encounters are difficult. I've been challenged, live on television and in face-to-face debate, with just about every view about Israel one can think of, and some harsh ideas about Jews and Judaism as well. No doubt this also reflects some of the misguided and unjust conceptions of Islam my interlocutors feel they have experienced in the West. I've learnt that even what we consider the most basic facts and narratives of our history cannot be assumed to be shared. I understand this not purely as an indication that my interlocutors are wrong, though I not rarely consider that they are. Nothing has brought home to me more forcefully the reality that every narrative, everyone's story, including my own, is a construct; none is solely 'the truth and nothing but the truth', and all demand serious critical interrogation. I'm also aware that my partners in these debates are informed by different pressures and realities than those which impact most powerfully on me. They too have their 'street' before which they must render account. I recognise and respect the fact that for them engaging with a rabbi constitutes a serious step towards seeking to understand Jews. It may in some circumstances exact a significant price from their fund of credibility or even put their standing at risk.

I've returned home from these meetings, be they live or virtual, humbled, angered, touched, and occasionally in despair. When I sense that a session may be difficult I think of my grandfather's calm face and tell myself to be measured, not to flinch, not to be angry and not to betray my people or my faith. I've learnt, too, that even in the midst of the most difficult encounters, there may be unexpected moments of closeness. Once, on Al-Mustakillah television, an Arabic network broadcast from London to the Middle East and Europe, a woman called in after we'd discussed the killing of a father and daughter in a Jerusalem café; they were murdered on the day before her wedding. 'I always understood Palestinians were human beings,' she said. 'You've made me realise Israelis are people too.' We all need to be reminded of the humanity of others.

Such meetings are difficult from one's own end as well: what does one's own community think about its leaders becoming involved in the world of Islam? How might such connections be manipulated by either 'side'? Many in Europe are quick to feel threatened by its Muslim populations, parts of them already radicalised by an Islamist agenda often driven by movements originating in the Arab world, Iran or the Subcontinent. For Jews, engagement is even more difficult. Is one undermining Israel, or one's own largely pro-Western values, by meeting at all? How does one really know the political views of one's partners in such dialogues? Or, a charge frequently levelled, by maybe inadvertently sharing platforms with clerics who might have expressed radical opinions elsewhere, is one undermining emerging moderate voices within the Muslim community itself?

Yet we have to take risks in our willingness to engage with each other. The Jewish community will be weaker if we all shelter within a comfort zone behind a border fence labelled 'They all hate us out there.' Europe will continue to feel threatened if it cannot find successful ways to engage with its Muslim populations. Only by both listening to and working with each other can we create a strong civic society and promote understanding, justice and peace.

❖ Through the good offices of Dr Lemmen, who works in Catholic–Muslim relations, we go to see the Muslim Women's Centre in Cologne. The ladies who take us round are full of enthusiasm: we see the kitchens, activity rooms, computer labs, babycare facilities, children's day centre. We're shown pictures of the staff who work in every department, the certificate of recognition by the state. There are notices in German everywhere (almost no Turkish or Arabic), there is plenty of material about integration. Indeed integration is the overriding theme.

It's all wonderful, but I feel I'm on a Cook's Tour. I don't need to be convinced that this centre does important work; that's obvious from the outset. So when we're sat down to a beautifully arranged tea with cakes and savouries and I see the inevitable power-point all set up and ready, I decide to take the initiative. I ask, 'What is your ideal as Muslim women? Is it integration? Do you want to be fully German? Or is the study of Islam equally important?'

The response is immediate and forceful: 'Our ideal is certainly not that we will become totally absorbed in German culture and our identity as Muslims will disappear. The agenda of the state is broadly assimilation . . . ' But these women are guarded in what they say. They explain to me how having a head covering (not the hijab, just a simple kerchief to cover their hair, such as many moderately orthodox Jewish women also wear) is taken as a sign of extremism. One of them told me she'd been asked to chair a discussion group at a conference but had then been 'uninvited' on the grounds that a woman who covered her hair couldn't possibly be entrusted with such a task. Another said that she received unpleasant comments in the street, that it was a regular occurrence that people said to her, quietly but firmly, as she passed: '*Ekelhaft!*' – 'Disgusting!' I was shocked.

The women comment on how a leading statesman has recently said that Jews and Christians, with no mention of Muslims, have been a part of the German past. However, he did, if I understood rightly, acknowledge that Islam would play a part in Germany's future, thus giving rise to much debate.

I persist with my questions and the conversation develops into a warm discussion. I talk about the German-Jewish experience. One of the women notes that Jews were fully integrated here, that they even served, and died in great numbers, in the First World War. Only later were they marginalised and then annihilated. I comment that this is not entirely the case. Even during the Great War there were issues. Jews were accused of failing to serve their country in sufficient numbers. A census was undertaken in the army, but the results were never published because they proved that high numbers of Jews were fighting with distinction in the ranks of the German forces. My grandfather recalled in his memoirs constantly having to exercise diplomacy to defend his co-religionists against the charge of cowardice. Maybe one never belongs.

It seems that what these women want is to be both Germans and Muslims, to be able to live and contribute as Germans precisely through their values as engaged Muslims. But the current reality feels very different to them. Yet at least here is a place sponsored by the state where women can come, children, young girls, Muslims from many different backgrounds, and study German while their babies and young children are well cared for, receive good food, learn computing and other skills and meet role models of highly competent and successful Muslim women living in Europe. The place is vital to the core.

'Write about us,' they tell me. 'It has a far greater effect when others than ourselves speak out about the xenophobia we encounter.' But they refuse to be filmed; the issues feel too sensitive, their vulnerability is too great. I leave feeling troubled. Later a friend who helped me organise this walk and who's joined me for a couple of days in Cologne tells me that she is well aware of these realities. Such racism, she feels, is a direct continuation of the xenophobia which led to the Third Reich. Recently Jews have once again been targeted too. It's part of the reason why she prefers to live in Britain.

The issue of the openness of society to the other (the very word begs the question of who constitutes that 'other' and for whom), of whether it is even possible to create a truly plural and interactive yet cohesive and communitarian society, challenges me from almost every corner of my life. It goes to the heart of the issue of light and darkness. I often find myself thinking about the words of my teacher Rabbi Hugo Gryn as he looked back on what the experience of being deported in 1944 from his Hungarian home town of Berehovo and taken to Auschwitz had meant for his life and values:

I realise now that of Berehovo's three big and beautiful churches, I had never been inside any of them, and the chances are that none of the Christians ever set foot in any of our synagogues. And when the chips were down, I do not know of a single instance of a Jew [from Berehovo] being saved or hidden by a non-Jew. That I spend so much of my time working for better understanding between religious groups and fighting racism as hard as I can is partly because I know that you can only be safe and secure in a society that practises tolerance, cherishes harmony and can celebrate difference.[2]

What is a multicultural, or a pluralist, society and how should it, or can it, function? This, together with the welfare and protection of our environment, may constitute the most significant challenge of our time.

Even my passion for gardening proved no escape from the issue. You wouldn't have thought one could get into political trouble at a horticultural exhibition, but a couple of years ago that is precisely what happened. I was invited to a preview of the prestigious Chelsea Flower Show, which for the first time featured a garden of faiths intended to portray in horticultural form the vitality and diversity of spiritual expression in Britain. I noticed that the small beds representing Hinduism, Judaism, Christianity and Islam were laid out as four rectangles and that the paths between them formed the shape of the cross which thus emerged as the organising principle of the design. I reflected that this arrangement could well be taken as an apt image for multiculturalism in Britain; it did indeed exist, but under the jurisdiction and beneath the toleration of the historical priority and numerical predominance of Christianity. I hadn't intended the observation to be critical, though unfortunately it was reported as such. I simply meant to point out that the design mirrored a crucial issue in the debate on pluralism: was there a future for multiculturalism or was it simply too weak a framework to foster any kind of social and national cohesion? In the latter case, should we look rather to developing and sustaining cultural and religious diversity under the protective shelter of a dominant discourse, the proof of the strength and durability of which would be precisely its capacity to provide safe space for others?

I first heard the word '*Multikulti*' when I was crossing the bridge over the Mosel in Koblenz; it's the dismissive German term with which the death of multiculturalism is heralded. *Multikulti* has got us nowhere, I was told. This comment came in the wake of a speech by Angela Merkel to a large gathering of young Christian Democrats in which she declared that *MultiKulti ist absolut gescheitert*, thoroughly kaput.[3] I was to hear her opinion quoted several times in the following days, both with evident agreement and with horror. One obviously had to take into account the politics of the constituency she was addressing, but even then her comments seemed exceptionally forceful. What, I wondered, was she suggesting that we should put in its place?

In fact, Merkel was following, rather than setting, a trend. The debate had come to the fore with unanticipated fury earlier in the year after the well-known banker Thilo Sarrazin, a social democrat, published a book in which he accused Muslim immigrants of being unwilling to integrate into German society. 'I do not have to acknowledge anyone who lives on social benefit, doesn't care for the education of his children and constantly produces new little headscarf-girls,' he wrote.[4] He also commented on the genetic heritage of Jews. He was attacked by some for being xenophobic and sacked from the board of the Bundesbank, but the book sold hundreds of thousands of copies bought mainly by those to whom his words arrived like long-awaited truths.

Subsequently the German President, Christian Wulff, observed in a seminal speech that Christianity and Judaism had long been an established part of German history and the German narrative. Now, he added, Islam was too: 'Christianity belongs undoubtedly to Germany. Judaism belongs undoubtedly to Germany. That is our Christian–Jewish history. But Islam too now belongs to Germany.'[5] His comments were greeted with scepticism by a Jewish friend with whom I discussed them in Cologne. 'For a thousand years we were the Antichrist,' he observed wryly, 'and now we're suddenly heralded as partners in the German story, primarily so that we can serve as allies in the exclusion of Islam.'

But non-Jews also greeted his words with dismay. Was the president offering an olive branch to Shaaria? The capacity to accommodate other faiths, noted the American historian Russell Berman, lay precisely in the distinction drawn between Church and State:

Liberals like the historian Wehler [who fiercely criticised Wulff] or the German-Syrian political scientist Bassam Tibi emphasise the democratic values of modern society. Tibi has dubbed these values the *Leitkultur* or defining culture – by which he does not mean the culture of German literature and the arts, but the bedrocks of modernity: equal rights, the dignity of individuals, the rule of law, and the separation of Church and State. Immigrants are welcome, but society should insist that they accept these cultural principles.[6]

A group can only be included if it abides by these ground rules of democracy. The question being asked across Europe, fairly or unfairly, is: Is the Muslim community really willing to do so?

It would be absurd and dangerous to deny that a society is entitled to have expectations of people who seek to settle within its borders. Host societies are right to require that certain fundamental values, such as peaceful tolerance of religious, cultural and social diversity, democracy, freedom of speech and the rights of women are respected by all immigrant communities, as well of course as those long settled in the land. Indeed, Jews have generally sought entry into such societies precisely because they have understood them to be more democratic, more just and more open, not simply more prosperous, and have often been among the most vociferous proponents and the most tenacious defenders of those values.

Over two hundred years ago Moses Mendelssohn weighed this issue in his *Jerusalem*, a book which more than any other Jewish text may be seen as the harbinger of entry into the modern world. Following his then radical proposal that 'With respect to civil rights, the members of all religions are equal', he made an explicit exception of those

whose opinions run counter to the principles of human and civil duties. Such a religion cannot lay claim to any rights in the state. Those who have the misfortune to be attached to it can expect tolerance only as long as they do not disturb the social order by unjust and harmful acts. If they perform such acts, they must be punished, not for their opinions but for their deeds.[7]

A few months after Angela Merkel's speech, David Cameron joined the debate on multiculturalism, interestingly enough while he was visiting Germany. A genuinely liberal country, he said, 'believes in certain values and actively promotes them . . . Freedom of speech. Freedom of worship. Democracy. The rule of law. Equal rights, regardless of race, sex or sexuality . . . It says to its citizens: This is what defines us as a society. To belong here is to believe these things.' Communities within those countries must be judged by their adherence to these core values: 'Do they believe in universal human rights – including for women and people of other faiths? Do they believe in equality of all before the law? Do they believe in democracy and the right of people to elect their own government? Do they encourage integration or separatism?' Multiculturalism had failed, he argued, because in its heedless promotion of difference and diversity for their own sakes it had mindlessly given succour to extremism and radicalism at the same time. Liberal society was effectively funding its own destruction from the inside. This had to stop. A new policy of 'muscular liberalism' was required.[8]

Merkel and Cameron were both exercised by the failure to curb violent extremism; to deal with violence, Cameron argued, one had to tackle extremism as well. They are certainly right to oppose blind support for every group and faction regardless of its relationship to core democratic values.

But that doesn't necessarily amount to a compelling case that multiculturalism is dead. What did Merkel intend to put in its place? We are de facto religiously, ethnically and culturally diverse societies. Not only can there be no return to the status quo ante but it is a dangerous fiction to imagine that there ever once was such a thing as racial or national homogeneity. Precisely that perverse notion lay at the heart of Nazism. Nor can assimilation alone provide the answer. Even if, for reasons of self-protection, or for the sake of anonymity, or because of the advantages of getting on in the wider society, sections of any particular community may wish to silence the voices of its own identity (apparently Rabbi Lord Sacks once wittily described the ethos of the Jews of Britain as 'incognito ergo sum', though that attitude has changed substantially over the past twenty years), no people with a serious history and culture is capable of simply submerging itself in the ideology of another. As Gary Younge argued in his critique of Cameron's speech: 'National identity is just one among many identities and may well not be the primary one;' it was therefore important to support 'an affirmation of plurality against calls for assimilation that attempt first to invent and then enforce "British values" and other national orthodoxies'.[9]

How should the voices of these different aspects of our identity find their balance within a truly democratic, plural, tolerant and open society? What can be asked of a minority, and what may not be demanded?

As I pondered my visit to the women's centre in Cologne, two observations from Jewish history kept returning to my mind. The first was the much quoted dictum of Samuel (died *c.*257CE), founder of the Talmudic academy in Nehardea in Babylon, that 'the law of the land is the law'. Though it originally referred specifically to taxation, it came to be applied far more widely to the whole domain of civil, as opposed to ritual, law.[10] This ruling therefore broadly defined the border between religious matters, in which the Jewish community had always shown remarkable tenacity in striving to preserve its autonomy, and conformity with the law of the land, such as it was, in all areas of civil jurisdiction. It was by holding to this line of demarcation that Jews had managed to exist, and often thrive, in the numerous lands of their dispersion for over two thousand years.

The second was the famous comment by the Count of Clermont-Tonnerre, made on 23 December 1789, when the place of the Jews, and other minority groups regarded with suspicion, was being debated in the new France:

The Jews should be denied everything as a nation, but granted everything as individuals . . . It is intolerable that the Jews should become a separate political formation or class in the country. Every one of them must individually become a citizen; if they do not want this, they must inform us and we shall then be compelled to expel them. The existence of a nation within a nation is unacceptable to our country.[11]

The Count of Clermont-Tonnerre's distinction still strikes a note of discomfort today. No doubt it also has its contemporary proponents who would agree that the price of belonging to the nation must be the complete dislocation of all public religious allegiances which could be construed as constituting an alternative or, worse, a preferable form of identity.

A few years later Napoleon convened an Assembly of Jewish Notables and required them to respond to a series of questions concerning the relationship of Jews to France and of Judaism to French law. In August 1806 the Notables responded:

> *Sixth Question*: Do Jews born in France, and treated by the laws as French citizens, consider France their country? Are they bound to defend it? Are they bound to obey the laws and conform to the dispositions of the civil code?
>
> *Answer* . . . The love of a country is in the heart of Jews a sentiment so natural, so powerful, and so consonant to their religious opinions, that a French Jew considers himself in England, as among strangers, although he may be among Jews; and the case is the same with English Jews in France.[12]

Was this answer the whole truth and nothing but the truth, or was it even then partly disingenuous? Would the answer to Napoleon's question be expressed in similar terms by Jews today? It reminds me of the account of a Jew I heard from his relatives almost a century after the event. He had been serving in the front line of the German army in the First World War when all of a sudden he was confronted by a French infantryman with his rifle at the ready. It was a case of 'shoot first or be shot'; he fired, and as the Frenchman fell he heard him cry out, '*Shema Yisrael* – Hear, O Israel, the Lord our God, the Lord is one.' Is this the *ad absurdam* of that answer to Napoleon? Or was that terrible war an exception from which little can be learnt beyond its horrors?

How would Jews and Muslims respond to a contemporary Napoleon? Is regional or national allegiance as powerful a factor today in the self-understanding of individuals and groups as religious identity? If not, are there disadvantages? Might this herald a new era of desecularisation, of the resurgence of religion as the primary determinant of identity, entailing the diminishment or perhaps even the collapse of what has been regarded for over a century and a half as the safe civic space in which, in Western societies at their best, believers and unbelievers of every religion and creed have been able to relate to one another, protected by the largely faith-neutral institutions of the secular nation-state?

What does the garden look like in which different faiths and cultures can truly flourish, prospering all the better precisely because of their interaction with each other?

From Mitzpah's Blog

The first half of today was really exciting but then it got extremely boring.

Personally, I think inter-faith meetings are overrated. There's lots of talking, but nobody ever does anything afterwards. I have to lie on the floor for hours and hours pretending to sleep.

In my opinion we should have inter-species meetings instead. If people listened more to dogs, horses and other animals the world would be a far better place. There would be less pollution, less cruelty, more grass and more trees and everyone would be happier. People go on and on about religion and identity and politics and all that rubbish. All we animals want is to be allowed to live in peace.

Daddy didn't have any of my proper food with him. I was very hungry, so he went into a shop and bought some pizza just for me. I ate it up right outside and the owner came out and thought it was very funny.

Lots of people stop and chat to me and they all say, '*Braver Hund*'; I don't know what it means but they say it in a kind tone and it sounds approving.

Love,
Mitzpah

Day Eleven – In Wuppertal

There's only one way to bridge the divide, to live together, to realise the goals of two peoples: we have to find the light to guide us to our goal. I'm not talking about the light of religious faith here, but light as a symbol of truth. The light that allows you to see, to clear away the fog – to find wisdom. To find the light of truth you have to talk to, listen to, and respect each other. Instead of wasting energy on hatred, use it to open your eyes and see what's really going on.

from Dr Izzeldin Abuelaish, *I Shall Not Hate*

A message to his daughter Aya, who was tragically killed in Gaza by an Israeli shell, written by her sister Raffah

Aya, you were the light of our home.
What's happened to the home that was lit up by you?
Where has the beautiful light gone . . . ?
Where have you disappeared to, Aya?[1]

I have brief and convoluted memories of that first evening in Cologne. I recall the sudden realisation that I'd totally forgotten to feed Mitzpah and a sense of guilt at going into a baker's shop to buy a pizza just for the dog. 'The owner will feel insulted,' I remember thinking. But I was wrong; he stepped outside with a beaming smile to watch Joe filming the dog devouring his product with such relish that it seemed scarcely more than a single mouthful. We climbed up the stairs to the Domforum, opposite the Cathedral, where the film-maker, now friend, Günther Ginzel, chaired a three-faith dialogue. Our Muslim partner referred us to a most beautiful description of light; I know that he sent me the text afterwards and search through all the files on my computer but sadly cannot find it.

We arrived late at our hotel in a grim quarter of the city, past the vast

164

halls of the Messe. 'Are you able to do washing, as we'll be staying here again at the weekend?' 'No, I'm sorry we don't have the facilities.' 'Can you kindly tell me when there are trains to Wuppertal in the morning and where I need to go to catch them?' 'Of course.' But in the event the information wasn't forthcoming and I raced off at half past six towards the nearest station, uncertain how to find it, unsure which train to take and panicked that I'd be late. I was due at half past nine in Wuppertal where I'd been invited to lecture at a theological college on the meanings of light in Judaism. Just as I was running along the platform a man stopped me, 'You've left the torch on in your rucksack pocket.' I thanked him hastily; I knew I ought to have stopped and explained but I just didn't have the time.

Wuppertal was not directly on my route and I hadn't intended to visit the city. But one morning about six months before I was due to set out and when I was close to despair that I would ever succeed in developing contacts in Germany, the phone rang. It was Professor Klappert. 'I was a friend of Rabbi Friedlander,' he explained, before inviting me to speak to his department. He had the whole day carefully planned, the seminar, a visit to the church, then he would take me to the site of the former concentration camp at Kemna, from where I would be able to walk back to his home where he and his wife would be happy to host me and the dog for the night. I thanked him profusely, put down the phone and sat on the floor in disbelief. It was the first time anyone had taken the initiative and contacted me. It was the turning point; I realised that the whole plan for this journey was actually going to work.

For the next two days my route took me far from the Rhine but close to the footsteps of my teacher Rabbi Dr Friedlander, or Albert, as we all used to call him. Our families had been intertwined for generations. My grandfather had taught him rabbinics; he had taught me. He had given the eulogy when my grandfather died, aged 92; I gave the eulogy when he passed away, sadly only in his seventies. I remember him as an invariably kind and gentle presence, a tender-hearted man with a wry and quiet sense of humour. He and his father had left their home on Kristallnacht, wandering the streets of the poor quarters of Berlin for days. They fled the city, eventually arriving, via Cuba, in the United

States. Marriage brought Albert back to Europe, where he represented the values of German Jewry, a profound understanding of history and a deep immersion in culture and art. He was a frequent speaker at church seminars in Germany, a soft-spoken but firm guide through the vast cemetery of communities, personalities, poets, writers, painters, musicians, critics and ideas, always compassionate but never amenable to insubstantial or generalised pleas for pardon and forgiveness. He wasn't taken in by either *Versöhnungsromantik* or *Versöhnungskitsch*.

I missed Albert greatly and felt like a disciple wearing shoes several sizes too large. Almost all my teachers had died in the past few years and I realised with feelings of contrition and inadequacy that virtually the entire row of scholars and rabbis who had stood in front of me, in whom I trusted and to whom I could put all my questions, intellectual, pastoral, historical and spiritual, was no more. Nor are there many rabbis alive anywhere in the world today who carry the spirit of German Jewry not on their bookshelves alone but in their closest family history and memories, in their values, endeavours and affections. I owed all the contacts for the next phase of my walk to his legacy and to the helpful kindness of his wife Evelyn.

❖   Professor Klappert took me to see the church of Barmen-Gemarke. I knew nothing whatsoever of its story and had never heard the name of its pastor Karl Immer before. But now this ignorance leaves me ashamed. Immer was to die of the effects of a stroke in Berlin's Moabit Prison in 1944. A proud Prussian, he couldn't come to terms with the fact that the Nazi regime regarded him as a traitor.

He and the seminal Protestant theologian Karl Barth were the moving spirits behind the statement of the Confessing Church known as the Barmen Declaration, made public on 31 May 1934. 'Karl Bath was the theologian behind the ideas; Karl Immer put them into practice,' Professor Klappert explained. The declaration, addressed primarily to German Christians and to the Church in so far as it was all but incorporated into the apparatus of the state, stressed the overriding duty of following the teachings of Scripture and Jesus. It was not just a religious but also a political document in that it rejected the right of the state to determine moral and spiritual matters beyond the province of its concern:

> We repudiate the false teaching that the state can and should expand beyond its special responsibility to become the single and total order of human life . . . [2]

Thus the Confessing Church went further in its protestations than any of the other churches in Germany. Karl Immer went further still; he lived out, and died for, the consequences of the position he took. On the Sunday after Kristallnacht he came to his church without donning his official robes. A few hundred metres from this church God's word had been burnt, he declared; how in such circumstances could he possibly preach it here? Instead, he recited the Ten Commandments in Hebrew and German and invited all those who understood the nature of his message to join him afterwards in the sacristy. I shall return to these events later.

I asked to see a photograph of Immer; it showed a man of strong character, determined, focused on something far beyond, or deep within, the immediately visible, a man profoundly troubled.

His conduct had an immense impact on his students. One of them was Johannes Rau, a future Bundespräsident of Federal Germany. He had grown up in Immer's household almost as one of the family. He was the first President of West Germany to speak in the Knesset in German; apparently Golda Meir determined that, given his background and his teacher, he should be invited to address Israel's parliament and be allowed do so in the German language.

I stood in the church with mixed feelings, with profound admiration, and also with the awareness that the terrors happened anyway, happened with little active opposition. I was told that there were just three pastors across the whole of Germany who were known to have spoken out after Kristallnacht. I write 'just', but this was a matter of life and death: what would I have done in such a situation?

Yet one person who stands up and objects, who calls upon his or her congregants to act, who sets an example, and who as a result causes the rescue of a single person, has, according to the second-century Jewish code the Mishnah, 'saved an entire world'.[3]

Ashamed that I had never even heard of Karl Immer, once I was back home in London I made a point of researching his life. Extraordinarily, I couldn't find a single entry on the Internet, but mercifully Professor Klappert and his colleagues had written about him. A contemporary of my grandfather, Immer had, like him, been awarded the Iron Cross for his service during the First World War. A Prussian and a patriot, he died, a supposed enemy of his country, on the very day the Western Allies landed in Normandy.

The Nazi rise to power found Immer ministering to the community of Elberfeld, effectively a suburb of Wuppertal, in the Confessing Church of Barmen-Gemarke. He was a friend and colleague of Karl Barth, by whose theology he was deeply influenced. At a critical gathering in Elberfeld on 26 June 1933 Barth outlined five principles which he believed should define the position and direction of the Church, from prayer and preaching to spiritual resistance and preparation for martyrdom. When Barth was compelled to leave the country in 1935, Immer, always the more practical partner, effectively became the executor of his programme inside Germany.

In his New Year's sermon for 1934 Immer declared: '*Die Kirche ist zu Hure des Staats geworden* – the Church has become the whore of the state'. Challenged by the authorities, he defended his position by maintaining that his words were directed not at the state, which wasn't his immediate concern as a minister of the Church, but rather at the latter for failing in its responsibilities: 'In the state there may indeed be a Führer; that is not up to us; but . . . the Church must not allow its . . . message to be determined by the state . . . The Church can only serve the people and the state when it follows the path of direct obedience to its Lord.'[4]

His distinction brings to mind the traditional tripartite division of power in Judaism as expressed in the Mishnaic tractate *The Chapters of the Fathers*: 'There are three crowns, the crown of Torah, the crown of priesthood and the crown of kingship.'[5] The implication is not only that no two of these crowns must ever be worn by the same head, but also that their independence ensures that they exist in a necessary tension through which each is both limited and critiqued by the others. It is generally considered that one of the key reasons why the later rabbis partly disapproved of the Maccabees, who defeated the Seleucid Greeks and restored the independence of Judaea in the first half of the second century BCE, is that they combined their inherited station as priests with the self-appointed role of king. The function of the priest, and more especially of the prophet, was to tell truth to power, a challenging but essential task if the state was to be protected from moral corruption, but one rendered impossible if those entrusted with fulfilling it themselves became part of the political establishment. This Mishnaic declaration may represent one of the earliest instances of the separation of Church, or rather Synagogue, and State.

Despairing of the official leadership of the German Church after its acceptance of Hitler's overtures in January 1934, Immer looked to the *Gemeinde*, the community, as the active unit of spiritual integrity. He taught, preached, wrote and organised meetings and conferences, culminating in the declarations of Barmen and Reformed Barmen in 1934 and 1935, in which, boldly critical of *Deutscher Christen und der gegenwärtigen Reichskirchenregierung* (the German Christians and the current leadership of the official State Church), the Confessing Church committed itself solely to the authority of the teachings of Jesus Christ.[6]

But the political consequences of defending the Church's moral independence soon became clear. The very assertion that any institution could, and indeed must, maintain its spiritual and ethical autonomy was in itself a form of defiance of the state's claim to absolute power. Hence Immer's assertion, 'Responsibility obliges us to state clearly where the total power of the state has its limits,' could not but be understood as a form of political activism. It was this step towards spiritual resistance which in 1935–6 came to distinguish the 'committed' Confessing Church (*die bekennende Kirche konsequenter Prägung*) from its passive wing, which in practice appeared to do little more publically than tow the National Socialist line for the duration of the Reich.[7]

Thus in a key letter, intended also for Immer, Barth wrote on 30 June

1935 to his colleague Hesse of the failure of the Church to take action beyond the limited confines of its own institutions: 'It has as yet no heart for the millions suffering injustice. It has said not a single word about the most blatant issues of public integrity. It speaks, if it speaks at all, only about its own concerns.'[8] Barth's regret that he did not do more while in Germany was an obvious message to Immer.

It was during this period that the local SA daubed the front of his house with the words 'Here lives Immer, traitor to his people' in giant Gothic script. Of this insult Johannes Rau, who described Immer as 'his second father', wrote that he could only dimly begin to imagine the pain it must have caused his mentor.[9]

The events of Kristallnacht shocked and horrified Immer. The following Sunday he asked his whole family to accompany him to church. As Professor Klappert told me when we stood in the very place where his congregants would have sat listening to his message, he replaced his sermon with carefully selected texts in both Hebrew and German. He quoted the parable of the Good Samaritan, turning what can be read as an anti-Jewish polemic, only partially concealed within the seemingly benign intentions of the story, into an implicit indictment of the German people, and the Church, for ignoring the suffering of the Jews, and into an invitation to his hearers to become actively involved in caring for the victims. H. Albertz, who was a vicar in Gemarke at the time and present at the service, recalled how Immer then called on all those who had understood his words correctly to join him in the sacristy after the service: 'As I remember, some forty or fifty members of the community came. Over the following days we helped a number of Jewish citizens to escape the German Reich with false passports.'[10]

Consulted on 2 September 1939, following the British and French declarations of war, on the question of what special prayers the Church should say for the state, Immer is said to have responded, 'God, make us lose this war. Do not grant the German people victory . . . Otherwise the whole of Europe will become a concentration camp.'[11]

In 1943, after the almost total destruction of Wuppertal in Allied air raids, and in marked contrast to the Bishop of Hanover who referred to the strikes as 'terror attacks' and prayed that they should not deter the

German spirit from determined prosecution of the conflict, Immer interpreted the resultant destruction as a judgement over Kristallnacht in particular and on the Reich's treatment of the Jews in general.

Immer died following a stroke he suffered due to his treatment in Moabit Prison on 6 June 1944, a proud German who found it impossible to reconcile himself to the conduct of his own country.

I haven't yet met anyone other than Professor Klappert who has even heard of Karl Immer. It is important that his name becomes known, not only because this is the very least that can be done to honour his memory, but chiefly because of what must be learnt from his conduct. If religion is to preserve any integrity and moral credibility it has to speak out in the name of justice and human dignity against the abuse of power. Otherwise it fails in its responsibilities and betrays both God and the generation before which it is called upon to testify. The appeal to moral courage, which Immer heeded and which eventually cost him his life, is always contemporary and whoever wears the cloth must duly take note.

*   *   *

❖ Later that day I'm taken to see the memorial at Kemna. Kemna was one of the earliest, if not the very first, of the concentration camps created by the National Socialist Government after it came to power in January 1933; the site was already in use by July of the same year. In the short time it was in operation eight thousand people were interned there. Most of them were Communists, as indeed were the majority of those arrested and imprisoned elsewhere in the early phases of Nazi suppression.

Why was the camp closed down so swiftly? I'm told it was because it was too close to the city and local people knew too much about it. I'm puzzled. This explanation doesn't feel sufficient. After all, Dachau is close to the small town of that name and not far from Munich, yet it was never shut down.

A memory flashes through my mind. Eighteen years ago Nicky and I went to Dachau to see where my grandfather had been interned. Afterwards we met up with a close Catholic friend in a café in the town. We ordered tea and coffee, but a long time went by and we were not served. At length I saw the girl responsible for our table standing in the corner in tears. I became aware of an argument: it seemed as if the proprietor felt that too many Jews were coming to see the camp; let them wait for their food and drink. Or maybe I misunderstood? Or was it easier to think the latter?

The memorial is on the opposite side of the road from the site of the former camp. I'm shown the one house from that time which still stands, then I turn to the memorial. It depicts railway lines, still present, barbed wire, and, in the middle of the sculpture, a huge hand reaching down, palm facing outwards, fingers open. I'm puzzled by this hand. Is it asking for help? If so, why is it reaching down from above? Or is it a hand offering assistance, a hand descending from heaven? If so, was there ever such a thing? The monument disturbs me. It was designed by a local school; I would like to find out more about it.

Back in London I google 'Kemna Concentration Camp'. A minimal entry under 'Second World War Monuments' provides no further information. But then I come across the deposition of a former inmate:

I hereby undertake to refrain in future from any political activity hostile to the state, in particular from any form of high- or state-treasonable machinations. It was explained to me that protective custody will again be imposed on me, moreover for an unspecified period, if I again engage in anti-state activity. I further declare that no claims will be made by me on the grounds of the political measures taken against me. It was also explained to me that, if the case arises, I may again choose protective custody voluntarily.

Duisburg-Hamborn, 16 October 1933
Signed Karl Ibach[12]

'Protective custody' was one of the euphemisms employed by the Nazis from very early on to mask the actual reasons why they imprisoned and tortured their political opponents. It will have fooled nobody.

I believe my grandfather had to put his name to a similar declaration before being released from Dachau. I remember hearing him say that he had to swear that he had not been ill-treated in any way and that he would not lie to anyone by claiming that he had been so abused. I doubt if the form he was forced to sign to obtain his release contained anything about political activity; he was punished simply because he was a Jew. No specific actions had to be associated with that particular crime.

Ibach's statement confirms the fact that Kemna was created to lock away political opponents of the regime, as were the other 'early' concentration camps, Dachau, Oranienburg and Sachsenhausen, all of which were subsequently used to intern large numbers of Jews after Kristallnacht.

Searching further, I came across the following testimony from the Nuremberg Trials. It is part of a report of the Inspector of the State Secret Police (i.e. the Gestapo), dated 12 March 1935, concerning how and why prisoners were beaten. It acknowledges that the motive was often nothing more than pure sadism. The document is quoted by Dr Gürtner, the Minister of Justice, in a letter to the Minister of the Interior to prove that, at least in the early years of the Reich, Gürtner was concerned about the issue of Gestapo cruelty and tried to initiate criminal proceedings against them. The letter was brought as evidence during the cross-examination of Dr Hans Bernd Gisevius by Justice Robert Jackson on day one hundred and fourteen of the Nuremberg trials, Thursday, 25 April 1946. Dr Gisevius had been concerned by the activities of the Gestapo from the early thirties onwards and provided important evidence against the Nazi leadership at Nuremberg:

The experience of the first revolutionary years has shown that the persons who are charged to administer the beatings generally lose their sense of the purpose and meaning of their actions after a short time, and permit themselves to be governed by personal feelings of revenge or sadistic tendencies. Thus, members of the guard detail of the former concentration camp at Bredow near Stettin completely stripped a prostitute who had an argument with one of them, and beat her with whips and cowhides in such a fashion that the woman two months later still showed two open and infected wounds. In the concentration camp at Kemna near Wuppertal, prisoners were locked up in a narrow clothing locker and were then tortured by guards blowing in cigarette smoke, upsetting the locker, etc. In some cases the prisoners were first given salt herring to eat, in order to produce an especially strong and torturing thirst. [13]

*   *   *

❖   Afterwards I walk for over an hour through the woodlands above Kemna until it's completely dark and I have to use the spotlight of the *Ner Tamid* to find my way back down to the road. Is this a profanation? Perhaps, but I think of the verse: 'A light by my foothold are your commandments . . . ' I ponder the fate of the eight thousand people imprisoned here. They are cut off from hope and help; their cry is not heard. I wonder what their futures hold; is it already, at this early stage of the Third Reich, death? Their families turn desperately for assistance to the few from whom they can safely seek it, to Pastor Karl Immer, to friends abroad. I learn that some of the first deportations in the whole of Germany are from these regions. The Jews are taken east from here in 1941.

Later on I descend from the forest and find myself walking parallel to the railway tracks. There are no overhead gantries; maybe the siding is in disuse. I consider walking along it; Mitzpah would feel happier a little more distant from the busy road with its many headlights bearing down upon us. But I cannot bring myself to use the railway line as a hiking route. Mitzpah hates the traffic so much that I eventually catch a bus to the nearest station on the Schwebebahn, the unique hanging railway which follows the course of the Wupper river through the town.

Guy has been asking me what I imagine God must have felt during the Third Reich. Who can know what God feels up in heaven, or even if God feels in such a human way at all. But I believe strongly that God is present in every person, in their hopes and dreams, in their nerve ends, in their sense of pain and betrayal, in their despair lest they never ever see again those they love most in all the world. God weeps in many thousands of moments of human hopelessness. That

174

is enough for us to know on earth. If we truly understood it, we would not rest until we had changed the world. What happens in heaven isn't our concern.

I stay tonight with Professor Klappert and his wife, kind, gentle and deeply learned people. She explains to me why she finds such joy in life. Last year she had a bypass operation. It was discovered that without it she would have just three more weeks to live. 'I was ready to die,' she said. 'I'd accomplished all I wanted; I was happy with my life, I was prepared to go. Operate on younger people,' she told the medical team.

'You'll have a whole new life ahead of you about which as yet you know nothing,' her doctor replied.

'And so it has been,' she acknowledged, 'and I find such joy in everything.'

Professor Klappert asks me what I'm going to speak about on Shabbat. The weekly reading from the Torah focuses on the life of the patriarch Isaac and I say that I will probably talk about his blindness. This leads to a discussion of how the rabbis understand the precise expression used by the Torah, 'His eyes were dim from seeing.' In Vietnam, he tells me, he met mothers who witnessed their children killed by the Americans before their very eyes. Many of them are literally blind today, blind from seeing, he says.

The dinner table is soon covered with books, articles, texts we debate together, passages set aside for me to take home. I thank my hosts for their kindness. 'We love having guests,' they say; 'we both grew up in Indonesia where it's simply a part of the culture.' I cannot adequately express my appreciation for the degree of courtesy with which I have been welcomed in so many places.

Mitzpah sleeps on the bed behind me; I keep him with me upstairs as the Klapperts have put their cat in the cellar for the occasion and I do not want Mitzpah sniffing and huffing through the gap beneath the door. Poor dog, he's only had about five miles of walking today; it's simply been so full of conversations and encounters that we've made little headway north. The bad news is that it's nine o'clock at night and a certain quadruped has too much energy.

In the morning a diplomatic crisis is narrowly avoided. I take Mitzpah for a short walk to do the necessaries and come back earlier than anticipated. The poor cat had been allowed up from the cellar to eat his breakfast and is promptly whisked away as Mitzpah puts his eager head around the corner. 'Interfaith encounters,' we joke over breakfast.

It's only incidentally that I learn how much of Wuppertal, and Elberfeld especially, was destroyed by Allied bombing. On reflection I find it strange that I should have pushed to the periphery of my mind the many references to the destruction wrought by the war. They grew more frequent the farther north I travelled, through the Ruhr and towards the border with Holland, where, after the failure of Operation Market Garden, the area remained a battle ground until the final days of the war. 'Ninety per cent of the town was destroyed in the bombing,' I was told in Kleve. I heard exactly the same comment a day later on the Dutch side, near Arnhem. Yet, extraordinarily as it seems to me now, I didn't give a great deal of thought to what the bombing of Germany might have meant to its inhabitants, or to what the landscape through which I was walking would have looked like in the late 1940s, or even the 1950s, or possibly still later than that. 'The Germans endured the bombing of their cities with much the same stoical patience as had the British,' I once read somewhere. But I had never really considered in depth what this might actually have meant for either population.

The major raid on Wuppertal took place on 29 May 1943 and involved over six hundred planes. 'No industrial city in Germany has ever before been so completely wiped off the map,' the London *Times* reported the next day. [14]

Over twenty local industrial targets were listed in the British Ministry of Economic Warfare's 1943 *Guide to the Economic Importance of German Towns and Industries*, the book nicknamed by the RAF 'The Bomber's Baedecker', which located the town as lying 51° 15´ North and 7° 15´ East, and at a distance of 318 miles. Presumably this was measured from London, though most of the aircraft would have taken off from fields in Lincolnshire (still known to many today as Bomber County) and elsewhere in East Anglia. 'Wuppertal was formed in 1929 by the amalgamation of the towns of Elberfeld and Barmen,' the *Guide* begins, before listing the key information about all the local industries, including what they manufactured, the numbers employed in their workforce and the acreage they covered. The most significant targets in the Wuppertal region were the I. G. Farben oxygen and pharmaceutical works in the west of Elberfeld and the G. and J. Jaeger plant which made ball bearings, a critical component for the war effort: 'The factory is thought to be specially important for the manufacture of tank bearings for turrets and other heavy applications,' said the *Guide*. It occupied a 45-acre site, again in Elberfeld. The *Guide* also described the unique Schwebebahn and its eight-mile route down the narrow valley along which the two sides of the town extended.[15] Mitzpah and I travelled in one of its swaying carriages, sitting behind two voluble youths dressed in paramilitary gear, one of them drunk and the other still sufficiently sober to chastise his friend for imbibing too much beer, both of them making an equally intimidating impression.

The key industrial targets may have lain in Elberfeld but that May night in 1943 the bombs fell on Barmen. They destroyed a part of the very church in which Karl Immer had so courageously protested; I remember noticing the join between the new structure and the old, the line where the bombs had blasted the ancient masonry apart.

Joerg Friedrich describes the raid on Wuppertal in the opening of his harrowing work *Der Brand* (*The Fire*). By the late spring of 1943 the RAF had carefully researched and honed its method of attack to ensure maximum damage to the target. Through the disastrous first years of the war and until the opening of the second front in Western Europe, the only way the British could seriously strike back at Germany was from the air. Mosquitos, directed by a Master Bomber circling high above, indicated the target area with red flares; they were followed almost immediately by a wave of planes leaving green markers. Next came 55 fire raisers, dropping incendiaries, and finally 600 further bombers. 'At 1.20 a.m., Barmen was sealed off by a fire stretching from the theatre to the Adler Bridge . . . The typical half-timbered buildings, the narrow and twisted alleyways, the valley basin – which acted as a chimney – and a treacherous wind all served to fan the flames.' [16] Eighty per cent of the residential area was destroyed, Friedrich claims, and 3,400 persons killed. His book reveals the immense destruction of German lives, architecture and art in the Allied bombing campaigns. What he all but omits to mention is that these are not simply wanton acts of unprovoked aggression. The RAF, and later the USAAF, were conducting a bitter campaign in a war not of their making but instigated by the extreme greed and brutality of Nazi Germany and had refined tactics which, in their earlier stages, had been forged and deployed by the Luftwaffe during the Blitz on London and other British cities. Notwithstanding these very major failings of the work, it is impossible not to be horrified by his description of the results of the massive bombardments and the vast, sweeping fires, purposely created by the careful timing and sequence of incendiary and blockbuster bombs, in which many thousands were to perish, most notoriously in the attacks on Hamburg in 1943 and Dresden in 1945.

The scenes Friedrich describes in the aftermath of the bombing, as fire encompassed the town and the asphalt melted beneath the feet of its fleeing citizens, while the small Wupper river, one of the most polluted of all the Rhine's tributaries, proved too shallow to provide protection against the raging heat, can be comprehended, if at all, only by those who have passed through similar experiences and somehow survived.

After it was all over, what was left of the civic administration began to gather together the dead:

Heinrich Biergann, a sixteen-year-old trainee with the German railroad, had a truck driver's licence and was assigned to recover corpses: 'They'd say: here are six corpses, here are twenty, etc. Sometimes the people lay there totally at peace, as if asleep. They had been asphyxiated due to lack of oxygen. Others had been completely incinerated. The charred bodies measured about twenty inches. We recovered them in zinc bathtubs and washtubs. Three fitted into one washtub and seven or eight in a bathtub.'[17]

The Westend-Synagoge: the only one of all Frankfurt's many and beautiful synagogues to survive Kristallnacht

My grandfather, Rabbi Dr Georg Salzberger: probably one of the last pictures taken of him while he was still in Frankfurt

The visa issued by the British Consulate in Frankfurt, which saved my grandfather's life

Brian Berelowitz, my good friend who got me to the synagogue on time

The old Jewish Cemetery in Bingen, where a soldier killed for the fatherland in the First World War lies near a memorial to a woman murdered by the same country in the Second (*courtesy of Anna Wiehl*)

Mitzpah, eager to move on,
while I enjoy a short rest
(*courtesy of Anna Wiehl*)

Mitzpah's turn to relax after a
hard day's walk
(*courtesy of Anna Wiehl*)

On previous page: The beautiful River Rhine (*courtesy of Anna Wiehl*)

Left: The rock of the Lorelei, about which Heinrich Heine wrote his famous poem which was subsequently declared 'anonymous' by the Nazis (*courtesy of Anna Wiehl*)

Below: With my good friend John Schlapobersky outside the tiny synagogue in Saffig (*courtesy of Anna Wiehl*)

Adam von Trott zu Solz, at his trial by the 'People's Court' on 15 August 1944
(*courtesy of Renata von Trott*)

Karl Immer, a leading minister of the Confessing Church, who spoke out after Kristallnacht, and was branded a traitor by the Nazis

The glow of a rainbow: a symbolic moment? (*courtesy of Anna Wiehl*)

The Eternal Light burning in our new synagogue (*courtesy of Michal Mcewen*)

Friedrich refers many times in the course of his harrowing work to this shrinking of the bodies of the dead in the terrible heat.

W. G. Sebald's essay on the bombing of Germany in *Towards a Natural History of Destruction*, published in 2003, explores the silence in which the past and its devastation had been wrapped: 'I had grown up with the feeling that something was being kept from me; at home, at school, and by the German writers whose books I read hoping to glean more information about the monstrous events in the background of my own life.'[18] He quotes an entry from the diary of one Friedrich Reck for 20 August 1943, after the bombing of Hamburg, in which the writer describes how forty to fifty refugees are trying to force their way on to a train at a station in Upper Bavaria when a suitcase 'falls on the platform, bursts open and spills its contents. Toys, a manicure case, singed underwear. And last of all, the roasted corpse of a child, shrunk like a mummy, which its half-deranged mother has been carrying about with her, the relic of a past that was still intact a few days ago.'[19] Sebald finds this account so disturbing that it is impossible to credit; it is simply too terrible for the mind to comprehend. But many years later in Sheffield he meets a woman who was on duty as a helper at Stralsund Railway Station when a special train came through carrying refugees from Hamburg. There were several women, she told him, who 'actually did have dead children in their luggage, children who had suffocated in the smoke or died in some other way during the air raid.'[20]

In a sermon delivered not long after the bombing of Barmen, Karl Immer, whose church had largely been destroyed in the raid, took as his text a verse from the maledictions in the book of Deuteronomy: 'You will be afraid by night and by day' (28:66), to describe the horrific devastation as the just reward for Germany's own conduct. He regarded the destruction of his own city as bound morally to the events of November 1938 and what followed from them, and thus interpreted the bombing as divine punishment and a call to repentance. Sebald indicates that Immer was far from alone in understanding the attacks from the air in this manner. Trying to penetrate the historical and literary amnesia amid which he grew up – 'There was a tacit agreement, equally binding on everyone, that the true state of material and moral ruin in which the country found itself was not to be described'[21] – he notes that, 'It is also possible . . . that quite a number of those affected by the air raids, despite their grim but impotent fury in the face of such obvious madness, regarded the great firestorms as a just punishment, even an act of retribution on behalf of a higher power with which there could be no dispute.'[22]

Immer's interpretation brings to mind once again those words my grandfather heard as he walked through the crowds which had gathered to watch Frankfurt's main synagogue burn down on that morning of 10 November 1938: '*Das wird sich rächen* – This will be avenged.' Yet though the belief in ultimate moral justice is appropriate, and even to a degree courageous in the circumstances, I find little consolation in a theology based on retribution. It is surely blasphemous to argue that God was patiently watching the vicious destruction of Europe's Jews, and many millions of other citizens besides, while biding the divine time before finding the right moment to reassert authority and intervene once more in the disastrous course of human affairs. I take no theological comfort in the view that God wanted or needed the tens of thousands of civilians who perished in the bombings and firestorms across Germany to lose their lives. However deeply guilt and responsibility for the evil of Nazism did indeed penetrate through German society, and I believe it penetrated far, most of them were presumably innocent of direct involvement in serious crime, above all the children. Yet I feel a certain awe before the depth of the moral instinct which rightly understands, and indeed requires, that wrongs must not, and shall not, go unpunished.

But most of all I feel a dreadful horror before the incomprehensible, unimaginable cruelty of war.

In *Bomber County*, Daniel Swift follows the fortunes of his grandfather, by this stage in the war a highly experienced Lancaster Bomber pilot. After describing the raid on Wuppertal, he quotes from a letter his grandfather wrote to his wife on landing safely back at base in the early hours of the following morning: 'I had a job of work to do . . . ' The chances of surviving an entire year as a bomber pilot were less than one in two; scarcely more than a month later, during an attack on Munster on the night of 11/12 June his plane was lost. His body was recovered five days later at Callantsoog on the Dutch coast and buried nearby.[23]

It is hard not to be struck by the disjunction between the statement 'I had a job of work to do' and the suffering and dying taking place below. His wording is no doubt affected by a number of constraints: the wish not to make his wife more afraid than she no doubt already was, the limits of what it was permissible for him to disclose, the almost inevitable dissociation of his thoughts and feelings from the effects of his own actions, the fact that it was only through violent deeds and courage that a long, vicious and bloody war could possibly be won.

I often think of a story Isca used to tell about a friend in the RAF who always took his dog with him on missions. One night the animal refused to enter the aircraft and the man was obliged to leave his furry friend behind. Dogs, it is often held, have a sixth sense and know what human beings are unable to perceive. That night the plane was shot down. The man did not have the same options at his disposal as his dog; no soldier or airman ever does.

From Mitzpah's Blog

I didn't like that place we went to see this afternoon. I don't know why but it made me feel frightened. I could tell that it was making daddy unhappy too. He kept me on my lead, but I began to tremble all over. I wanted to get away and when he did let me free I ran and ran through the forest and all the way up the hill. I didn't like that old railway line either, or walking in the dark along the busy road with the sound of cars coming from behind me.

Later we climbed up lots of stairs and went in a very strange machine. My daddy says it's called a Schwebebahn. I only know that it hangs from a rail, goes very fast and swings a bit as it travels. It was very exciting. After we got out I barked and barked at the next one which went past.

I wonder how long we're going to be away from home. I don't really miss it, but today I wished the children had been here to play with me and take me away from that sad place.

Love,

Mitzpah

Day Twelve – From Wuppertal to Imshausen

After breakfast Professor Klappert drove me into town to meet up with Guy, Anna and Joe. On the way we parked for a moment near a busy junction so that he could show me the statue of the poet Else Lasker-Schüler, the 'black swan of Israel'. I had always loved the few poems by her with which I was familiar and had made a point of bringing a number of them with me. They possess a compact, compelling and sometimes strangely frightening beauty. Gottfried Benn, with whom she had a short and tempestuous love affair followed, unusually, by a faithful friendship, described her as 'the greatest lyrical poet Germany ever had'. 'The subject matter of her poems was mainly Jewish,' he noted, 'her imagination [was] essentially oriental, but her language was German'. [1] That 'but' was to prove fateful when the Nazis forced her into exile both from the land of her birth and, even more painfully, from the language of her art.

City records reveal that Else Lasker-Schüler was born in Elberfeld on 11 February 1869, though she herself concealed her true date of birth, this being just one of many ways in which she created for herself a range of sophisticated personae. She died an impoverished exile in Jerusalem, the place where all exile is supposed to end for ever, in January 1945. My father, who fled to Palestine as a teenager in 1937, remembered seeing her wandering through the streets of the city, alone, destitute and to outward appearances seemingly half crazy. A friend from those days, Heinz Politzer, described her as 'a broken old woman who looked like a solitary, exotic night bird, with enormous eyes in an ageless face'. [2]

'People did their best to support her,' my father recalled; she wasn't left in the streets to starve. She lived, and died, in her one room, which she would clean by tying oiled rags to her feet and skating across the floor. But even the most devoted of friends, who included the philosophers Martin Buber and Ernst Simon, as well as the publisher

Salman Schocken, couldn't help the poet back to her familiar landscape, her German-speaking readership, or her dreams.

Perhaps it was my father's memories which led me to form an early image of the poet as a brooding, haunting presence, as if she were somehow able to perceive, from beneath the garb of her exotic androgynous identities and the rush of sensuous impulses which flowed through her, the deaths of ages and nations:

> There is a weeping in the air
> As if the beloved God himself had died,
> And the leaden shade which has descended
> Weighs heavy as the grave.
>
> Come, let us conceal ourselves more closely;
> Life lies in every heart
> Like in a coffin.[3]

The poem is titled 'Weltende' ('End of the World'). I had assumed that these lines were written in 1933, after her flight from Germany, or maybe even later. It was a shock to realise that this poem was first published in 1903, predating not only the Nazi era but also, and by over a decade, the commencement of the First World War. Who could have foreseen then that thirty years later the God of humanity was indeed to die again in Germany and that it would prove impossible for the poet, or any of her co-religionists, to conceal themselves from the consequences, however 'closely' they tried?

Else Lasker-Shüler had blossomed in the world of Berlin cafés, where, twice divorced and often penniless, she created what she described as 'our nocturnal home . . . our oasis, our gypsy caravan, our tent in which we can rest after the painful battles of the day', unless, that is, she slept, as she often did, on park benches.[4] Here 'in this milieu where the intellectual establishment and the avant-garde of Gentile and Jewish society met, she blossomed as the friend of intellectuals and artists of all walks of life, philosophies, and backgrounds'.[5]

She adorned herself not only in strange garments but with exotic titles, referring to herself as the Prince of Thebes, claiming she was born in Egypt, or as Tino of Baghdad, or as Prince Yussuf. 'It was impossible to go anywhere with her without everyone stopping to stare,' Gottfried Benn recalled, remembering 'her flowing skirts or pants, incredible capes, her entire being bedecked with gaudy fake jewellery, necklaces, earrings, rings . . . '[6] Amidst these colourful but fragile identities she created a poetry of vivid expressionist imagery, lyrical purity and, frequently, a compelling simplicity which strikes straight at the heart. It is hard in translation to avoid a certain banality, which, as the sheer beauty and limpidity of the language attest, is entirely absent from the original. Thus the following lines from 'Mein Liebeslied' ('My Lovesong'):

> *O, ich denke an dich –*
> *Die Nacht frage nur.*
> *. . . Wenn du da bist,*
> *Bin ich immer reich.*

> Oh! I think of you –
> Just ask the night.
> . . . When you are there
> I am always rich.[7]

Or consider equally these lines from a poem 'An Mein Kind' ('To My Child') about her son Paul, a gifted artist who died of tuberculosis in 1927, which was published in Palestine in 1943 in her final collection, *Mein blaues Klavier* (*My Blue Piano*):

> *Darum weine ich sehr, ewiglich . . .*
> *In der Nacht meines Herzens.*
> *Die Liebe zu dir ist das Bildnis,*
> *Das man sich von Gott machen darf.*
> *Wenn der Mond in Blüte steht*
> *Gleicht er deinem Leben, mein Kind.*

> Therefore I weep greatly, eternally . . .
> In the night of my heart.
> Love of you is the only likeness
> One can make for oneself of God.
> When the moon is in blossom
> It is like your life, my child.[8]

After the Nazi arrogation of power in 1933 she was beaten in the streets by a mob. Without so much as returning to her room she boarded the first train out of Germany for Zurich, never to go back to the country of her birth. In 1939 the Swiss authorities refused her the right of residence and she was obliged to seek permanent refuge in Palestine. It was at once the land of her dreams and of her ultimate suffering. She had never hidden the fact that she was Jewish and had famously responded to an offer to translate her poems into Hebrew by exclaiming that they were already composed in that language. Perhaps her best known collection was the *Hebräische Balladen*, which included poems on numerous biblical figures, Abel, Abraham and Isaac, Moses, Saul and, most importantly, on many of the women of the Bible – Ruth, Esther, Abigail and Shulamith, the great lover, with whom she evidently identified:

> O, I learn from your sweet mouth
> To know too many blessings!
> Already I feel Gabriel's lips
> Burn upon my heart . . . .
> And the night cloud drinks
> My deep cedar dream.[9]

'My soul burns itself out in the evening colours of Jerusalem', she concluded. But the actual land proved alien. She had lost her language, the milieu of her creativity and most of her audience; she was left old, poor, lonely and in mourning. In a conversation with a friend shortly before her death she gave expression to an irony which she was surely not the only refugee-immigrant to feel: 'The same Jerusalem over which I fought with my friends when I was little and because of which I was expelled from school, the same Jerusalem that I have glorified in my poems offers me no home . . . '[10] 'I do not know the speech of this cool land', she wrote in a poem entitled 'Homesickness'. She dedicated her final collection of poetry not to the future, but to the past: 'To my unforgettable friends in the cities of Germany and to those, like me, exiled and dispersed throughout the world, in good faith!'[11]

She was a 'victim of the illusionary German–Jewish symbiosis', but she assessed its realities honestly, concluded Dagmar Lorenz: 'The destruction of Germany as she knew it caused the breakdown of her inner reality. There was no substitute in Palestine for what she had lost.'[12] But did that world of the German–Jewish symbiosis ever really exist any more than the Prince of Thebes or Tino of Baghdad? Or does the creative energy often burst through the earth's surface at just those fissures and conjunctions which, like so many borders, are both extraordinarily fertile and intrinsically unsafe, the meeting place of volcano and plain, land and river, which, when their raw powers are let loose, either drown their inhabitants or burn them alive?

*　　*　　*

❖　Today the weather has turned. At first the rain is light, but then it sweeps in wind-driven gusts against our faces. Guy walks with me. Conifers half hide the brilliant colours of the birches and beeches but cannot entirely obscure the glowing amber and gold still visible in the distance.

We lose our way – the map is harder to study in bad weather – and find ourselves back beside the same log pile next to which we had stood an hour before. This is not the way to bring anything home from Frankfurt to Finchley.

We stop beside a grove of thin, tall beeches. They sway in the wind like a quorum at prayer, sometimes all together, sometimes each in its own direction. Birds of prey dance in the wind; no doubt they are hunting but it feels as if there is a joy in them. Joe observes a honey buzzard, white beneath its wings.

Mitzpah is delighted when we leave the small roads and disappears off ahead. I only wish he wouldn't race quite so far in front of me; I call and call and just as I'm worrying where he's got to (perhaps the Dutch coast by now) he reappears, galloping with all his strength. I finally persuade him to stop. Later as he lies on the bed next to me his legs still move in some dream race.

I remember feeling troubled all through that day. A scene from the church in Barmen-Gemarke was bothering me. We had met a local guide, a friend of Professor Klappert, and he had been talking with her about how the Post Office had hurried to deliver letters containing a message from Karl Immer before the Gestapo could prevent them from being sent out. 'Oh, the resistance of ordinary people,' she had said, and he had nodded in agreement. The inevitable thought had passed through my mind: 'If there had been that much resistance by ordinary people maybe it would all not have happened.' I felt angry. But immediately afterwards I found myself wondering if this was fair. My grandfather recalled in his memoirs how, as he left the city gymnasium where he had been cooped up after Kristallnacht with hundreds of other Jews before being taken to the railway station from where they would be transported to Dachau, a man had handed each of them a bottle of milk. 'For that act of kindness I remain thankful to him to this very day,' he had written. At first I had thought that this was just a small gesture of humanity and consideration, but on reflection I realised that this was not so. It was no random, unpremeditated act. The man must have thought carefully about where to stand, bought the many bottles of milk, transported them to the spot and, above all, known as he stood there potentially visible and vulnerable to the Gestapo that he was putting himself at risk. But such deeds seem to have been the exception, while compliance was the rule and complicity and participation were frequent.

Few speak out against the abuse of human rights even in times of peace and relative safety. One thinks to oneself, 'Maybe I'm only seeing part of the picture,' or, 'It'll get me into too much trouble,' and says nothing. Perhaps one even secretly feels, without wanting to admit it to oneself, 'It serves those so-and-so's right; they've had it coming'. Thus one's own prejudice, or cowardice, or simple silence renders one complicit. To speak out in the hour of engagement, when one may be putting one's own life and, worse, the lives of one's family, in danger, demands a very significant degree of courage.

I think of the passage in which Sebastian Haffner, a German non-Jew, describes how men from the SA visit for the first time the law library in which he and his colleagues are preparing for their professional exams. He has always loathed the new regime and is later compelled, like several of his friends, to flee Germany:

The door was thrust open and a flood of brown uniforms surged in. In a booming voice, one of them, clearly the leader, shouted, 'Non-Aryans must leave the premises immediately.' . . . [A] brown shirt approached me and took up position in front of my work table. 'Are you Aryan?' Before I had a chance to think, I had said, 'Yes.' He took a close look at my nose – and retired. The blood shot to my face. A moment too late I felt the shame, the defeat. I had said, 'Yes!' . . . What a disgrace to buy, with a reply, the right to stay with my documents in peace! I had been caught unawares, even now. I had failed my very first test.[13]

Would I have acted differently? Or would I, too, guided by the impulse towards obedience and safety, have supplied the convenient answer and then regretted it in seemingly compliant silence a few seconds later?

But there is no need to transport oneself hypothetically into the past. How often do we ourselves speak out unambiguously about the injustices within our own society, or faith, or community? Or do we prefer to enjoy the relative peace of our own lives? 'There is no peace for the wicked!' declares the prophet (Isaiah 48:22). But surely it should be the other way round: the just person should find no peace because of the urgent and ceaseless demands on the conscience to challenge the wrongs of the world's order. Indeed, declares the Talmud, there is no complete rest for the righteous in this world, and the person who takes it, other than on Sabbaths and sacred days, diminishes his or her portion in the world to come.

The question of resistance was to occupy me more deeply later that day.

❖   We travel far off our route to near Imshausen, the home of the von Trott zu Solz family. It's especially important to me to come here to honour the memory of Adam von Trott, who was executed by Hitler after the failure of the July Plot in 1944. I first read about him in a book I saw on my grandfather's shelf when I was a teenager, and which I used to take down to read because the title moved and puzzled me: *Dying We Live*. In it are recorded the final letters from prison of those men and women who opposed the Hitler regime and paid for their principles with their lives. Among them are the letters of Adam von Trott zu Solz. ('Solz', I learn later, is the name of the small river which flows past the family estate.) Adam writes home in the last days of his life with a deep affection for his family, agitated about the state in which he is forced to leave his loved ones and his country, but at peace with his spirit in the knowledge of having done what is right and just.

I've been invited to give an address at the Johann Sebastian Bach House in Bad Hersfeld, not far from Imshausen, where a programme about light has been created involving remarkable music. (I'm worried that Mitzpah, who is also included and who has somewhat limited tastes in this area, will bark during the recital, so I carefully tickle his tummy to keep him calm. In the event, he behaves impeccably.) When my turn to speak comes I talk quietly about my project, the importance of memory, testimony. The music includes the sounding of bells reminiscent of those which were heard from afar by prisoners in Rome before their execution. They sound pure and clear, the very antithesis of violence.

After my talk several people come up to me. 'I remember the flames on the Reichspogromnacht,' a man tells me. 'I used to play with the Jewish children next door. Then suddenly they were gone.' A moment later he adds, 'And there are people here who say they knew nothing. Terrible!'

Another man asks me: 'You've been talking about light, but what of all the darkness? Are you also mindful of that?' 'Every day,' I tell him, meaning not just every day here while I'm in Germany, but almost every day of my life. Certainly I think about it on this walk. But I add that it's important to me to seek out and acknowledge the light as well.

'There was a sewing lady we knew. She had many Jewish friends and colleagues. When they were taken to the Ostbahnhof in Frankfurt to be deported, this lady walked on the other side of the street and prayed for them.'

'Are your community positive about your walk through Germany or are some of them angry that you're doing this?'

I don't know what to make of these various comments. Like

yesterday, ambivalent feelings arise in me: the wish to acknowledge the good that was done and listen thoughtfully to those who approach me, alongside the consciousness that all around so much evil was perpetrated and that these examples of humanity do not refute that reality.

Although it's already late, the main conversation of the evening is yet to come. We are all invited to dinner and I sit between Katharina, the daughter of Adam's brother Werner, and her sister-in-law Renata, wife of her brother Heinrich. Katharina was a child when the war ended, but she has many memories. She tells me:

> Those were terrible times. They were all Nazis round here. I mean after the war as well. There were houses we could go to as the family of a man who had been executed for trying to kill Hitler, and there were houses to which we could not go. Some people were Nazis but still gave us food. It wasn't always black and white. The silence after you spoke tonight, I couldn't stand it. It wasn't the silence of attentiveness, but of not wanting to know, of embarrassment, of self-protection. That's why I made my comment that it may be all right for you to be gentle in what you say but we Germans need to be more outspoken with one another. [As it happens, neither Anna, Guy, Joe nor I agree about this interpretation of the response to my talk. But Katharina has spent long years pondering the thick blanket of silence in which the past is so often wrapped; her sensitivity may be more finely attuned.] Even now, we had a gathering a few days ago and we all came, even the children of former Nazis. But there's a distance; one is aware of who was who. Is what happened during those times really talked about? Among historians and researchers, yes of course. Among the population, no, almost not at all.

We sense the pain of people surrounded so much of the time by others with whom they cannot really communicate. Later, at the family home in Bauhaus where all of us are invited to stay, I'm shown pictures. A group of eight children stand outside the door of a large house; the photograph was taken in 1948 or 1949 at Imshausen.

Those two girls are Adam's daughters Verena and Clarita. After Adam's arrest in July 1944 the Gestapo took them and their mother away from Imshausen. For a long time the family didn't know where they were or if they too were going to be killed. It was terrifying. But they eventually came back. This boy is Wilhelm von Halem, the son of Nikolaus von Halem, an extraordinarily courageous man who was tortured for two years and gave nothing away. They used to send his clothes back home covered in blood. At the end of the war the house was briefly full of soldiers. This was the front line, between the Germans, the Americans and the Russians. My grandmother gave them civilian clothes so that they wouldn't be shot by either the Russians or the Americans, or worst of all by the Nazis. They were all trying to get away with their bare lives. You can't just leave people to be shot. You need to understand that in the years after the war this was not just a family home. Many families lived here, aunts, uncles, refugees from the east.

The next day we are taken to see the house at Imshausen. Renata and Katharina show us a small church nearby and tell us that it contains a commemorative plaque for Adam: 'It wasn't easy putting it up; at first the local people were against it.' On the hill above the house stands a large cross, placed there by his brothers at the end of the war. 'This too wasn't simple. It aroused local opposition. But what else could Adam's brothers do? It was a basic act of loyalty, remembrance, love, despair.'

I feel a deep kinship with these people. They and I come from families traumatised by a past which lives on in our stories, our thoughts, our most essential understanding of who we are; a past the moral consequences of which define all our values and significant relationships. Yet most of those around us do not share this same history. Among those who know, who do partake in it, there is an immediate and intuitive empathy. This family also lives the experience of being a minority, perhaps even more so than I.

Months later Katharina and I are still in correspondence about these conversations. She weighs my words and finds them wanting, makes me sharpen them, urges me to confront the silence more directly. In the film her moral passion cuts through the screen: 'What they did to the Jews! They murdered them, they gassed them: it's incomprehensible!' Her concern is not confined to the past alone. She writes to me that the search for truth involves 'recognising where we ourselves are also guilty because we've been insufficiently vigilant or lacking in courage in analysing situations with proper acuity. For even the inhabitants of the Third Reich were so-called "normal" people (whatever that's supposed to mean). That's just what's so terrifying and disturbing.'

At the time of my visit all I really knew about Adam von Trott was derived from those final letters. Back home I read eagerly about his life. He was one of three sons of the Prussian minister for culture August von Trott zu Solz. After studying law and writing a thesis on Hegel's concept of the state and international justice he took up a Rhodes Scholarship at Oxford. I later learnt that he was one of the only Germans to be honoured with a plaque to his memory at Balliol, his former college. Returning to Germany he described Nazism as an 'appalling disaster' for his country, and refused, despite considerable pressure, to join the Party. He loathed Hitler and the entire Nazi regime and warned against the persecution of the Jews, but maintained a deep love for his country – Germany as it could and should have been. The Rhodes Scholarship subsequently enabled him to spend long periods of time in 1937 and 1938 in America and China, developing friendships and diplomatic contacts. A dynamic personality with a compelling presence, he strove to cultivate relationships at the highest level in both England and the USA, even after the outbreak of hostilities, in order to convince them that there was a viable opposition in Germany and that, with the removal of Hitler, war might be avoided. 'War,' he would say, 'solves nothing.'[14] But both the British and American authorities, warned to distrust his intentions, viewed him with suspicion. In 1940 he accepted a position in the *Auswärtigen Amt*, the German Foreign Office, using his membership of the Nazi Party, which at this stage he was unable to avoid, as a cover for opposition activities. A fascinating insight into his activities at this time is afforded by the remarkable war diaries of 'Missie', Marie Vassiltchikov, who effectively became his personal assistant and worked closely with him on many matters. She recalled that when she started her employment by attempting to clear his desk his secretary came in and said, 'Mr von Trott is a genius, and you cannot possible demand that a genius be tidy as well.' Aware of the nature of his activities and friendly with the wide circle of opponents to the regime implicated in the July Plot, she was critical of what she saw as the over-emphasis on what was to happen to Germany after the Führer's death rather than how and when Hitler was to be killed.[15]

Adam von Trott became a key member of the Kreisauer Kreis, a conservative circle around Helmut James Graf von Moltke, which stressed spiritual and intellectual resistance and took a leading role in the debate about the nature of the new Germany to be created after the war. His attempts as the group's spokesperson on foreign affairs to persuade the Allies that there was a different Germany with whom they could negotiate came to nothing in the face of their – readily understandable – demand for unconditional surrender. When the key precondition to any progress with the Allies, the assassination of Hitler, failed, von Trott's fate was sealed. In the years of ruin which accompanied Germany's utter defeat, those few among his fellow thinkers who did survive were largely ignored in the creation of the new order.

*   *   *

I remember that after all this we were worn out. Mitzpah wrote nothing in his blog that night. I can still see him slowly climbing the steep wooden stairs of the beautiful Engelsburg, Henner and Renata's home, to curl up on the bed and fall instantly asleep. No doubt the thoughts and scents of the day had exhausted the poor dog. He probably dreamt of the sound of bells.

Day Thirteen – From Imshausen Back to Cologne

❖   Over breakfast we continue the conversation for hours. This is more important than a few extra kilometres along the Rhine.

We ask Katharina to tell us more about her uncle. 'That's difficult,' she explains, 'I can't do that spontaneously in just a few minutes.' She feels a deep responsibility to do justice to the many different facets of his personality and activities and this makes her reticent. Yet at the same time we sense that it is important to her to speak.

> He was a brilliant man; he was also very handsome. You knew when he entered the room. He travelled greatly before the war, to England, to China, to America. He was opposed to Hitler from the start; he understood that he was a criminal. But the resistance was complex; there were many different political directions, communists, different Christian groups. He sought to build bridges.

> I cannot adequately describe the conversation. I can only testify to a mutual feeling of closeness, to that bond created between listener and speaker when their values connect.

We look together at the last picture of Adam; it was taken when he stood before the so-called *Volksgericht*, the People's Court, and knew what the judgment would be. Seven separate references to his address in the log-book kept by von Stauffenberg's chauffeur had incriminated him. The Gestapo filmed his hanging, all those hangings.

Another family memory: Katharina's mother was once in the nearby town of Bebra where she saw a train full of Jewish children; they had no food and nothing to drink. 'At least give them some water,' she said to a soldier. '*Ich kann nicht mehr* –I can't cope with this any more; leave me alone,' came the reply and the man turned away.

I part sadly from this family. Heinrich, Adam's younger brother, as well as Renata and her husband Henner were very close to my teacher Rabbi Dr Albert Friedlander, may his memory be for a blessing, and to his wife Evelyn, who visited them many times. I owe this important contact to them.

As a parting kindness, Renata gave me a book about Adam written by his wife Clarita. Its core consisted of documents about his activities lovingly and painstakingly compiled by her over many years, around which she had woven the narrative of her husband's short life. She was no longer young when the book was first published and was ninety-two when the second edition appeared. I was sorry not to have had the opportunity to meet her on this visit.

I immediately read the chapter describing Adam's final weeks of life after the failure of the July Plot and at once found the letters I had been looking for earlier:

MY BELOVED WIFE, DEAR CLARITCHEN . . . Memories of Imshausen too have filled me over and again with peace and happiness, memories of the valleys and the heights, the woods and fields through which we wandered together, of the deer, of all those movements, sounds and scents of nature untouched by human hand – just as our beautiful home will always bestow on you and the little ones its consolation. Whenever you climb our heights, alone or with the children, we shall be close together. [1]

Adam wrote this letter on 15 August, knowing that he was due to be sentenced the next day. A picture shows him sitting between two soldiers, presumably Gestapo or Kripo, who look like clowns in their absurd helmets, but clowns viciously armed with the power of life and death. I find the letter even more moving for having been to Imshausen and seen the views of which he speaks, for having met and been befriended by his family. On 26 August, the day of his death, Adam wrote to his wife from Plötzensee prison:

DEAR CLARITCHEN – This is now sadly the very last letter. Hopefully you have received my previous long letter. Most of all: forgive me for all the deep pain I've had to cause you. Know for certain: in my thoughts I remain with you and die in deep trust and faith. [2]

These letters are heart-breaking. They testify not only to a good and loving human being, but to the moral greatness of a man who remained true to his values despite knowing that he might have to pay for his integrity with his life, and who accepted his fate with courageous and unbroken faith.

Yet at the same time I cannot but think of what it means to have the opportunity to write a letter at all. We have a final card from my great-grandmother which she sent from Theresienstadt to relatives in Switzerland probably on 22 November 1943 (the date is hard to decipher), prior to being deported to Auschwitz where she was gassed. She had to write with an eye on the censor; it was all part of a ploy to deceive the world into thinking that life in the town, in which many tens of thousands died, wasn't so bad after all. But at least the letter proves that until that date she was alive. It also testifies to her undefeated spirit and selfless concern for the welfare of her family. However, the vast majority of murdered Jews, gypsies, communists and all those who perished in the camps had no opportunity to write anything whatsoever. To be able to tell your loved ones what you feel, where you are, indeed that you are – would have been an unimaginable luxury to them. Who, in those moments before death, even knew whether his nearest and dearest were still among the living? After all, it is love which makes our lives worth having. To live, and to die, when you know that somewhere in the world there still exists someone you love, and that maybe, just possibly, your last words and thoughts may eventually reach them, is different from living and dying in utter loneliness, already robbed of everything which endows life with purpose, and which, in happier times, used to fill it with joy.

After my grandmother died I inherited a number of my grandparents' books, including that volume *Dying We Live*. The clear faith expressed in so many of those last letters, the courage and serenity of those who knew they were dying in God's hands, their testament to a profound inner love and even happiness, made a great impression on me. 'These Romans, these wretched creatures, this Schultze and Freisler [the president of the People's Court, by which he had been condemned to death] and whatever the names of the pack of them may be – they would not even understand how little they can take away,' wrote Count von Moltke to his wife on 10 January 1945, less than two weeks before his execution at Plötzensee.[3] 'Christianity and we National Socialists have one thing in common,' Freisler had said to him at the trial, 'and one thing only: we both claim the whole man.'[4] But how very differently they each claim him, the one for love and the other for hatred. Precisely that is what makes any kind of fascism a form of idolatry. God, von Moltke wrote to his wife in what appears to be his final letter, had humbled him, freed him from anxious attachments to all earthly matters and given him 'time and opportunity to put in order everything that can be put in order, so that all earthly cares can fall away'.[5]

Once again I experience a kind of double vision. Since I first picked up that book I have led four groups from my community to visit Auschwitz and Birkenau. The sight of the ruins of the crematoria at the end of that long railway spur in Birkenau comes between me and these final letters. Last time I was there, frogs sang so loudly from the pool next to the broken masonry of Crematorium Three, still full of the ashes of the dead, that it was almost impossible to complete the memorial prayer. I imagine my great-grandmother walking from the railway track to those chambers alongside the electrified fence, descending perhaps into that very bunker next to the remains of which I stood, breathing in the gas. 'My deep faith,' she said, according to the testament of her friend Recha who offered to go in her place to Auschwitz and managed to survive the war, 'remains intact.'

*   *   *

With typical generosity Renata von Trott came to London for the lighting ceremony of the *Ner Tamid* in our new synagogue. The following day we went together to the Jewish cemetery in Hoop Lane where Rabbi Albert Friedlander is buried, a few rows away from his friend and congregant Jacqueline du Pré, whose conversion to Judaism he had overseen. Renata explained to me how, after a difficult experience in the church where a plaque was finally placed in Adam's memory, they had gone together to the cross on the hilltop overlooking Imshausen where Albert had led a moving service for the family. I could well believe it; he had a particular gift for bringing healing.

My father, mother, grandparents and aunt are all buried in that same cemetery in Hoop Lane. Renata asked me to take her to visit them all; I was touched by her quiet attentiveness and her courteous respect for the sleeping generations in which our hearts have their roots.

At my request Renata had written to me about her mother, Maria Mercedes von dem Bottlenberg. During Maria's year studying art at the Frobenius Institute in Frankfurt she had become friendly with Dr Hilde Lion, who later became the headmistress of a school established for Jewish refugees, Stoatley Rough, near Hindhead in Surrey. I replied that this was the very place to which my aunt Ruth had been sent soon after her arrival in England in April 1939. Renata wrote back:

> From 1937–9 our mother was in Britain, at Haslemere, in the school Dr Hilde Lion opened there for immigrant Jewish children. She taught the children German and drawing for free, in return for board, lodging and pocket money. It was there that she met the Summerville family and fell in love with and became engaged to their son Mark. He was a British airman and was stationed in Casablanca after the outbreak of war. He was shot down by the Germans that same year . . . My mother had always been eager to know what became of the children she taught.

So my aunt and Renata's mother might have known one another? Indeed, it seemed impossible that they wouldn't have met, especially as my aunt had loved drawing. How delighted Ruth would have been by this strange re-crossing of paths! I could hear her puzzling over it, mentally placing different people in her memory. But I learnt of it all too late; I wished I'd known about the connection just a couple of months earlier, before the horrible stroke which removed my aunt to that lonely island of consciousness from which she could no longer communicate in any manner we could accurately comprehend. Meanwhile I replied that I would do my best to trace some of those 'children' Renata's mother had taught and arrange for Renata to meet them at my home. I placed an advert in the newsletter of the AJR, the Association of Jewish Refugees, and promptly received an email from a lady who explained that she was the official historian for Stoatley Rough. Sadly, she couldn't find any records of Renata's mother's service at the school and I found myself unable to keep my well-intentioned but rash promise. I would have loved to listen to the life stories of those 'children', and learn more about her mother. Only much later in the war did she meet Renata's father. I never learnt the full story. It was obvious that Renata had adored her mother and missed her very deeply.

Thinking of Renata and her mother, and of the fate of those children for whom she cared, and of that whole community of refugees amidst whom I grew up, I went back to the cemetery in Hoop Lane and wandered among the graves.

Here lay Dr Ellen Littman who had studied Judaism at the Hochschule in Berlin (where my grandfather had gone to become a rabbi) and then taught Bible at Leo Baeck College in London. She was no longer alive by the time I became a student there, but my brother and I remembered her as a regular visitor to our grandparents' home. She had the painful habit of squeezing our biceps to see if we were growing up healthy and strong; then she would correct our pronunciation of the Grace after Meals. But she was a great and warm-hearted personality and we loved her all the same. She died during what should have been a routine operation. She had previously conveyed her apprehension to Isca: 'If you have misgivings don't go ahead,' Isca had advised, but perhaps she felt that she had no real choice.

Had these refugees ever come to feel at home in this foreign land where they now remained for ever? One grave after another proclaimed their fate: 'Born in Hamburg'; 'Born Vienna 1920, died London 2007'; 'In memory of my family who perished in the Holocaust'. In one large grave were buried five family members, two separate generations, who had all been born in Breslau. Perhaps they had known my father? I wished we had recorded on his grave the different lands in which he had lived: 'Breslau, Jerusalem, Glasgow, London', the inscription would have read. 'Berlin 1927, London 2004', Rabbi Friedlander's gravestone stated simply. He became a great supporter of Queens Park Rangers football club and was a regular fan at their matches. But did he feel at home, truly at home, in England, or was he also at the same time always somewhere else, in a different world?

'It's a very interesting question,' replied one respondent, interviewed for the fascinating book *Changing Countries* which addresses that very issue: 'If I go to Central Europe, I'm crying out for England. If I am anywhere else, I'm so happy to come back . . . I like to be here, but I am different from the English people, my language, my food, all sorts of things, but we are such good friends, because we tolerate each other.'[6] Others felt strangely, disconcertingly at home in Germany when they visited many years later.

I stop by the triple grave of a mother and her two children, all born in Germany. Did they flee here together before the war? Or did the children come first and manage, by knocking on every door they dared, finally to obtain the necessary papers to enable their mother to join them? Or did she remain behind but survive the camps, losing her husband and all her wider family, to rejoin her children after the war, from whom she nevertheless remained separated by experiences too frightful to articulate?

Here they had all come to rest, a community reconstituted in death, protected by the familiar inscriptions on Jewish gravestones concluding with the traditional abbreviation in Hebrew letters for the words: 'May his [or her] soul be bound up in the bond of eternal life.' The brief words were worlds: what flight and terror, what struggle to recreate an existence, to re-establish a family, lay between the 'Born in Hamburg' and the 'Died in London'?

My heart aches for their fate, and because I feel at home among them, at home with those who lost their home and perhaps only truly found it again in the company of one another, fellow exiles inhabiting the same story, speaking the same mixture of languages often in the very same sentence: 'Would you like some *Milch* in your *Kaffee, und* some *Kuchen* with *Schlagsahne?*'

'People ask me where I belong,' says Isca; 'I answer that I'm Jewish.'

*   *   *

That afternoon we drove back to Cologne for Shabbat. Frustrated by having accomplished so little walking, I took Mitzpah on a quick recky of the area between the hotel and the river before we returned to our room to prepare for the Sabbath.

From Mitzpah's Blog

Where we stayed this Shabbat was a long way from the synagogue. Part of the walk to get there was down a wild path by the Rhine which I loved because I could play with sticks all the way. Daddy didn't like it because at night it was pitch dark and he kept calling me because he was frightened. But we also had to cross a huge bridge with lots of traffic and I found that part scary. So we both helped each other.

On Friday night daddy put a large packet of old cheese in the bin. I fished it out and ate it all up. I can't understand why he's just rushed to open the window. It isn't very warm in our room.

I got a lovely letter from my friend Eva in Sweden. She sent it specially for me. It says:

Please take care of your dad and his friends, tell him to eat and sleep properly and above all to rest now and then.

What should I do? He even works on the Sabbath giving sermons and all that sort of stuff. If he doesn't listen when God in heaven tells him to rest, he's hardly likely to pay any attention to me – though I think he loves me more.

Shabbat Shalom,
Mitzpah

Shabbat in Cologne

❖   A sermon on Friday night, another on Shabbat Morning, teaching after Kiddush – I feel totally at home. This lovely community in Cologne, Gescher Lamassoret, is most welcoming. All the prayers on Friday night are sung and a combination of warmth and *kavvanah*, inner engagement, envelops us all. Mitzpah too is made to feel quite at ease. (I have to say that his behaviour so far through services Jewish and Christian, in monastery and synagogue, has been exemplary. Not for one single moment has he disturbed the worship, neither through his front end by barking nor through his nether end by somewhat different means. Instead he has been quiet, and, when spoken to, affectionate and calm. It must be the effect of the Hebrew and the German: instant boredom – 'I know that during this I'm supposed to sleep.' How many humans feel the same way?)

On Shabbat morning I speak of Isaac's blindness, or rather, about the more accurate meaning of the Hebrew, '*Vatich'hennah einav meire'ot* – His eyes were dim from seeing' (Genesis 27:1). I focus on the rabbinic explanation that, bound upon the altar and lying on his back waiting to be sacrificed, he has seen his father raise the knife above his outstretched neck. This fate, with no angelic intervention, befell the Jews of Cologne during the First Crusade.

According to a further rabbinic account, the angels in heaven wept at the sight and their heavy tears, dropping directly into Isaac's eyes, impaired his vision for ever after. 'Post-traumatic stress disorder,' someone in the congregation says. Absolutely. Afterwards Isaac can only perceive the world through the obscuring film of the terrifying experience which has befallen him. But what is it that, thus injured, Isaac is unable to see? Perhaps it is the distinct world of each of his children, their different lives, their separate realities and needs. Perhaps he can see that of the one son, but not that of the other. Perhaps he is aware of neither of them clearly.

The crucial moral issue in all our societies is whether we hear, and how we respond to, the narrative of those who are different from us, especially in culture and religion. Can we see and feel how their world looks? Do we care?

Isaac cannot see clearly because of the trauma to which he has been subjected; tragically, alienation and hatred result from this blindness. Have our tribulations as a people, the ways in which we have been victimised and made to suffer, made us too 'blind from seeing'? I think of the tragic and unnecessary conflict between Israelis and Palestinians and pray for a resolution. I recall a passage by Amos Oz in which he notes that brothers who have been similarly oppressed often see 'in the other not a partner in misfortune but in fact the image of their common oppressor'. [1] If only, instead, we could understand our shared humanity, our struggle for freedom, justice and security.

This journey makes me daily aware of the need to hear the other, of the necessity of being engaged with that other, of not saying 'I do not see,' 'We never knew,' or, worst of all, 'I just don't care.'

On this the future of the world depends.

I find myself rereading these words while visiting Israel to teach for a few days some months later. I love this country, have many family and friends here, and ever since my twenties the fact that I do not live here has always felt, even in the best years, like a semi-silent reproach. On this occasion I visit a friend who has devoted the last several years of his life to working with refugees from North East Africa, mainly from Eritrea and the Sudan. They make the dangerous journey across the Sinai Desert to enter Israel; sometimes the phone number of a friend or family member who has made it safely to Israel is all the 'travel information' these destitute people have.

We sit in the lane on a couple of chairs Nick has taken out of his tiny office which is mainly filled with bags of nappies. 'Seconds,' he explains, 'delivered by a kibbutz factory, but perfectly usable with a little care . . . These women and children come here directly from detention centres in the Negev; their husbands are generally kept there for far longer. They stay here for between three to six months before moving on.' I'm not quite clear what 'moving on' means; they are mostly given three-month renewable visas which don't allow them to work. 'But the authorities don't prosecute them or their employers if they do,' Nick observes. 'They can get jobs cleaning or washing up or sometimes cooking for parties and events.' What hope there is for them in the long term, whether they will ever be able to climb out of destitution and attain a better life for themselves and their children, remains unclear. In the meantime they live in these small rooms, each a few metres square, beds all around the edges, all now furnished, thanks to my friend's efforts, with a basic sink and a couple of electric hobs for cooking. Where do they get enough money to feed and clothe themselves and their children? 'Lots of people help,' Nick explains. 'The Israeli Gay and Lesbian Society has been amazing.' No doubt they understand all too well what it means to feel like outcasts.

It's the last day of June and the summer holidays have commenced. The next challenge is to find the funding to run a summer programme, otherwise the children will be bored and frustrated. 'Play with us,' they say when they see Nick. But the most immediate project is to get rid of the rats. Apparently they're breeding somewhere in the plaster walls which divide these meagre rooms and only a couple of days ago one of them bit a child. 'We'll have to evacuate the area for a week to get the job done.'

Nick is paid a half-time salary by the UN for which he puts in a double-length day. 'My parents are proud of me,' he says. 'My grand-mother came to England on the Kindertransport.' I'm proud of him too, proud that he grew up in our synagogue and youth movement Noam, and I'm moved by what he does and how deeply he cares. I still believe that, for all its issues, Israel contains a very great deal of remarkable and whole-hearted idealism.

But then I see myself standing on a rooftop in an Arab village just outside Jerusalem; it happened some three years ago. I'd been driving past with a colleague who runs Rabbis for Human Rights when we saw what was taking place and stopped. With us on the roof was the Arab family who owned the property; from rooftops opposite others were watching, equally silent, in shock. Below, a vast bulldozer looking like some pre- Ice Age monster with its long, agile neck and small, prehensile armoured head was devouring a house, slowly, section by section. Apparently the owners had built an extension without obtaining the requisite planning permission. But this was in dispute; unusually, it seemed that they may in fact have possessed the necessary documents. In most such cases householders, who simply want to add on a few more rooms to accommodate an expanded branch of the family, have given up the unequal endeavour to obtain the appropriate papers. Piece by piece this dream of many months or even years was being destroyed before our eyes. What seeds were being sown by this outrage, what pain and anger? On the way back to the car a couple of hours later we passed the local children returning home from school: they too were not to be spared this horrible scene.

What lay behind such actions? Underneath everything presumably was fear, fear of being outnumbered, fear of being set upon once again, fear of the other who tells a different story, who belongs to a different narrative.

Yet I love this country, created with so much courage, tenacity and hope in the wake of so much horror, then attacked by its neighbours within hours of declaring independence (with the support of the United Nations), in a war which has never completely left it at peace since. In Dresden at the Kirchentag I watched a film of the first service held by returning survivors at the Roonstrasse synagogue in Cologne. Such people were the builders of Israel and created out of disaster and destitution a fertile land, full of the love of the arts and learning, of Torah and science, as a response to so much hate. If only their dreams of peace and justice could also be fulfilled.

*   *   *

Walking through Cologne, I found myself thinking about the work of the Jüdische Kulturbund which had an important regional centre here. The Kulturbund was formed in Berlin in 1933 under the leadership of Dr Singer (he was to die in Theresienstadt in 1944) when Jewish actors and musicians were banned by the Nazis from the theatre, opera and the entire entertainment industry throughout Germany. Until its dissolution on 11 September 1941, the very date on which Jews were obliged to wear the yellow star, it not only provided jobs to hundreds of Jews connected with the stage and music, but allowed tens of thousands to forget for a few hours the oppression to which they were constantly and increasingly subject and find spiritual consolation in the world of art and ideas and in the companionship its performances provided.

The Rhine–Main branch was based in Frankfurt, where my grandfather was on the organising committee. I remember him talking about one particular episode which occurred during a lecture on Heine. A young SA man who was present to 'oversee' the proceedings (Nazis were in attendance at all public Jewish events, including synagogue services, to ensure that nothing offensive to the regime was said) turned to him and asked him quietly, indicating the speaker, '*Ist das der Herr Heine?* – Is that Mr Heine?'

Intense debate surrounded the question of what kind of plays the Jewish theatre should perform. The director of the Cologne branch, Willibald Fraenkel-Froon, wrote optimistically in the November/December 1933 issue of the *Mitteilungsblätter* that:

> The goal of our stage is to bring joy and the courage to face life to all by letting them participate in the eternal values of poetry or by discussing the problems of our time, but also by showing light hearted pieces and not rejecting them. We intend to keep up the connection with the German *Heimat* and to form, at the same time, a connecting link with our great Jewish past and with a future that is worth living.[2]

The editor of the Zionist-leaning *Jüdische Rundschau* disagreed, arguing for a robust Jewish content so as to deepen the national consciousness of the people:

> They must feel that they have joined the Kulturbund as Jews, and in their capacity as Jews are to enjoy art and other spiritual treasures. Open to the world, yet from a Jewish point of view: this differentiates the new Judaism from the era of assimilation.[3]

In the event, Lessing's *Nathan der Weise* was chosen to be the first production in Berlin, to criticism from both sides: Didn't this represent a head-in-the-sand hankering after a spirit of tolerance which was plainly gone for ever? Was there any point in trying to teach the Germans how they ought to behave? Was this the way to encourage Jews to develop a more independent identity? Shouldn't the very first play have reflected a more Zionist ideology?

Strangely, the same drama was selected when the Deutsches Theater was reopened by the Allies in Berlin on 7 September 1945. The director was Fritz Wisten, born Moritz Weinstein, a survivor of the concentration camps, while the part of the dervish was played by Alfred Balthoff, who had managed to survive the war underground in Berlin. To engage with that very same play in what must have felt not so much like a different Germany as a different universe must have been the most perplexing, ghostly and surreal experience for them both.

Money was a constant problem for the Kulturbund, as were the frequent interventions of the state. After 1935, the different Jewish cultural organisations across the country were united under one single authority, partly, according to Hinkel, who represented the Nazi regime in their dealings with it, to prevent local Gestapo officials from interfering unnecessarily in its work. Hinkel may have had a degree of genuine respect for Dr Singer, who in turn felt that, amid the numerous difficulties placed in the way of the organisation, here at least was a man it was not impossible to work with. Yet Hinkel, who had joined the Nazi party as early as 1921 and whose membership number was as low as 287, devoted much of his career as a journalist to attacking the Jews as 'masters of lies'. It was his regular boast that the Kulturbund was proof of the Nazi's generosity towards their greatest enemy; on the eve of its dissolution in 1941, he threw a party to celebrate twenty years of his membership of the NSDAP.[4]

Over the eight years of its existence the Kulturbund arranged hundreds of plays, operas, concerts, cabaret performances and lectures. As the economic and political situation of the Jewish community deteriorated and the persecution of those Jews remaining in Germany intensified, its work became ever more difficult, but also ever more important.

The authorities placed increasing restrictions on its artistic repertoire. Schiller and the German romantic dramatists and poets were the first to be banned. The works of Beethoven could not be performed. As long as Austria was out of favour Mozart was permitted, but this changed after the *Anschluss* in March 1938. The Kulturbund was forbidden to transfer royalties abroad, so all productions of foreign plays were prohibited unless the texts were out of copyright or the dramatists specifically waived their fees. The writings of authors known to have said anything critical of the Nazis could not be touched. Even Shakespeare was subject to censorship. A further 'difficulty' was that more and more actors and soloists managed to flee the country, leaving less Jewish talent available in Germany.

Immediately after Kristallnacht Jews were banned from visiting all regular places of entertainment; performances by the Kulturbund thus became the only source of spiritual respite and artistic inspiration for an increasingly beleaguered and desperate community. The Kulturbund itself was temporarily shut down in the wake of the outrage, but within three days the Nazis ordered it to resume its work. This placed it in the most extraordinary and painful position. Herbert Freeden described the reaction among the actors in Berlin:

> The smoke was still rising from the burnt synagogues and the debris of the pogrom lay in the streets – ring up the curtain: the Jews must go on play-acting! A wave of indignation went through the small gathering. But it would have been suicidal to resist the order . . . In innumerable homes, women were waiting for some news of their arrested husbands and sons; in innumerable homes, people were sitting among the ruins of their existence . . . And in the Jewish theatre the lights went up again . . . At 7.25 the first bell rang . . .[5]

Details of performances as well as reviews were publicised through the only organ now permitted the Jewish community, the *Jüdisches Nachrichtenblatt*, which Jews were more or less compelled to buy in order to keep up to date with the endless stream of Nazi decrees with which they had to comply. One reader who, exceptionally, managed to obtain a copy of the paper in Palestine, wrote as follows in a 1938 issue of the Tel Aviv-based *Mitteilungsblatt der Hitachduth Olej Germania* – the *Newsletter of the Association of Immigrants from Germany*:

> Approximately one third of the paper is devoted to the Jewish Kulturbund . . . At a time when most Jews do not even know what they are going to have to eat the next day and no one has a proper income of any kind, the impression is being created that Jews have recently developed a special interest in the theatre . . . It is quite likely that a large proportion of Kulturbund members are in no position to attend the performances – even if one might assume that these tormented and harried individuals would certainly like to do so.[6]

What the writer did not acknowledge was the contribution to morale made by the Kulturbund. Thus Dr Auerbach, rabbi of the district of Rechlinghausen, wrote as early as December 1934 in praise of the organisation, stressing that:

> By the Kulturbund's not restricting its performances to the large communities but coming also to the medium-sized and small communities, there serving in addition the surrounding tiny communities, we are all united by a great bond . . . It is precisely the individual Jew in the small communities who feels in a double way the heavy economic and psychological struggle for existence and who is dependent on the work of the Kulturbund and owes to it a debt of gratitude for its efforts.[7]

There is no reason to believe that this need for solidarity and support would have diminished in the intervening years.

On 11 September 1941, the activities of the Kulturbund were banned, its property confiscated and its staff arrested. Most of the latter were to perish in the extermination camps of Eastern Europe.

The work of the Kulturbund astounds and moves me; I find the creativity and dignity of this response to persecution humbling and inspiring. Through its activities that Jewish artistic energy which had seemingly found freedom from the ghettoes in the new and supposedly liberating cultural spaces of nineteenth-century Europe came back home to try to sustain and comfort its own beleaguered family. In so doing it not only returned to the depths of its own spiritual traditions but sought at the same time not to abandon the best of that wider cultural vision by which it had been so utterly betrayed. Were the events organised by the Kulturbund a luxury, as the *Mitteilungsblatt* suggested? Surely not! My father used to say of the hungry and embattled 1930s and 1940s in Palestine, later Israel, that people wouldn't have been able to survive had it not been for the music.

*   *   *

That night after the Sabbath had ended, I went with Guy to a laundrette in the centre of Cologne. There, in the last half-hour before the place closed and with Mitzpah comfortably curled up on the seat opposite, he asked me about God. 'I won't let you get away with anything,' he warned me, 'so tell me exactly what you mean when you use that word "God".' I remember watching the washing spin round in the machine and thinking of the earth turning on its axis in the vast, immeasurable and unimaginable universe. God? A personal God whose will we could influence through prayer? Was it possible to believe in such a being any more? Or were God and our God stories not rather part of our 'myth', central to the way we talked to ourselves about the world in order to render life meaningful, in order to circumscribe existence with moral rules so as to save us from an opportunist nihilism, but not true, at least not 'true' in that pre post-modern sense meaning 'out there and actually, empirically, existing'?

I don't precisely remember what I told Guy in that launderette, though the film is my witness as the scene is included in full, but this is what I believe I said: God is the sum of and transcends all the energy in the universe in its constant process of transformation from energy into matter and back again into energy. God is the totality of the as yet unexplained vitality and consciousness within it, which animates all life in its unendingly varied forms and is yet a profound unity, and of which my own awareness (which I call 'me') is a tiny, fragmentary spark that will, after my death, be reunited with the whole.

This God inspires the love which, in my best and purest moments, fills my heart. This God inspires the awe which sometimes sweeps through my soul with fear and beauty, humbling and fulfilling me at once. The awareness of the very existence of God is in and of itself the source of the constant and overarching commandment from which all the others can be derived: 'Love and care for life and strive to do nothing which hurts any living being.'

That's what I think I mean by God. But like the washing spinning round in that machine, my thoughts are always provisional, turning and changing before the vastness of this unbounded reality which absorbs me into itself and bears me wherever it wills.

Guy then asked me whether God was there to be a source of comfort. I answered both yes and no; yes, because God inspires the love in our hearts and unites all consciousness, thus turning life into a great bond of companionship; but no, because, in the words of the mediaeval *Adon Olam* hymn, 'After the end of all things, God will reign alone in awe.' When the earth dehydrates, or the sun explodes, or our entire solar system is sucked into some black hole, God will still exist. Ultimately God is not for our comfort; God is because God is.

*   *   *

That night I again found myself questioning the meaning of walking through Germany carrying a light:

❖   For two weeks I've been travelling with this torch. Right now it's plugged in so that the battery can recharge. Each night it shines like a half moon against the wall in the room where Mitzpah and I sleep. By day I tie the torch to my rucksack and, for double security, place it firmly in a side pocket as well, but in such a way that the light remains visible.

What does this light mean? Once again this is a question to which I have no ready answer. It gathers riches as I go. It contains the autumn beauty of the trees, the thick yellow drifts of birch leaves on the woodland floor, the fire of amber beech trees filtered through the rows of intervening pines. It holds the lights of those many lives about which I've learnt, Karl Immer and his companions, the hopes of the people imprisoned in Kemna. It is the flame which burns in the

211

Ner Tamid in Frankfurt, and in the small glass lamp above the space left by the Ark in Saffig, destroyed on Kristallnacht, and in the synagogue along the Mosel which that family devoted twenty years to restoring. It is the light we seek to find in our own soul but which life's confusion and our own complexities conceal from us. It is the light of friendship and courageous companionship between those of different faiths who struggle for the same ideals – the freedom to be human, to care for others and to contribute to the wellbeing of all life. It is the joy in the dog's first dance when, released from the lead, he spins in wild circles across the grasslands above the Rhine then hurtles himself forward in the sheer happiness of running. These are some of the colours which merge in the seemingly simple white of the lamp's single beam. All my life long and throughout the lives of us all, their different tones and shades transmute into each other and reveal themselves in gleams and shadows day by day.

But what if I should turn the flame inward and shine it on my heart? What do I see there?

Guy asks me again about God. The great commandment which addresses us from all being, from the vast consciousness to which our heart and mind belong and to which our tiny fragment of awareness will one day return, at once in that moment bringing the fulfilment of our lives as part of the all, and taking from us the notion that we are ultimately a separate distinctive 'I' or 'thou' at all – the overriding command which God trusts our sensitivity to comprehend from life's wonder and life's sorrow – is that we must not hurt or wound or injure or destroy. Both in beauty and in pain life commands us: love me and be filled with awe before me. Or perhaps we cannot even say 'before me' because we belong to that very same life which illuminates us from within and interrogates the heart. There is only that life.

And what do we see there by this light? All our faults and all our hopes, the love within us striving to be free, the joy within us striving to serve life in everything it encounters every day.

Once, as my cousin and I were searching through letters found in Jerusalem after my father and his sisters had died, we came upon the eulogy delivered at my mother's funeral. I was five when she died and, according to the wisdom of that time, it had not been considered appropriate that I should be present at the burial. Nor should I have remembered the exact words had I been there. But I had never seen this eulogy before, delivered by my grandfather's close friend and colleague from German days and during their shared exile in London, Rabbi Dr Eschelbacher. The text was taken from Psalms and consisted of no more than half a verse, *Lev tahor bera li* – 'Create me a pure heart, God' (51:12). I had always loved those words and the Psalm from which they came. Evidently there are causes why we treasure certain phrases and melodies, why they speak to us more than others, even if we no longer know the precise reason why. So my mother too had loved this very verse, had also set at the centre of her life the struggle for a heart which was neither obtuse nor opaque, through which God's light would shine in purity.

From Mitzpah's Blog

The Shabbat service today went on for a very long time. But they put out the Kiddush food early so I thought it would be a good idea to help myself. After all, the Talmud says that animals should be given their food before their humans are allowed to eat. So I don't understand why my daddy stopped me. He's going against Jewish law. Those challah breads looked so delicious and I was just about to take one. It really isn't fair.

Often I have to wait for a very long time while daddy sits and thinks. Sometimes I get bored and run off to play, until he calls me back. But at other times I can tell that he's sad and wants me to stay next to him. Occasionally he hugs me and then I lick his face. But more often I roll over so that he can tickle my tummy because that always makes him better. I'd never do it otherwise.

I know he loves me, even when his thoughts are a long way away. I can sense his feelings and my heart always tells me when he's scared. We dogs are all heart. Humans think too much. We dogs smell our world and feel it; that's why we always know whether others are happy or sad.

Love,
Mitzpah

Day Fifteen – From Cologne to Duisburg

❖   Poor Mitzpah; six times while we are in Cologne we have to cross one of those giant bridges over the Rhine. Traffic is ceaseless and he pauses and stares up anxiously at me when he sees where we're heading. But after a few words of encouragement and a scratch behind the ears he follows me and plods steadily along the pavement, looking behind him only when an exceptionally large or loud item of traffic roars by.

Down on the grass verge he encounters many dogs; everyone seems to be out today with their hounds. I watch with a wary eye. Mitzpah greets his fellow quadrupeds briefly, then hurries on with a cheery wave of his tail. I have the sense that he's telling them, 'Sorry, I'd love to play but I really haven't got time. I must be moving on to London. Bye!' Then he runs a couple of hundred metres farther down the path. Only once do I intervene. Mitzpah has attracted the attention of a huge, growling Alsatian-cross. And cross seems to be the word. I call Mitzpah away, whispering into his ear, 'Just remember, last time Germany and England met at football, England lost four one.'

Ahead I see a large wall or pile of grey-brown stones. From half a kilometre away I begin to wonder what they are. Who's put them there? Are they a former river barrier? Are they architectural remains? Surely the river cannot have washed them up in such a tidy formation? It's only when I'm almost alongside that I realise what the monument actually is: these are not stones, but sheep. They simply stand there, motionless as in a game of statues. I wonder how this can be possible when so many dogs, including Mitzpah, frolic all around them. Then I see one sole Alsatian guarding them all. Not a single sheep stirs; even the Lord's skills as a shepherd could scarcely be better. But don't ask me what they're doing here, herded into a virtual compound between a huge industrial complex and the river. I still can't quite believe it, but the animals look to all intents and purposes perfectly alive and real.

214

Today is Rosh Chodesh, the festival of the New Moon, inaugurating the Hebrew month of Kislev which includes the festival of Chanukkah, and I find great joy in singing the Hallel to myself, the collection of Psalms which forms part of the liturgy for such festive days, as I walk along the empty streets which for the moment separate me from the Rhine. I don't know why this brings me such pleasure. Partly it's because I love the Hallel and I've no need to rush the words since I hope to walk another ten kilometres at least along this stretch before I stop for a rest. Maybe it's some assertion of Jewish life, 'I shall not die, but I shall live', because over the last week my thoughts have often been preoccupied with death.

On that sad note I come to a verse which has long puzzled me: 'Precious in the eyes of the Lord is the death of his loved ones' (Psalm 116:15). Of late it makes me think about my father. But 'precious' is a strange and challenging word to use about death; can death really be so valuable and important to God? Surely this can't be what the verse means; it isn't death which is so precious, but God's 'loved ones', each and every single person. All living beings matter to God and God is present in them all.

When I rang Isca from Cologne, she said to me, 'I'm sure you must be thinking about Adi [my father] he used to go there often for work.' Actually I found it hard to do so. The part of Cologne in which I was staying was behind the Messe, the enormous series of halls which host the trade fairs, hardly the most attractive side of a generally beautiful city. The vast, often deserted buildings, the derelict warehouses, the inhuman scale of it all, had a profoundly depressing effect on me. I wasn't surprised to learn later that it was from this district that the city's Jews were deported.

I do however think of my father as I say the Hallel. I remember how these songs used to bind us all together; they were at the heart of his *girsa de'yankuta*, the learning and knowledge he had absorbed in his childhood. He knew as if by instinct all the *nuschaot*, every inflection of all the melodies of the Jewish year. I shall never forget how, at the close of the Rosh Hashanah meal at Nicky's and my home when he was already very ill and could only walk with great difficulty,

Isca stood on one side of him holding his arm, and my brother and I on the other, and we all sang the evening prayers in the beautiful and haunting modality of the New Year.

Nor will I forget how, close to the end of his days, when he was lying in a state somewhere between deep sleep and unconsciousness, he twice raised himself up in his bed, just far enough for his head to be clear of the pillow, and said, without to my mind being wakefully conscious of what he was doing, a line from the thrice-daily prayer: '*umekayyem emunato lisheinei aphar* – God keeps faith with those who sleep in the dust', before falling back into a deep slumber. So, for all the fact that he never once spoke about it openly, or even offered any indirect sign that he knew what lay so close before him, he was indeed deeply aware that he was dying.

Is dying 'precious in the eyes of the Lord'? I find it hard to bring myself to think so, unless dying should bring a particular closeness, perhaps even tenderness, between ourselves and God. But life most certainly is precious to God, every life and every living being, for God's presence fills us all.

I arrive a little late for my meeting with the Jewish community that evening and am full of apologies; we were stuck in a vast queue on the motorway (the distance from Cologne to Duisburg is too great to walk in one day, and Mitzpah and I are proud of the many kilometres we've covered). Around the table are just half a dozen people. There follow apologies in the other direction, 'There's so much on today . . . '

I recall an initial feeling of disappointment; I had hoped to meet with leaders of the local Muslim, as well as of the Jewish, congregation. Duisburg is after all one of the largest Muslim communities in the whole of Germany and a new and important mosque had recently been completed. But this feeling is quickly forgotten in the warmth of that small circle; it was a wonderful evening. This friendly group of people told me the stories of how they had come from Russia to live here in Germany. I was of course aware of the 'Russian Jews'; I had often heard about how they had swelled the numbers of the new German-Jewish community to over one hundred thousand souls, approximately three times its pre-1991 level. New synagogues had opened; there was an on-going search for Russian-speaking rabbis; prayer books had to be produced with a Russian translation or transliteration. I also have to say that there was at times something of a disparaging tone to the way those words 'Russian Jews' were spoken, with the emphasis on their widespread unawareness of their heritage. For this, seventy years of Communist repression, not just of Judaism but of all active religious life in the former USSR, was to blame, not the Jewish community or its members. Indeed, many Jews and Christians had risked severe punishment and the Gulag for the sake of keeping faith with their religion and their God, not to mention the thousands of refuseniks who had often suffered prolonged threats and severe discrimination because of their desire to leave the country and create new lives in Israel. I was therefore grateful for this opportunity to gain an initial insight into the world of Russian Jewry, or rather, into one or two of its many different and complex worlds.

'I spent three years in a ghetto,' an elderly man began. 'I was born in 1935; back then our birth certificates were in Yiddish. 1948 was a terrible year; all the Jewish newspapers were shut down, the great Yiddish writers were all shot. By Stalin.' He lists many names. 'I was in Transnistria, between the Dniester and the lower Bug Rivers. My grandmother was a Hasid; she scrupulously kept all the rules and traditions.' 'And you're becoming a Hasid now again,' the others tease him. He explains to me that there were four camps in Transnistria where Jews were murdered. He and his family were awaiting their turn to be deported. 'Then the Russians were victorious at Kursk and Orel and they liberated us. But there was no Jewish school when we went back in 1944, only a Ukrainian school.' There was no Jewish community left either.

I ask a lady who until now has been completely silent about her story. The family tradition is that her great-great-great-grandfather came to Russia with Napoleon, and stayed. 'He must have met a pretty Russian girl,' I joke. She nods her head and laughs. More stories about Napoleon follow, one telling how a pious Jew had saved him when he was fleeing from the Cossacks by covering him with his *tallit*, his prayer-shawl, and pretending that they were *davvening shacharit*, saying the morning service, together. I ask them if they know the story of the Alter Rebbe, Shneur Zalman of Liadi. Questioned whether he supported Napoleon or the Czar, he said that he was for the Czar. Napoleon would be better for the Jewish body, he acknowledged; but the Czar, in refusing to offer the Jews equality and the alluring opportunities which would no doubt accompany it, was better for the Jewish soul. His attitude was forcing Jews to remain Jewish.

Tanya, who leads the group and works as a teacher in the community, explains that there is uncertainty about her family name. Does it derive from the fact that the family lived in Smolensk; is the surname related to the Hebrew *smol*, left (there is no obvious explanation for this), or does it come from a term meaning 'of dark complexion' because the family were originally Sephardim from Spain?

I love listening to all these memories and reflections so warmly and openly shared. How much history there is around this small table.

Then I learn about Rabbi Neumann, the liberal rabbi of Duisburg, who refused to flee because he felt responsible for his community and who as a result was deported to Theresienstadt in 1942 and perished. I'm shown a lane named in his honour and told that on the anniversary of Kristallnacht there will be a candle-lit procession along it. He protected the orthodox Russian rabbi of the community of Ostjuden from the Gestapo and saw to it that he obtained a position in Switzerland, thus saving his life. But he himself died, as did so many of his congregants.

*   *   *

As we drew nearer to the border with Holland, I found myself reflecting more and more on the whole history and destiny of the Jews in Germany. When did the modern experience of dual identity begin? Had it really been a total failure? Yet was it not precisely this that so many of us were, whether Jews or Muslims, Hindus or Sikhs or countless others living far from the land of their birth: were we not all somehow hyphenated, both one person and another, striving to live with integrity both as a citizen in the land of our residence and as a member of the peoplehood of our faith? Indeed, whose is the identity which is not somehow multiple, complex, conflicted, even if only by virtue of the fact that we are all composed of two genetically different sets of parental genes?

In his masterly book *The Pity of It All*, Amos Elon opens his account of Berlin Jewry at the moment when Moses Mendelssohn enters the city through the *Rosenthaler Tor* in 1743. Was it Mendelssohn's cultivated friendship with the writer and dramatist Ephraim Gotthold Lessing with which the 'German–Jewish symbiosis' began? Was it his ability to refute, in lucid German, with firm courage and with subtle yet cultured argument, the Swiss minister Johann Kaspar Lavater's challenge to him to become a Christian and instead demand, as he proceeded to do in his *Jerusalem*, the equal status of different religious faiths within the basically rational and secular space of the tolerant state?

It was in 1781 and at Mendelssohn's behest that Christian Willhelm von Dohm wrote his influential pamphlet *Über die Bürgerliche Verbesserung der Juden*, 'On the Civic Improvement of the Jews'. It is not accidental that the very title is ambiguous. On the one hand the tract was a plea to remove a whole series of oppressive and unjustifiable burdens from the Jews; on the other, it argued that the Jews had much to do in order to better their own selves and prove themselves worthy of such treatment. Dohm did however maintain that the amelioration of their civic status had to precede such internal changes; the faults so widely associated with the Jewish character, he argued, such as parochialism, obstinacy, preoccupation with money and dishonesty in business, were not endemic to it but were rather the natural result of centuries of exclusion and maltreatment:

> More than anything else a life of normal civil happiness in a well-ordered state, enjoying the long withheld freedom, would tend to do away with clannish religious opinions. The Jew is even more man than Jew, and how would it be possible for him not to love a state where he could freely acquire property and freely enjoy it.[1]

Dohn was courageous enough to balance his argument by noting that there was bigotry on both sides: 'With the moral improvement of the Jews there should go hand in hand efforts by the Christians to get rid of their prejudices and uncharitable opinions.'[2]

Less than a year later, on 2 January 1782, Joseph II, Holy Roman Emperor and King of Germany, issued his Edict of Tolerance. It allowed Jews to attend Christian primary and secondary schools and learn all kinds of trades, abolished head tolls and extra taxes, permitted Jews to choose their own place of residence in the cities where they lived and removed all requirements of distinctive dress. The edict applied to the category of 'tolerated Jew' and initially affected only Lower Austria. It was one of a number of enactments, including the prohibition against using Yiddish or Hebrew in business and public records, the requirement of adopting secular surnames, the banning of the autonomy of religious law and the inclusion of Jews in military service, which removed barriers and drew Jews into the mainstream of society. 'Since by these favours,' the Edict continued, 'we almost place the Jewish nation on an equal level with adherents of other religious associations in respect to trade and employment of civil and domestic facilities, we hereby earnestly advise them to observe scrupulously all political, civil and judicial laws of the country to which they are bound as inhabitants . . . '[3] It is difficult for the contemporary reader not to be struck by the word 'almost'.

Though the decree was regarded with great suspicion by the Jewish masses as threatening their traditional way of life, and as a subtle way of compelling Jews to serve in the Austro-Hungarian army, it nevertheless opened the door for a rising and growing middle class to enter European culture, to which it quickly began to contribute.

In 1783 Mendelssohn's *Jerusalem* was published:

Principles are free [he argued]; by their very nature, attitudes do not suffer constraint or corruption . . . Thus neither Church nor state is entitled to subject the principles and attitudes of men to any form of coercion . . . Whoever does not infringe public happiness, whoever honestly observes the civil laws, let him speak as he pleases, let him call to his God in his own way or the way of his fathers, and let him find his salvation where he hopes to find it.[4]

Little more than a decade later Napoleon's victories brought the core concepts of the French Revolution, emancipation and equality, to Germany. In July 1796 his troops set siege to Frankfurt and bombarded the Judengasse; in 1811, after almost 350 years, the requirement that Jews reside within it was finally abolished. Though his humiliation in Russia and his defeat at the Battle of Leipzig in 1813 were to mean a swift shrinking of the horizon of hope and a retraction of rights gained and promised, especially in Prussia, nevertheless there was no return to the status quo ante. The intellectual and social currents were already working powerfully from within which would, over the next hundred and twenty years, until the collapse of the Weimar Republic in 1933, move Jews to the centre of German life and letters.

Jews, including those who fought with patriotic fervour in the Prussian army against Napoleon, broadly welcomed the opportunity to enter European society. They embraced the new ideal of *Bildung* with its emphasis on the moral development of the individual irrespective of origin; as Georg Mosse wrote in his troublingly titled *German Jews beyond Judaism*: 'Here was an ideal ready made for Jewish assimilation, because it transcended all differences of nationality and religion through the unfolding of the individual personality.'[5] At the core of the concept was the belief that the development of the intellect activated a person's moral sense, while the aesthetic sensibility expressed a moral and spiritual harmony, an ability to control and harness the passions. Berthold Auerbach, considered one of the most representative German Jews of the nineteenth century, wrote: 'Formerly the religious spirit proceeded from revelation, the present starts with *Bildung*.'[6] It would be the degree of a person's *Bildung*, not whether he or she happened to be born a Jew or a Christian, which would henceforth determine the question of civic status. Here then was a path which led to new vistas of opportunity, and Jews were eager to follow it.

This ideal was embraced not only by the early reformers, but also by the new orthodoxy exemplified by such a figure as Samson Raphael Hirsch. Born in Hamburg in 1808, Hirsch received rabbinic ordination from Rabbi Yaakov Ettlinger and studied at the University of Bonn. He was a lifelong admirer of Schiller, whose spirit was seen by some, even more than that of Goethe, as lighting the way to a new age.

In 1836 Hirsch published his *Nineteen Letters*, an impassioned response to an imaginary interlocutor, Benjamin, who, on the point of deserting Judaism for a free life in the wider world, had turned to his rabbi friend for urgent guidance: 'What shall become of us, dear Naphtali?' he pleads.[7] Naphtali, who is of course Hirsch himself, exhorts Benjamin to re-evaluate his understanding of Judaism. *Nineteen Letters* is one of the first Jewish works to address the central dilemma posed by the advent of modernity and increasing civic opportunity: why remain Jewish, bound by all its seemingly illogical and unnecessary restraints and subject to the prejudices and disadvantages which being Jewish still entails, when a wider world beckons with all its intellectual and cultural riches? In response, Hirsch coined the phrase *Yisroel-Mensch*, the 'Israel-Man', the person who was both fully a *Mensch*, that is, a citizen in the surrounding world, yet remained an observant Jew. In this way he balanced a remarkable universalism with an eloquent defence of traditional Jewish practice. Thus he defined the Mitzvot, here one of the six headings under which he described the commandments of the Torah, as 'Precepts concerning love towards all living things without distinction, purely because it is the bidding of God, and in consideration of our duty as men and Israelites.'[8] In his Torah commentary on the verse from Leviticus, 'Love your neighbour as yourself', he observed that this was 'something that is expected from us towards all our fellow-men in the name of God, who has given all men the mutual calling of "neighbours".'[9]

Meanwhile, increasing numbers of Jews were in fact following Benjamin's path without taking the trouble to ask their rabbis. *Bildung* became their goal, an ideal which, pursued through a deep and sustained engagement with the humanities, combined the ethical and the aesthetic, and, it was believed, would inspire all human beings, irrespective of their faith, to work together in harmony for the good, the beautiful and the true.

This was the cultural and spiritual ideal which I was fortunate to inherit from my mother's side of the family. My grandfather expressed it through the study of the classic rabbinic tract *The Ethics of the Fathers*, accompanied by relevant quotations from Goethe and other German poets, as well as through his special love of the wisdom literature of the Bible. For me, the symbiosis was Talmud and Shakespeare; the rabbinic commentaries on the stories of Jacob and Joseph together with discussions of the novels of Thomas Mann and Dostoevsky. But I also inherited, and I'm equally glad of it, a more traditional and observant Judaism from my father's family.

Yet this process of acculturation soon came to have its detractors, both outside and within the Jewish community. The German historian Heinrich von Treitschke (1834–96) observed that 'on German soil there is no room for dual nationality' and in 1879 created the slogan I had always assumed to have been one of the (milder) inventions of Goebbels: '*Die Juden sind unser Unglück* – The Jews are our misfortune.'[10] Precisely at the same time as Jews began to feel increasingly at home in Germany, counter-currents within the country were generating a political anti-Semitism which would come to a head in the 1880s. It would re-emerge in the pernicious census of Jews serving in the German army in 1916, designed to prove – as it failed to do – that they were cowards who shirked front-line service. When in the short-lived Weimar Republic Jews once again championed the liberal cause of *Bildung*, they were arguably less aware than they might have been that dangerous forces were carrying this term in a different direction, popular, nationalist forces rooted in ancient myths of Germany and the German spirit as predicted a century earlier by Heine. In this mood Jews would never share, even if the increasingly punitive and murderous legislation of the Third Reich had permitted them to do so.

If new and wider cultural horizons looked attractive to some Jews, how did they in turn look to their non-Jewish fellow citizens? How did the latter perceive this process of the increasing acculturation and integration of the Semitic other? The answer to this question is of course as diverse as society itself. But in few places, prior to the literature of Nazism, can there be a more disturbing depiction than in the novella written by Oskar Panizza, *Der Operierte Jud – The Operated Jew*. It recounts the fate of one Itzig Faitel Stern, the perfect caricature of the *nouveau-riche parvenu*, the wealthy, spittle-spitting, breast-beating, bent-forward, talking-with-his-hands, but liberated and German-speaking ex-ghetto Jew. Panizza's account is at once sophisticated, brilliant and vicious.

There was also unease inside the Jewish community itself about its new place within German culture . In March 1912 Moritz Goldstein, a young scholar of Jewish literature, published an article entitled 'Deutsch-Jüdisch Parnass' ('The German Jewish Parnassus'), in which he declared that: 'We Jews are administering the spiritual property of a nation which denies our right and our ability to do so.' He continued: 'Among ourselves we have the impression that we speak as Germans to Germans . . . But though we may after all feel totally German, the others feel us to be totally un-German . . . ' Still, his own ambivalence was all too apparent, or he would not also have written:

> The German spring is our spring, as the German winter is for us winter . . . Were we not raised on German fairy tales? Are not the German forests alive for us? Are we not also allowed to behold its elves and gnomes? Do we not understand the murmur of its streams and the song of its birds?[11]

I believe my grandparents would have shared these sentiments entirely.

Kafka was more blunt: 'Most [Jews] . . . wanted to leave Jewishness behind them, and their fathers approved of this, but vaguely . . . But with their hind legs they were still glued to their father's Jewishness and with their waving front legs they found no new ground.'[12]

Perhaps it was this sense that, having left the familiar territory of traditional Judaism, they had failed to secure another, which led to the Jewish revival which began to gather head in the wake of Germany's defeat in the First World War. What was needed was a return, as Rosenzweig expressed it in his address at the opening of the Freies Jüdisches Lehrhaus in Frankfurt in 1920, 'from the outside in'.[13] Its true leaders and teachers would be the alienated, indeed the more alienated the better, he argued, for they were now the only group of people capable of leading their lost brothers and sisters back home.

The process was cut short by Nazism and destroyed in Germany by the Holocaust, though elsewhere it would continue to inspire a return to Judaism even many decades after the war.

*   *   *

❖ This evening after my meeting with the community I search the streets of Duisburg for somewhere to eat. I find a stall selling delicious dried fruit. I approached the vendor eagerly: 'Sorry, it's too late; it only brings us trouble if we sell anything now.' I could have fancied some of those apricots. There are several indications that the friendliness we encountered farther south is not the universal rule up here. I finally go into a Chinese restaurant and, after finding something vegetarian for myself, order a bowl of rice for Mitzpah. We've done almost thirty kilometres together today: why should he have to watch while I alone eat? The lady who serves us is charming, 'No, no,' she says, 'not fried rice; plain rice is best for dogs.' I'm evidently not the first crazy customer to order a portion for his canine companion. He's so hungry that I have to stop him from trying to eat the foil dish in which his meal is served.

Here then is the outline of Oskar Panizza's story. Panizza, a writer touched by genius, of which this particular tale is a prime example, was at once physician, poet, Bohemian and outrageous iconoclast. His lively interest in prostitutes is presumed to have led to his contracting syphilis. His play *The Council of Love* on the subject of how the disease first came down to earth, an affair in which God, Jesus, Mary and the Pope were all declared by him to be implicated, led to ninety-three charges of blasphemy being lodged against him, a notorious trial and a year in prison. The disease evidently only added to the mental illness of which there was already a history in his family and he spent the latter part of his life in an asylum near Bayreuth.

The tale in question is called *Der Operierte Jud*, translated into English by Jack Zipes as *The Operated Jew*. Written in 1893, the story itself is deeply anti-Semitic. 'The worshipper of Luther and Wagner eagerly embraces his mentors' racial prejudices. His bias is especially evident when discussing the Jewish "race",' noted Peter Brown, who wrote a full-length study of Panizza.[14] But can an author who also fiercely attacked both Church, especially the Catholic Church, and state, and who was later to write, though evidently grudgingly, of the Jews that 'their monotheism is one of the most powerful spiritual forces that has ever been of service to humankind', solely be summed up as an anti-Semite?[15] The tale has other tragets as well, among them the whole notion of change and adaptation, either through social integration or by means of eugenics. 'We cannot be anything other than what we are,' he wrote on the latter subject.[16]

The story concerns one Itzig Faitel Stern, a close friend of the author, or rather of the persona the author adopts. The name is not a creation *ex nihilo*; rather, it is taken from Friedrich Freiherr von Holzschuher's parody of Jewish efforts to attain equal rights, 'The Emancipation of the Praiseworthy Royal Bavarian Jewish Community: An Address to the Honourable Gentlemen of the Parliament, delivered by Itzig Feitel Stern', written in 1834. Panizza devotes the opening pages of his account to a depiction of Faitel's physical characteristics: his squat, unbalanced body, his bow-legged gait and his spluttering, over-enthusiastic, bastardised German, punctuated by strange expostulations sounding like 'Menera!' and 'Deradang!' and accompanied by the ejection of large quantities of saliva. The narrator's tone as he describes his friend is one of bemused contempt mixed with a mentor's voyeuristic solicitude: 'I observed with astonishment how this monster took terrible pains to adapt to our circumstances, our way of walking, thinking, our gesticulations, the expressions of our intellectual tradition, our manner of speech.' [17] It is worth noting the 'our' with which the 'friend' claims prior ownership of the true and pure German culture. Faitel is presumably only one of many similar Jews

> who emanated directly from the stingy, indiscriminate, stifling, dirty-diapered, griping and grimacing bagatelle of his family upbringing, and as a result of a hasty decision, with his pockets full of money, was suddenly thrown on to the great pavement of life in a European city, and there he began to look around, ignorant, with blundering movements.[18]

This then is at least one view of how the prolonged and painful Jewish struggle for emancipation and civil rights was perceived from the other side. The story, however, does rather more than simply pander to the then popular theories of race or the currents of late-nineteenth-century political anti-Semitism; it is clear that the latter is not the author's sole intention.

The narrator tells Faitel that he really must do something about his manner and appearance if he wishes to be accepted on the social scene. This advice falls on willing ears and there follow for Faitel many months of painful operations and numerous lessons by leading experts in how to relearn the basic skills of walking and talking, this time with a straight back and with no objectionable accent to betray his unseemly Jewish origins. For all these unpleasant procedures Faitel and his father pay gladly through their noses. (Panizza never tells us how this apparently endless supply of money has been generated.) Everything takes place under the scrupulous direction of the outstanding Professor Klotz. *Klotz* means 'lout' or 'clod' in German and, as Panizza presumably knew, 'clumsy dolt' or 'inept idiot' in Yiddish. As a keen student of medical developments Panizza was *au fait* with the growing literature on the subject of ethnic characteristics, racial improvements and eugenics of which this story has been read as a mocking *reductio ad absurdam*. The process of Faitel's betterment culminates when, on this sole occasion against medical advice, he opens his own arteries, an operation which he performs in a warm bath so that sufficient blood will be lost to make room in his veins for the welcome receipt of eight litres of pure Christian elixir supplied by seven hearty Aryan girls from the Black Forest.

Last but not least, Faitel seeks to acquire a new spirit. He 'had heard about the chaste, undefined Germanic soul, which shrouded the possessor like an aroma. This soul was the source of the possessor's rich treasures and formed the *shibboleth* of the German nations, a soul which was immediately recognised by all who possessed one. Faitel wanted to have this soul.'[19] It is difficult to assess the level of irony in Panizza's writing at this point. Is the subject of his critique the very notion of this ethereal German *Geist* and its supposed superiority, or the desire of so many Jews not only to assimilate themselves to it but to become its champions and connoisseurs? In this domain, however, it is determined that no operation can be of any avail; Faitel is left to his own intuitions. Yet he manages well, exhaling to great effect in the very best salons such sweet nothings as, 'Oh, I must confess, when I reflect about this, when I consider this, everything seems gloomy to me, and my heart shudders.'[20] Is it too much to see in these details the mockery of such observations as Goethe's, that, for reasons he cannot fathom, it is his Jewish readers and specifically the women among them, who have the greatest emotional and spiritual empathy with his writings?

His hair now blond and straight, Faitel reappears on the Heidelberg scene as Siegfried Freudenstern, the perfect Christian German. Or so at least it seems. Yet the author shares with his readers his fear that beneath his friend's outward manner there remains something amiss about this new hybrid creation:

> During the day he was in the European corset, harnessed, supervised, under great surveillance. But in the evening when he was no longer bound, when he took off the barbed belt [which he wore to maintain a perfect, erect posture] and lay in bed, I'm sure he rocked as he formerly did, the pelvis moving back and forth, his hands spreading into the vest pockets, his tongue gurgling and bawling, 'Deradang! Deradang!' And the entire Palatinate-Yiddish deluge could not be checked.[21]

In other words, for all the effort and expense involved, the project of acculturation is doomed to specious superficiality. Beneath the deceptive garb a Jew is always a Jew and the other remains the inveterate, irredeemable other.

Meanwhile the time has arrived for Faitel to be married, 'to be grafted with the finest Occidental sprig'. Matters move forward swiftly, the match facilitated by the Stern family's ample supply of money. The ceremony duly takes place and Faitel and his uneasy bride, who boasts the name of Othilia Schnack, are declared man and wife. It is only afterwards during the celebrations at the White Lamb Inn that matters get out of hand, due partly to the excessive quantity of alcohol Faitel keeps imbibing. He is observed sitting rigid and staring under the table for a number of minutes. He then audibly rehearses a lesson from the Talmud, which he has already shared with his author friend prior to his efforts at self-improvement, concerning what the blessed Jehovah does during the course of the day. Reminding himself that in the late morning God presides over the copulation of the men and the women (in less coarse language, creates arranged marriages for them), setting aside nothing less than three hours for this activity, Faitel 'jumped from his chair, began clicking his tongue, gurgling, tottering back and forth while making disgusting, lascivious and bestial canine movements with his rear end . . . [and shouting], ' "Mine bridera! Geeve me mine bridera! I vant you shood know dat I'm jost a Chreesten human bing like you all. Not von drop of Jewish blud!" ' [22] The tale comes to its miserable end when all the guests flee the room, leaving the bridegroom a stinking heap on the floor in the sole company of the renowned Professor Klotz, who stares at the failure of his handiwork, 'a convoluted Asiatic image in wedding dress, a counterfeit of human flesh, Itzig Faitel Stern'. [23]

Here then is the figure of the lascivious Jew, ready to pollute the pure German stock with his vulgar, untamable blood. There doesn't appear to be too much left for Josef Goebbels or the cartoonists of *Der Stürmer* to add. Once a Jew, always a Jew; all the Jewish money in the world cannot buy a place in German culture.

Yet it needs to be acknowledged that the message of Panizza's story may be broader than the anti-Semitic stereotyping for which the Nazis tried, unsuccessfully, to revise his work forty years later. The author, who was also thoroughly to mock Christianity, may have had more than one target in mind: those who saw themselves as the predestined proprietors of High German culture; the contents of that culture itself as being little more than indulgent sentimentality; and through the figure of Dr Klotz, the pseudo-science of racial improvement and eugenics as unable to alter the plain bare facts of who is, and who isn't, an Aryan. No one would want to argue that the novella makes comforting reading.

From Mitzpah's Blog

We crossed the Rhine twice today. I'm so glad we went in a boat the second time as I hate those huge bridges. If I look one way there are lots of cars; if I look the other way the water seems so far below.

I don't really want to admit it but I do get a little frightened at times. What if daddy leaves me here? What if I should get lost? That's why I don't play very much with the other dogs I meet. I was much less scared in the woodlands, before we came to these big cities. I sense that my daddy feels the same.

But this has been my best day for food. Daddy hated his lunch, for which we waited for ages, so I got his whole baked potato filled with cheese.

In the evening we went out to eat together and I was given my own special plate of food in a restaurant. This has never happened before. The lady brought it in a shiny tray which didn't taste very nice.

Someone very kind gave lots of Euros today just to sponsor me. It makes me very proud. I hope there's going to be a special dog corner for me in our new synagogue. But I'm giving most of my money to train guide dogs. People need to know who's really in charge.

Love,
Mitzpah

Day Sixteen – From Duisburg to Kleve

❖ It's early in the morning here in Duisburg. Today's plan is to set off by car for the beautiful town of Xanten which has an old Jewish cemetery and to walk from there the twenty-something kilometres to Kleve where there will be a ceremony to dedicate a number of commemorative plaques on sites which belong to the Jewish history of the town. I've also been invited to speak at an unusual inter-faith and cross-cultural gathering, Christians and Jews, Germans and Dutch: Kleve is only a few kilometres from the Dutch border.

It's a beautiful, freezing autumn morning when I walk through Xanten. I stop for just long enough to warm myself up with a cup of coffee and to post the last of the small parcels of chocolates and marzipan with which I've been trying to make up to my children for being gone for three whole weeks. Then I make my way across the attractive town square, through the narrow alleyways and out northwards past extensive Roman ruins into a maze of small lanes across the flat countryside in which I quickly become thoroughly lost. I feel ashamed to be leaving behind me in such cursory fashion a town which holds so much history and determine that one day I must come back here with the family. I'm not even able to visit the old Jewish cemetery. But all through this walk it has been necessary to make choices, and as it draws towards its close it feels as though it has all gone much too fast. There are so many places and, more importantly, people to whom I hope to return.

It is not my best day at map-reading and I make the further mistake of trying to follow small footpaths. In general I've found that cycle routes are actually ideal: clearly marked, easy for walking and traversed only now and then by the occasional cyclist. Mitzpah likes them too as I can generally let him off the lead without too much trepidation. But today I manage to take one wrong turning after another. However, my errors also bring their rewards – a short cut across fields alongside a stream allows me to see the most beautiful flock of geese. Later I surprise two deer grazing in a cornfield and Mitzpah gives chase (even more surprising is that I succeed in calling him off).

But the best of it is that I'm saved from my zigzagging meanderings by coming upon a long, fairly straight path which takes me all the way to my destination, and this same blessed and helpful lane boasts the name of Oyweg! I make sure to take a photo of the street sign.

The afternoon proves equally rich in unexpected gifts. I pass a field full of deer, then four goats come running up to me with such enthusiasm that I cannot even get the camera out to take their portraits before they try to eat it. Later we watch a kestrel hunting over a field, now gliding, now holding itself still with swiftly flapping wings, now folding them to halve its height in a moment. I've never in my life seen so many birds of prey.

Then, as the cold damp yields to a short late glow of sunlight, a rainbow, the sharpest, clearest rainbow I've ever seen, loops from one end of the fields to the other like a translucent hoop. Above and as if embracing it is another, fainter bow. Mitzpah breaks loose and races through the muddy grass, driving an entire flock of gulls upwards into the light, their white wings radiant against the brilliant sky.

However, a herd of cows expresses powerful disapproval of the poor dog's presence. They gather round to moo, kick and stare him out. Mitzpah barks fiercely back at them, 'Look at me; I'm bigger than you!' For once I'm grateful for the fence between us. The cows soon settle back down, but Joe, Guy and Anna try to persuade them to repeat their 'first, fine careless rapture' for the camera. They refuse; instead, one of them turns her backside towards us and in a torrent of brown liquid voices her opinion of us all.

It wasn't until I got home to London and began to read more deeply that I became aware of a particular event that occurred in Xanten in 1891, recently enough for my grandfather, who was nine at the time, and who well remembered the Dreyfus Affair which began only three years later, to have seen it mentioned in a headline during his childhood and to have been affected by the anti-Jewish tension surrounding it which spread across Germany.

On June 29 of that year, a five year-old Catholic child, Johann Hegmann, was found murdered in a barn: his throat had been slit from ear to ear. The next morning the Christian butcher Heinrich Junkermann accused his Jewish colleague Adolph Buschoff of the crime, asserting that the wound resembled the cut made by a kosher slaughterer and reminding the mayor of the familiar canard that Jews needed Christian blood with which to make their unleavened bread, their matzot, for Passover. (Weeks later the anti-Semitic conservative newspaper *Das Volk* was to report that the body had been found completely bloodless.) The stories swiftly grew: Buschoff had been acting suspiciously; he had seemed shocked when he heard the news and had that evening lacked his habitual verve; he had allegedly been overheard saying to his son, 'If they can't prove it, they can't do anything to us.' His refusal to visit the site of the murder, perfectly explained by the fact that he was a Cohen, a descendent of the priests who served in the Temple in Jerusalem and whom Jewish law forbids from entering the precincts where a dead body is present, was taken as a further indication of guilt. As Walser Smith showed in his book on a similar but later case, the blood libel in Konitz in 1900, the public response and the accruing accusations, based on no substantial evidence whatsoever, themselves followed an almost ritualised pattern.[1] But what they led to was real enough: window smashing, the taunting of Jews on the streets, threats to Jewish lives and to public order so grave that the police of both towns had to call in the army. The situation in Konitz eventually even necessitated the intervention of Kaiser Wilhelm II himself, who commanded that an entire battalion of troops be sent to the town to disperse the thousands of rioters who had congregated there from neighbouring villages and even farther afield.

On 14 October, three and a half months after the crime, Buschoff was arrested together with his family on the advice of an inspector sent by the government from Berlin, who evidently took the local tale-bearers seriously. Mercifully, Buschoff was subsequently released after the judge determined that the case lacked any substantial supporting evidence. But this was far from the end of the matter. On the contrary, renewed public agitation brought the affair to national attention. During a debate in the Prussian Landtag, a certain Baron von Wackerbarth-Linderode went so far as to assert that the acquittal proved only that the Prussian judiciary were in the pocket of the Jews. Buschoff was rearrested and the date was set for a ten-day trial in nearby Kleve, from 4–14 July 1892. By now the case had become the focus of sharp national and international interest. But it was once again dismissed, after even the district attorney responsible for the prosecution urged the jury to acquit the accused. Several members of the medical council for the Province of the Rhine had testified, first that no more blood was to be expected in a five-and-a-half-year-old child than had in fact been found at the place where the body was discovered, hence there could be no question of ritual murder, and second, that the cut in no way resembled that made in kosher slaughter, where the knife had to be moved horizontally, whereas here it had been inserted at an angle. Buschoff was freed from prison for the second time, but his life had been ruined. It was impossible for him to return to Xanten and, weakened by the trauma and his incarceration, he died a few years later in Ehrenfeld near Cologne, a district through which I had also passed on my journey.

I was struck, when I learnt of these events, to think that I had walked in blind and total ignorance down the very streets where they had occurred. But the pretty square, the cheerful coffee houses, the lovely town, had concealed all.

So perhaps they should. Ought the memory of what has happened and the ghosts of its *dramatis personae* be allowed to haunt a place for ever? After all, shouldn't new and innocent life be able to grow and thrive, free from the blood guilt of the past? If the earth itself could not forget, the whole world would by now be one vast graveyard. Or does it perhaps depend on the scale of the crime?

What arrested me when I first learnt of those events in Xanten was not that such libels had been levelled at the Jews. I knew that well enough; after all I had visited the Wernerkapelle in Bacharach. I had often thought about that brief but revealing comment by Rabbi Yisrael

Meir Kagan (1838–1933), known simply as the Chafetz Chaim, that, whereas it was generally to be preferred for all ritual purposes, the colour itself being considered one of its virtues, red wine was to be avoided in those locations where the blood libel remained a risk.[2] But in my mind I had bracketed all this as a mediaeval lie belonging to an age of primitive mythologies ended for ever by the Enlightenment. Yet it had been repeated here in Europe during the lifetime of my own grandfather. Nor were such events as the blood libels in Skurz in 1884, in Xanten in 1891 and in Konitz in 1900 irrelevant to his subsequent fortunes, in that they provided a timely opportunity for political anti-Semites to exploit popular prejudice to good advantage by claiming, in a manner which would later become all too familiar, that the Jews had far too much power, controlling, among other organs of the state, the police and the judiciary.

*   *   *

❖   It's ridiculous, but it's only when it's pointed out to me – 'That's the castle where she grew up' – that I connect Anne of Cleves with the pleasant town of Kleve. (By the way, I was once told that the manor house which used to stand surrounded by its moat on the site now occupied by our synagogue was where Henry VIII spent illicit weekends with Anne Boleyn prior to the annulment of his marriage to Catherine of Aragon. Given that Anne is considered to have had considerable political acumen, it seems unlikely that these ever actually took place.)

I'm very grateful to be taught something of the history of the Jews of Kleve. Nothing is known for certain about the Middle Ages, but from 1661 there is evidence of a Jewish community in the town. Its size varied but the congregation consisted on average of about one hundred and fifty souls, '*klein aber fein* – small but of quality', I'm told. Whereas nearby communities in the Lower Rhineland were mainly composed of poor peasant Jews, the central figure in Kleve was Elias Gomperts, a *Stadtlan* or *Hof-Jude*, a court Jew, who financed the Prussian princes. Gifted with immense wealth and a rare capacity to relate to people, among other achievements he founded a Talmud

Torah in his home, where rabbis were trained for the region. He was the first Jewish guest to be invited to attend a wedding at the Prussian court. His own son married one of the daughters of the famed Glückel of Hammeln, who recorded in her remarkable memoirs that she had known that Elias was wealthy, but when she arrived for the celebrations her eyes almost fell out of their sockets – the man lived like a king.

Thus the community became known as the stepping stone between Amsterdam and Cologne. For over a century and a half, until some point in the mid or late nineteen hundreds, a particular tolerance reigned between Jew and non-Jew. But during the Third Reich it was the same here as everywhere else in Germany. Among the Jewish families who fled the town was the creator of Tomor, a well-known brand of kosher margarine. Between fifty and sixty Jews from Kleve perished; we later saw the so-called *Judenhaus* where they were held before their deportation.

We arrived just in time to be present at the unveiling of the first of three plaques to commemorate the city's Jews, though, as the mayor told me, there had previously been other such events in the town. This plaque marked the location of the earliest synagogue, the second Elias Gomperts's home and the third the 'Jews' house' referred to above. A small crowd had gathered and followed the mayor from one site to the next. It was bitterly cold.

Not long after arriving back in London I received a copy of the guide-book which had been written to accompany an exhibition of Jewish life in Kleve. I was particularly struck by a group of letters because they reminded me of that card, which has strangely made its way into my possession, posted from Theresienstadt by my great-grandmother in the autumn of 1943. To the best of our knowledge it was the last message she was able to convey to her family before she was murdered in Auschwitz in December of that year.

The letters from Kleve were sent under the supervision of the Red Cross by means of slow and complex channels, yet they offered to men and women whose situation was hopeless the small but significant mercy of being able to communicate to their loved ones, through hints and suggestions only, something of their and their family's plight. Strict regulations controlled how those letters had to be composed. The message was limited to twenty-five words; even these could not be written in the handwriting of the sender but had to be transcribed by an authorised Red Cross worker before the paper was folded over and placed in an official envelope at a designated Red Cross station. The back of the letter was reserved for the recipient's reply. It took several months for such post to reach its destination, during which time virtually anything could have happened either to the sender or to the addressee. The book accompanying the exhibition explained:

> At first sight the content of these cards seems to give little away. Their limited length and the extreme conditions under which they were composed gave rise to brief messages in a telegrammatic style which makes them appear remarkably stereotypical in character. People were glad to be able to indicate that they were still alive and to express their good wishes. But a closer reading of the short texts allows one to discern individual details, some of which shed light on personal destinies and others of which, reaching beyond the personal, add to the general picture of those times.[3]

Bernhard Gonsenheimer was already living in the 'Jews' house' in Kleve when he sent his letter. Jews were compelled to move there in 1941, in the first instance presumably to isolate them from the town's Aryan citizens who were in this manner protected from the polluting effect of their company, and subsequently to facilitate their deportation. The house was formerly a hotel, the Klever Hof. A pretty pre-war holiday postcard shows an attractive building by the river with the characteristic steeply pitched roof of the Schwanenburg, the Swan Castle, visible behind it – an image of the sort of resort at which one might have been tempted to spend a quiet weekend.

Reading the letter reminded me of the dedication of that plaque attesting to the building's function during the terrible years of 1941 to 1943; after its occupants had been deported the town was no doubt deemed *Judenfrei*. The place was now a restaurant and I recall being struck by the dissonance between its dreadful past and its harmless present. I stood there in the freezing cold – the weather seemed to get windier and icier the farther north we went – puzzling over this strange and disturbing dissociation: an advert for food on one wall and a sign commemorating mass murder on the other. The plaque had been placed there to ensure that people would never forget. Yet the reminder itself felt strangely like an intrusion, as if the faces of the dead were somehow interrupting between starters and deserts the meals of people who weren't even alive at the time of the outrage. I couldn't decide what I felt about it and fled into a nearby café where, freezing in both body and spirit, I cheated on my diabetes and ordered a cake to accompany my coffee. I was sitting there sharing the pastry with Mitzpah and trying to thaw out my fingers, toes and thoughts, when Guy, Joe and Anna came in. Guy was troubled by similar reflections: you go to a riverside café for a Chinese meal and you see this sign telling you that the very room in which you are now enjoying yourself was a prison for totally innocent people, all of whom were murdered. What do you do with such a fact, with such an impossible juxtaposition?

Bernhard Gonsenheimer's card bore the date of 26 February 1942 and was signed 'Onkel Bernhard'; the addressee was his nephew Max, who had emigrated to Haifa. A small hexagonal stamp at the bottom indicated that it was approved by the censorship in Palestine. The message contained precisely twenty-five words in the original German, as prescribed by the Red Cross:

> Good wishes no longer reached mother; she's all right. No further news from Henny. Hear nothing from our children. Happy about your good news. Warmest greetings.[4]

The editor suggests that in this oblique manner Bernhard was able to communicate to his nephew the painful news that his mother was dead and that his sister had been deported. He himself would presumably have been taken to Theresienstadt, and, if he survived that harrowing journey – for which the Gestapo had scheduled a hellish nineteen days – he would probably have been sent on to the death camps and gassed on arrival.

Day Sixteen – From Duisburg to Kleve

The Gestapo's order for the 'evacuation' of the Jews of Kleve, stamped 'secret', was dated 11 June 1943. The report confirming the departure of the train bore the date 27 November. By then the Russians were advancing from the east and, though it would not yet be established for a further seven months, a second front was anticipated at any moment. Despite the cost in transport and personnel to the by then hopeless German war effort, deportations of Jews from the Reich continued unabated and were still taking place as late as the opening months of 1945.

The date my great-grandmother wrote on the card she sent from Theresienstadt was 22 November 1943, but it was postmarked 25 February 1944. She had addressed it to relatives in Switzerland, probably because it was a neutral country and the letter would have the greatest chance of reaching its destination. But a black stamp, next to the official red circle containing the Nazi eagle bearing the swastika in its talons, showed that the card had travelled via Berlin. Also in red was a further stamp warning the recipient that any reply had to be written on an open postcard and only in German. Such cards, of which many survive, testified to a final 'mercy' cynically permitted by the Nazis prior to the 'resettlement' of their victims farther east in those so-called 'family camps' which were in fact the barracks and ash heaps of Auschwitz. The sender was obliged to inform his or her relatives that all was well and was thereby forced to participate in the cover-up with which the Nazis so successfully deceived both their intended victims and most of the rest of the world. The message had to be written in German and was no doubt carefully censored. It could, however, be inscribed in the author's own hand and was not limited to quite so few as twenty-five words. My great-grandmother wrote:

MY DEAR ONES – I'm often together with Recha; we speak a lot about you and all our loved ones. I am most anxious about my beloved children. I've been in the old age home for a while and feel fine there. Heartfelt greetings from your faithful Regina Freimann.

By the time she sent this card two of her six children were almost certainly already dead. She herself was soon to be murdered in

Auschwitz. But Recha would survive and bear witness to her friend's inextinguishable faith.

*   *   *

A strange moment has remained in my mind from dinner that evening. My host invited a small group of us to have pizza together before our meeting in the town hall. One of his friends was an expert on the work of the great Yiddish poet Avraham Sutzkever, and the conversation turned to a poem he had written in the Vilna ghetto on 12 September 1943. It described how he and other members of the Resistance had made their way through the darkness to the Romm printing works, the most famous Jewish press in nineteenth-century Europe, to take the lead plates which had been used by the compositors to prepare what are still considered the finest and most accurate editions of the Talmud ever produced, and turn them into bullets:

> We were dreamers, we had to be soldiers,
> And melt down, for our bullets, the spirit of the lead . . .
>
> Letter by melting letter the lead,
> Liquefied bullets, gleamed with thoughts:
> A verse from Babylon, a verse from Poland,
> Seething, flowing into one mold.[5]

This image had long haunted me: centuries of inspired and sophisticated spiritual culture turned in utter desperation into lethal ammunition. It strikes me that sadly we have the skill to melt down letters and turn them into bullets, however risky and terrifying the operation may be. But as for the capacity to transform the weapons of war back into the instruments of culture, to turn our spears into pruning hooks and our bullets into letters, who has the wisdom to know how to do that?

Day Sixteen – From Duisburg to Kleve

From Mitzpah's Blog

Today I frightened away a whole herd of cows. I hope it was helpful; they didn't look friendly. I also chased a flock of gulls and when I reached them they all flew right up into the air. But the best moment was when I saw two deer in a field. I didn't know deer can run faster than dogs; it's just not fair.

Talking about being scared, sometimes we go to places with a strange sort of odour. I have to sniff very carefully because the scent is very, very old, but it smells of fear. Daddy can tell it too. I don't know how, because I can smell, hear and see better than he can and I can also run much faster. But he doesn't laugh or smile when we're in those places. He just looks sad. It's good he's got me with him.

One thing he does have more of than me is money. He bought me a special new kind of dog food. I hope they can get it in London too as it's delicious.

Love,

Mitzpah

PS When we get home I'm going to start a campaign to be allowed into cafés in England. I hate being tied up outside and when I go in over here I always get at least half a biscuit.

Day Seventeen – Across the Border into Holland

I'd thought for a long time about how I wanted to cross over into Holland. The story of the Kindertransport had moved me for as long as I could remember, the remarkable rescue of thousands of children, mainly but not exclusively Jewish, from across Germany, Austria and Czechoslovakia. I wanted to follow the route so many of them had taken, and to reflect on their fate. That meant crossing the border near Arnhem, going via Rotterdam to Hoek van Holland, then by ferry to Harwich and home from Liverpool Street Station, on the platform of which so many of those children had waited anxiously seventy years earlier to see who, if anyone, would come to take them into their home and family.

The exodus which came to be known as the Kindertransport was arranged as a result of an urgent request to the British Government after Kristallnacht: in the wake of these terrible events would it at long last relax its immigration requirements and allow the entry into the country of children in obvious danger of losing their lives?

On the 21 November 1938 the Home Secretary, Sir Samuel Hoare, met a delegation of leaders of Jewish and non-Jewish groups working together as the Movement for the Care of Children from Germany. 'Here is a chance,' he later told Parliament, 'of taking the young generation of a great people, here is a chance of mitigating to some extent the terrible sufferings of their parents and friends.' As a result of these discussions permission was granted for ten thousand unaccompanied children to enter the country. Visas would not be required, only a simple travel document and essential medical information.

Representatives were promptly sent to Germany to organise the registration, assembly and transportation of the children. Their offices were immediately besieged by desparate parents. A remarkable Dutch woman, Gertruida Wijsmuller-Meijer, managed to persuade Adolf Eichmann, then head of the Office for Jewish Affairs in Vienna, to

242

allow children to leave from Austria as well. In the event, the first train departed within days, just in case he should change his mind. Some nine months later, when the Dutch border was virtually sealed, Gertruida personally arranged for a bus to collect a group of children who would otherwise have been stranded in Cologne and had them driven during the night through country lanes and back streets to the ship which had been kept waiting at her behest. I later met one of the 'Kinder' who had been on that bus: 'If it hadn't been for that remarkable lady I would be dead,' he said, and wept. Recalling the scenes as they gathered in Berlin for the journey, he reflected: 'I had the impression that the children were, like me, unaware of what lay before them. But it was written in the parents' faces that this parting was for ever.'

Advertisements and articles were placed in papers accessible to Jews with titles such as '*Holt sie raus, bevor es zu spät ist!* – Get them out before it's too late!' Across Germany volunteers worked to the point of exhaustion, locating children, communicating with their anxious parents and preparing everything necessary for their travel. In England Viscount Hoare broadcast an appeal to the nation on 25 November for families to open their homes to these young refugees.

Strangely, it is only now, when faced with the necessity of explaining in a few brief lines what the Kindertransport was, that I research these facts. My thoughts have always begun from the other end, with the heart-rending decision to send one's beloved child away, with the packing of that small suitcase, with those terrible partings, in homes, on railway platforms. I've seen those exhibitions of teddy bears and prayer books, those few, small, special items through which parents strove to express an enduring love more important to them than their very lives. Even just thinking about this a voice coming from I know not where begins to speak inside my head in German, saying, '*Das konnte ich aber nicht* – I couldn't possibly bring myself to do that.' Yet those parents did part with their beloved children; they did so because they knew that this was their sole chance of saving them from the death which was encircling them and drawing closer every week and every day. And, of course, they would join them later; soon the whole family would be safely reunited in Britain. Or so at least they tried to believe; though what they actually knew must often have been very different. The great majority of parents never set eyes on their offspring again.

There were to be no scenes at the railway stations, in Vienna, Berlin, Prague, Breslau, Hamburg, Frankfurt; the children would enter the carriages in orderly fashion, the parents would not be allowed to accompany them on to the platforms. A letter sent to Karl Robert Würzberger informed him that his child was to be included in a transport leaving from Frankfurt on 24 August; the meeting place for families was the flower stall in the main hall of the central railway station. Each piece of luggage had to be marked with an official label on which the child's name and permit number were to be written in capital letters in red. [1]

Yet there were children who remember a sudden rushing as the train began to move; for one vanishing moment their mothers were alongside, waving, weeping, calling out to them. For the parents there now came the return to those empty rooms. Afterwards, there were letters: 'Be good to your English family; thank them for us. Be brave.' With the outbreak of war these too ceased, except where cards could be sent via relatives in neutral counties, or through the Red Cross. Then, in most cases, came silence.

When Vera Gissing, who arrived in England with her sister on the Kindertransport, returned to her home town in Czechoslovakia after the war, knowing that her parents had perished, she was handed a letter by a kind non-Jewish neighbour. Her mother had written it prior to her deportation:

> And now, my dear children, on behalf of your father and myself, I wish you . . . Be happy, be brave. We gave you love, we gave you the foundations of life, we wanted to give you more, so much more . . . Remember your home and us, but do not grieve. Your whole life lies before you, life which you will build at the side of your husbands. I give my blessings to them and to your children; I shall be watching over you from Heaven, and praying for your happiness.[2]

When I last met Vera she was off to celebrate the 104th birthday of her 'English mummy'. In that grim spring of 1939 she had been welcomed to her new home with the words, 'Here you shall be loved,' and with a request to be quiet around the house because her foster mother had a weak heart! Many children encountered a far colder and starker reception.

In 2008 we held a gathering in the synagogue to mark seventy years since the plan to bring the children to safety was born. We invited Kinder, their children and the children of the adoptive families who had welcomed them into their homes, many of whom had a Quaker background. The response was immediate and enthusiastic; one family came from as far away as Northern Ireland to join us. There was a warm and convivial atmosphere from the first moment; we felt connected not only by the bonds of history but by a sense of affection and appreciation. One small part of a monstrous tragedy had been turned into kindness, humanity and hope.

It was in preparation for this event that I had reread my grandfather's book and first conceived the idea of going on my journey.

I wanted to cross the German-Dutch border exactly where the trains of the Kindertransport had passed. They had halted at Emmerich, the last stop on the German side, assailed by a final fear that the children would be removed from the carriages just before reaching freedom. But when they stopped at the first Dutch station, usually Venlo, women lined the platform with food, drink and the most precious gift of all, a friendly welcome. The Nazis, who were able to observe these activities from their side of the border, later took a cruel vengeance on the people of the town for these basic acts of goodness.

I wanted to ponder those scenes by taking a train along the very same tracks, but somehow those plans didn't work out.

❖ In the end we cross the German/Dutch border in the simplest way and almost without realising it, since it traverses the cycle path we follow along the Rhine to catch the ferry at Millingen. Mitzpah crosses it about two minutes before us, as ever racing eagerly ahead. But as we stand in the boat, for which we have to run and which we catch only by the skin of our teeth, I am moved for many reasons.

I think of my grandparents. When they were finally able to leave

Germany, travelling by plane for the first time in their lives, my grandfather asked the stewardess to inform him when they had exited German airspace. Hearing that they were no longer over German soil, he, a deeply civilised man, said to his family, 'Now you can spit.' Guy asks me why; I can only imagine that it is the release of almost incomprehensible tensions, relief, outrage, disgust, the freedom at long last to express your feelings.

And, I have to say, I feel a sense of relief as well, that this part of the walk has been completed safely, and, for all the kindness and thoughtfulness I have encountered, an involuntary gladness that I have left the land where my family was persecuted.

I still remember the first time we came to Holland. It was in 1966, the day after England won the World Cup, and I was a young boy on holiday with my parents and my brother. Wherever we went people saw the GB sign on the car and gave us the thumbs-up. This was partly about the football, but more deeply about gratitude to the British for liberating them from Nazi occupation. Thomas, whom I met in Kleve, told me that it is only in the last ten years that there has been a real transformation in the Dutch perception of Germany.

Looking back, I see the scene in that boat crossing the Rhine vividly in my mind's eye. I remember that day's walk clearly; the dull, slightly drizzly morning, the few kilometres along narrow country roads before we picked up the path along the left bank of the Rhine; the moment when Mitzpah, chasing a stick, ran straight into Guy and knocked over his camera; how we passed the first Dutch flag as we began to realise that time was tight if we were going to make the ferry and changed our quick walk into a run. But just a few weeks ago I saw the film of the walk for the first time. By then I'd quite forgotten that Guy had interviewed me on that boat and asked me, as we crossed the rough grey water towards a small pier in the middle of nowhere, whether I was sorry to be leaving Germany. 'No,' I'd replied, 'I can't be sad to leave the country where the Holocaust was conceived and by members of whose population it was largely perpetrated.' But then I'd paused; 'We've encountered much kindness here,' I'd added, looking troubled. 'Will you miss Germany?'

'No,' I'd said. 'How can I miss the country where my family was made to suffer so terribly?' But in the end that line was edited out, the scene closing with, 'We've encountered much kindness here.'

However the question of whether I miss Germany stays with me and I wonder what the true answer really is. On one level it's simple: of course I don't miss Germany because I never lived there. I was raised in Scotland and England; Israel too is partly home. But Germany never was my homeland, so the notion that I might miss it can have no meaning.

Yet there is something which I do miss and for which I've been mourning since I got back to London. It isn't just the walking, the freedom and adventure out along the river with the dog, the opportunity to sit and read and write in cafés, the challenge and excitement of meeting different people. Being in Germany has helped me to feel closer to my family and their fate. For all the tragedy involved in the subject I find studying German-Jewish life gripping; it helps me to feel more deeply grounded in who I myself am. I therefore enjoy the fact that my German has improved and read about the history and theology of German Jewry as widely as other demands on my time allow. I turn appreciatively to my grandparents' editions of Lessing and Heine. I don't of course have to be in Germany to study these subjects; yet I know that I want to return there and participate in the deepening German-Jewish and Jewish-Christian dialogues. I sense that here lies part of my cultural destiny, that these are the roots of the particular kind of Judaism in which I was brought up. So the honest, if strange, answer is that, yes, a part of me does somehow miss Germany.

But I can also hear a critical voice which says, 'You're not going to tell me that you still believe in that failed one-way love affair which ended in Dachau and Bergen-Belsen?'

That there were profound flaws in this particular form of co-existence is undeniable. But does that mean that we have to give up on the very idea that people of different faiths can thrive in the same society and that different cultures can come together? Surely that's precisely how many of us live all the time; otherwise I wouldn't have stood with friends in Hampstead outside Keats's house one winter day reading his *Ode to a Nightingale* with my kippah on my head, nor would I quote

Shakespeare or Wordsworth in my sermons, alongside the Torah, the Talmud and Hasidic wisdom, just as my grandfather used to cite Goethe and Schiller. I know there are those who will say: have you learnt nothing from history? Yet to me that very question represents a form of despair. The reality is that we do inhabit multiple cultures; the issues are whether and how we can manage this wisely and honestly and enable others to do so as well.

Yet I am not without my own ambivalence. I recall the shocking impact of an exhibit I saw some years ago in the small Jewish museum in Fürth, a town which used to have a sizeable Jewish community. The visitor finds himself walking between two parallel rows of mirrors, so that he cannot help but observe his own image, and then watch himself observing himself. In those mirrors are inscribed a series of striking sentences from Jacob Wasserman's book *Mein Weg als Deutscher und Jude* (*My Way as German and Jew*):

It's pointless adjuring the nation of poets and philosophers in the name of its poets and philosophers. Each prejudice imagined overcome brings, like worms in carrion, thousands of new ones to light.

It's pointless turning the right cheek when the left has been slapped. It doesn't make them in the least bit more thoughtful; it doesn't affect them, it doesn't disarm them. They'll slap the right one as well.

It's pointless offering words of reason in the midst of the mad affray. They'll say: What? He dares to open his mouth? Stuff his gob.

It's pointless trying to offer an example. They'll say: We know nothing, we saw nothing, we heard nothing.

It's pointless trying to seek anonymity. They'll say: The coward, creeping around like that. It's his bad conscience which drives him to it.

It's pointless keeping faith with them, either as fellow fighter or as fellow citizen. They'll say: He's like Proteus; he can do anything.

It's pointless trying to help them remove the chains from their limbs. They'll say: He's making a tidy profit out of it all.

It's pointless trying to neutralise the poison. They'll cook up a fresh brew.

It's pointless living for them and dying for them. They'll say: He's a Jew.[3]

It turns out that the disturbing presentation of these sentences in the mirrors is not, as I had first thought, due to the inspirational genius of the museum's curator. It was Wasserman's own idea: 'I once dreamt of an analogy but I don't know how comprehensible it is. I set the frames of two mirrors opposite each other and it seemed to me as if the human images captured in both mirrors would devour one another . . . '[4] His book was not written just prior to, or during, the Third Reich, as one might have supposed. Wasserman died in January 1934. It was published in 1921.

I often think about those mirrors and the uneasy feeling of watching myself watching myself as I read the troubling text. I say to myself that they reflect the many facets of the person; the complex multiplicity of human identity. But inside I am also afraid lest they should have caught me in some act of self-betrayal.

*   *   *

❖   I remember very clearly the first hour in Holland. Guy and I were the only passengers on that small ferry which deposited us on the Dutch side of the Rhine. Within moments it had set off again across the grey and choppy waters for the other shore and we were left staring at a solitary signpost in a desultory stretch of dunes. We headed inland for the nearest town, some three kilometres away. It was futile to look for footpaths; there was simply too much water in every direction to risk anything more adventurous than following the road. It soon transpired however that what had seemed like a quiet lane was in fact the lorry route to a busy industrial depot. The trucks roared along, never so much as slowing down at the sight of two walkers with their dog, forcing us repeatedly into the mud at the side of the narrow tarmac strip. After a kilometre we emerged with relief on to a bridge over a small series of ponds linked by canals and filled with reed beds. Maybe, I thought, I can let Mitzpah off the lead for a little while to run, but I immediately spotted a sign informing the visitor that this was a nature reserve and that dogs were forbidden. 'Time for some filming,' said Guy; I remember feeling too cold to say anything coherent. The icy wind swept across the flat land and passed through my anorak as if it were made of tissue. I strove to distract myself by looking at the water birds; I watched them duck under in the icy pools. Only later did I learn that *onderduiken* is the Dutch term for those who went 'underground' into hiding during the war. Why, I wondered, does it feel colder here than in Germany? I had imagined that the very air would breathe its warmth and welcome on us now that we had crossed the border.

But it was not just for us that Holland proved less of a haven than had been imagined. The received story of the Dutch during the war is of a people who acted in the main with courage and compassion, who did their utmost to hide their Jews and, to the extent that this was possible, resisted the Nazis. After all, Anne Frank has been called the country's 'unofficial patron saint'.[5] Her story has been central in creating the picture of the humanity, bravery and warm-hearted practical compassion of a people just like the wonderful Miep Gies and her husband Henk who so reliably and selflessly brought the family food in the secret annexe. Miep opens her book *Anne Frank Remembered* with the memorable words: 'I am not a hero. I stand at the end of the long, long line of good Dutch people who did what I did or more – much more – during those dark and terrible times.'[6] Indeed more trees have been planted in Yad Vashem's Avenue of the Righteous of the Nations to honour Dutch people than in recognition of the members of any other country except Poland, which had a Jewish population thirty times the size of that of Holland. Almost every Jewish person I meet here had either been hidden, or was the child of hidden parents.

Yet a greater proportion of Jews perished in Holland than in any other country in Western Europe; over seventy per cent of Dutch Jews died. The causes of this shocking figure have been variously attributed: the Germans exercised more direct control in the Netherlands than in many other countries they occupied; the Dutch civil service was considered largely compliant, showing a deferential attitude to authority; the Jewish community was well organised, civic records were well kept and Dutch identity cards all but impossible to forge, all factors making it easy to round the Jews up in a flat territory of modest size where there were limited opportunities for hiding and no immediate borders across which to escape to non-Nazi states. But there is an uglier aspect as well; the Nazis were allegedly met with such a level of cooperation from certain parts of the state and its institutions that Eichmann is reported to have said that 'it was a pleasure to work with them'. It has been said that not a single Dutch train deporting Jews failed to run on schedule.[7] A friend I walked with on my second day in the country told me how someone, driving past the long queue of tourists waiting patiently along the Prinsengracht to see Anne Frank's house, shouted at them, 'That's not the truth. She was betrayed.'

An icy, cutting wind blew through us from the moment we crossed into Holland.

Yet I feel a painful reluctance to absorb these realities. Ever since my first childhood holiday in Holland I have loved the place. On my dozen or so visits since, I have basically felt safe as a Jew and welcome as a citizen of Britain. Among the Dutch there is an enduring gratitude to the British for the liberation of their country; after all, Holland was occupied by the Nazis longer than almost anywhere else, some parts remaining in German hands from May 1940 until May 1945. One thinks sadly of Anne Frank putting coloured pins in the map after D-Day to mark the Allied advance from Normandy in the constant hope that her liberators would soon arrive.

Perhaps my warm feelings are rooted in the recognition of the long and remarkable Dutch tradition of tolerance, dating back to the seventeenth century when Jewish refugees from Portugal were granted the freedom to create a community in Amsterdam. They are also based on the positive attitude towards Jews which I have several times personally encountered in Holland. Once I was stopped in the street in front of the Amsterdam railway station by a young man who asked me, 'Are you Jewish?' before going on to tell me that he was part Jewish himself and pouring out a stirring family story which I still regret having been unable to follow because of the hubbub in the street and the noise of the passing trams.

I therefore absorbed these disturbing facts about the more complex relationship between the Dutch and the Nazis with great reluctance.

Yet I cannot believe that it is over nations in general that God passes judgement. Would not God, free of the nationalist bigotry which so often afflicts us, consider each individual separately according to his circumstances and the pressures which acted upon him, her fears and the respective grounds for them, his courage, her capacity for empathy and his degree of determination to resist tyranny? I frequently reflect on the fate of the woman who was hidden in Holland by forty-seven different families, none of whom betrayed her. Numerous people risked their lives and those of their families to save Jews; others sold their fellow human beings for the price of a bag of sugar. And one always has to bear in mind the unanswerable question: what would I have done had I been faced by such circumstances? The only honest answer is: I don't know.

❖   With our walking for the day completed by the mid-afternoon, we head for Arnhem. We get thoroughly lost on the way and Isidor Nathans waits for us with great patience. He greets us warmly when we finally arrive; his daughter Lia is a member of my congregation in London and his grandson celebrated his Bar Mitzvah there on the very Shabbat before Mitzpah and I set off.

Isidor takes us to the synagogue. It is utterly beautiful. Used as a warehouse during the war (this is where the Nazis made the population bring their confiscated radio sets), it was recently restored with great care. It is bright and full of light, tasteful, with a classic harmony of design and a high white ceiling. I'm struck by the huge brass lamps and note that where the long cables from which they are hung meet the ceiling there is intricate circular tile-work which adds a typically Dutch grace and beauty. The Ark is made of solid hardwood, perhaps oak. Inside are at least a dozen Torah scrolls. I learn that many of them have been gathered here from small communities in the east of Holland which no longer have active congregations.

Isidor was hidden as a child. He tells me that he remembers watching from the attic window of the house where they were concealed, in a village only a few miles from Arnhem, and seeing the British airborne troops landing in Operation Market Garden for the bitter battle which was to be re-enacted in the film *A Bridge Too Far*. It was a disaster; although the British received late intelligence that crack German Panzer units were resting up exactly where they were intending to land, warning voices were not heeded. One interpretation of the over-hasty decision to proceed with the operation, which was to cost many hundreds of British lives and lose them vast amounts of equipment, was that Field Marshal Montgomery wanted to prove to his rival General Patten that the British could advance with equal speed as the Americans. Isidor remembers the sad sight of British soldiers filing past as prisoners of war. There are several accounts of the terrible and courageous fighting in the streets around the bridge. Many Jews landed here in the British army, and many died. In the end the region was not liberated until May 1945, seven long and bitterly hungry months after the abortive attack. Isidor shows us the bridge over the Upper Rhine where the fighting took place. It has been rebuilt since, yet *A Bridge Too Far* gives, he tells us, a very accurate impression of what happened. I want to see the British war cemetery, but have, to my shame, not enough time on this visit.

Isidor tells us about how he was hidden. After six months his parents joined him and his sister at the same hiding place. There they remained from 1942 until the end of the war. At first they thought that it would only be another few months, but this became a year, then two, and finally three. (That evening I stay at the home of Bert, whose mother was the lady hidden with her son in forty-seven different places. That means that there were at least forty-seven people, or families, prepared to risk their lives to take them in, whether for one night or a few weeks or months, all of whom kept faith with their secret. Bert tells me that until recently his mother could remember every single one of them and regularly wrote to them all each year.)

After the war Isidor celebrated his Bar Mitzvah in this very synagogue. He explains that a false ceiling was installed to allow the creation of offices above the sanctuary. But the building has now been restored to its former grace and beauty. I ponder how strange it must have felt in 1945 to return to a community which was once full of children and vitality, to find only memories and mourning. I ask Daan and Bert, with whom I stay later, whether the past doesn't feels like a constant presence, an inescapable undercurrent in one's Jewish consciousness. 'We're used to it,' Daan answers, then adds, 'It's changed now, but this was a community where no one had grandparents.' I recall Lia, Isidor's daughter, telling me how when she was growing up she was one of the only Jewish children there who had all four grandparents. Quite exceptionally, her parents had each been hidden, and survived, together with their own parents. Daan continues, 'We go to Amsterdam to buy kosher meat. There's only one kosher butcher in the Netherlands now. Before the war even here in Lochem there were four kosher butchers and three kosher bakeries.' Lochem is a small town in the east of the country, in the Medinah; Amsterdam was of course lovingly referred to as *Mokum Aleph, the* place par excellence.

I sometimes think of Isidor peeping out from the attic window and seeing the British paratroopers land and then, only a few days later, watching so many of them being led away as prisoners of war. It must have engendered a deep feeling of hopelessness. I read the memoirs of Louis Hagen, a Jewish glider pilot who took part in the fighting. The glorious moment had at last arrived in which he could help defeat the Nazis: 'The circle had been completed, justice was being done . . . and all this in my time. I was ready to take on anything and anybody that was German.' Preparing himself for battle, he recalled the treatment he had received before finally managing to flee Nazi Germany:

> Another flash brought me back to the concentration camp. Subconsciously I looked at my hands. They had been bloody and festering from carrying heavy latrine buckets which I was forced to empty with my bare hands. I remembered my seventeenth birthday at Torgau concentration camp just about ten years ago.[8]

He recalled too how SS men pushed a Catholic priest back into a muddy pond every time he tried to swim to the side, until finally the poor man drowned. Now at last Hagen had the opportunity to fight back. He survived the Battle of Arnhem by swimming across the Rhine to rejoin the British lines.

*   *   *

That evening was 9 November, the anniversary of Kristallnacht. I had thought to spend it at a memorial event in Germany but was unable to make the necessary contacts. At first I had felt disappointed. On this night above all I wanted to feel close to my grandfather; it therefore seemed strange not to be in Germany. Then I recalled the story of how a young woman from his former congregation in Frankfurt had been made to work in Holland as a slave of the SS. She was certain she would perish. But one day as she was cleaning their rooms she overheard a radio broadcast; the set had been left on and was tuned, illegally, to the BBC. The speaker was my grandfather, who had been invited to address in German the oppressed peoples of mainland Europe to strengthen their spirit and bring them hope. After the war she told the family that it was when she heard his familiar vibrant voice speaking to her in those SS quarters that she knew she was going to survive.

With no connections in Germany I was glad to receive an unexpected invitation to join the community in Haaksbergen in the east of Holland. The town's small synagogue was dedicated in 1828; the house next door contained the *mikvah*, the ritual baths. Remarkably, the synagogue survived the war intact. When the diminished community became too small to function as an active congregation the building was shut down and would have been destroyed but for the efforts of a local committee dedicated to saving it. It was eventually restored in 1982 and became the home of the Liberaal Joodse Gemeente Twente, the Liberal Jewish Community of the Twente Region.

❖   We arrive at the synagogue in Haaksbergen where we are given the warmest welcome. This is doubly important, partly because such things always matter (and I've learnt a lot over the last twenty days about both how, and how not, to look after guests) and also because we get there just five minutes before the time for the evening service and the talk I'm supposed to give. I've had no chance to change out of my muddy clothes, feed the dog or do anything at all to prepare. I whisk out Mitzpah's bowl, and while he has his nose in his dinner (he wakes me in the middle of the night to be taken out urgently with a dreadful upset stomach), I rush into the bathroom and try to transform myself from mud-covered hiker into respectable rabbi. It makes it all so much more comfortable when people say, 'Don't worry; take your time. Would you like some tea?'

Those present have come from all around the region. Some live many kilometres distant, but they come because they know that the very survival of the community depends on their personal commitment. It's what gives the group its warmth and good humour. This is one of several places where I've arrived tired and left hours later feeling awake, alert and very much alive.

There follows a beautiful musical memorial service for Kristallnacht in this simple, harmonious *shul*. Daan later explains to me how it survived the war: the Nazis asked who had the key and everyone replied that they had no idea; so the building stayed locked and the inside remained undamaged. This is something quite unique among the synagogues of Holland. The *shul* is small, with arched windows, a wooden Ark and *bimah*, and simple wooden seating. At the back is a small gallery. The thirty or so men and women (and one dog) present fill the place completely. Mitzpah is not simply allowed but actively encouraged to join me when I speak from in front of the Ark (on their requested topic of Jewish law today). The tiny platform is surrounded by what feels to all intents and purposes like a fence with a gate. You climb the steps, enter, and someone else closes the gate behind you. I wonder aloud if they ever leave rabbis whose sermons they don't like locked in here for ever. 'Yes,' someone replies from down below. 'You'll find the bones soon enough.'

Afterwards I have an opportunity to listen. A couple comes up to me; they live five hundred metres from the German border. The synagogue nearest us, they explain, was totally destroyed. Not a single stone was left standing. But some time after the war, when they were building an underground installation, one single piece of masonry was discovered. It was part of the stone tablets on which the Ten Commandments were inscribed: the words on the fragment read 'Thou shalt not murder.' It was turned into a memorial.

From Mitzpah's Blog

Daddy wouldn't let me off the lead very much today, so it wasn't a lot of fun. We had to walk along roads most of the time and there were lots of noisy cars.

I want to tell you something about walking. What dogs like me enjoy best is to be able to run. For myself, I like to run ahead, then all around you in circles. After that I like to hide behind a tree or a fence, where I can see you but you can't see me, so that I can jump out at you just as you go past. That's my idea of a good walk.

But I did have a nice evening. We were in a synagogue and it was very warm and I was tired. So I had lots of time to sleep. Besides, when daddy gave his talk from in front of the Ark, all the people told me I had to go up with him. I've never had an honour like that before.

Love,
Mitzpah

Day Eighteen – From Lochem to Amsterdam

I didn't attempt to follow the Rhine during my three days in Holland. That would in any event have proved impossible. At Millingen, where Guy and I crossed it, the river itself divides into the Waal and the Pannerdensch Kanaal which in turn becomes the Neder Rijn soon afterwards at Pannerden. This further subdivides at Arnhem into the Neder Rijn and the IJssel, the Neder Rijn eventually becoming the Lek. However, a full two thirds of the water remains in the Waal, which joins with the Meuse at Gorinchem and follows a complex route via the Merwede and Nieuwe Merwede before finally pouring, via the Hollands Diep and Haringvliet estuaries, into the North Sea. Following all those branches would have been a major project in itself.

For most of my – all too short – time in Holland I simply went where friends and communities invited me. This included a visit to the small town of Barneveld where my friend Daniel's grandparents had been imprisoned by the Nazis.

❖ Daniel brings me a poppy from England; tomorrow will be Armistice Day. I pin it on to my jumper; how can anyone not believe that it's important to remember?

Daniel takes us to the castle which is set in majestically beautiful grounds. A canal runs round a huge oblong lawn; on the far side of the water are tree-lined avenues, beyond them compelling woodland paths. This is dog heaven and as soon as I see other dogs off the lead I let Mitzpah run free. Mercifully he ignores the cows and other animals just visible behind the trees.

Not for the first time I experience a disturbing dissonance between the glory of the scene (even the sun has decided to come back from a week's holiday) and what transpired at this location sixty-eight years ago. For it was to this castle that the leaders of Dutch Jewry were brought, politicians, heads of communities, doctors, anybody with significant connections, in 1942 when round-ups of Jews were taking place across the country. Here they were held firmly out of reach of those whom they might have persuaded to intervene on behalf of their fellow Jews, prior to their own deportation east. The six hundred and fifty Jews kept here, including all Daniel's family on the paternal side, were locked inside the castle. They could not enjoy the glory of these grounds where we wander freely. Inside the walls there was a certain degree of autonomy. Lectures and concerts were arranged; Daniel tells us that he still has some of the invitations to these events. The place is thus a kind of Dutch Theresienstadt, though on a far smaller scale. From here, Jews were taken to Westerbork in the north of Holland and thence to Sobibor or Auschwitz.

The day came when the inmates of the castle were informed that they were due to travel to an undisclosed destination. Daniel tells us how his grandmother, then in her early twenties, had an instinct that they shouldn't go. His grandparents hid in the cellars and later managed to escape. They survived the war in hiding with a young doctor, who, when he built his home in 1939, had a double wall constructed in the knowledge that he might one day have to conceal fugitives. He was nominated after the war by Daniel's family for recognition in the Avenue of the Righteous at Yad Vashem. He refused to accept any such honour on the basis that he was merely doing his duty. The rest of Daniel's family went on the convoy; most of them perished.

We walk through the pretty town (the castle is well within it, undeniably in view of eyes which could see and remember) to the tiny Jewish cemetery. It is quiet and beautiful, a whole silent world of lives and time. Here Daniel's great-grandfather lies buried. He was an eminent doctor and it was because of him that the family were included in the list of leading Dutch Jews brought to Barneveld. He died of a heart attack in 1943. Next to him lies Daniel's grandmother; it was her particular wish that she should have her final resting place next to her father. As far as I can tell she is the person most recently interred here, in 2002. Daniel places pebbles on the graves and says the Kaddish. There is no *minyan*, no quorum; so we are his witnesses before God.

*   *   *

❖   As we walk through the wet but glorious autumnal forest, it feels as if history, like the paths we follow, lies only just beneath the fallen leaves. My friends talk about hidden children. The Dutch context is complex; thousands of people hid Jews, but there were collaborators too, and yet others who expressed sorrow when hidden Jews returned after the war. E. explains that she had a wonderful childhood in the 1950s; unlike in Germany, enough people came back for there to be at least some kind of continuity with the life which had existed before. Her parents, like most others, endeavoured to create a future for themselves and their children. Many did not speak about the past, not, at least, until they were far older, and even then often not to their immediate family.

But there were also those survivors who would say to their children, 'You're free to go out and do as you please. I was never able to do that; look, here's the number on my arm.' Many such second-generation children had to struggle with depression and needed help. 'There's an extensive system of Jewish social services and the state is very supportive,' I'm told. Every Dutch-Jewish family has its own story. That Anne Frank has become iconic (later I'm told that there's a feeling that her story is exploited by almost anyone who is against virtually anything they consider wrong) provides a convenient escape from the uglier realities of much of what happened here.

It must not be forgotten either that there was great suffering throughout Holland. The final winter of the war brought terrible hunger and much of the country was only liberated at the very end, in the spring of 1945.

The sun shines and the trees are beautiful. Mitzpah runs wildly; ducks waddle away with remarkable speed and launch themselves into the water.

*   *   *

Three months after my return from Germany I was in the middle of speaking about how I was guided round the beautiful synagogue in Arnhem when I became aware that someone in the lecture hall was weeping. I stopped and in the quiet which descended like a tribute to his sorrow began to ask him, 'Were you . . . ?' but before I could complete my question he explained that he too had been a child in hiding not far away.

The first conference about hidden children took place in New York in 1991; it was followed shortly afterwards by another in Amsterdam in 1992. For many 'children', by then past midlife, this encounter with others who had shared the diverse anguish of similar experiences proved an immense release. After all those decades here at last were voices in the loneliness; it was finally possible to begin the process of emerging from a more enduring and in some respects even deeper hiding which had begun at the very time one might have imagined that relief had finally arrived: 'After the war many were forced into another kind of hiding as parents made it clear that their children's pasts should remain concealed,' wrote Diane Wolf in an important study. 'Parents were joined by friends, teachers and schoolmates, none of whom wanted to hear about the children's experiences.'[1] The rest, their future lives, was to be silence.

When one thinks, in one's ignorance, about what it must have meant to be a hidden child, one is naturally drawn to the period of physical concealment and its many perils. How were safe places found amid such terrible dangers? Who were the remarkable students and resistance fighters who risked their lives to convey Jewish children to – comparative – safety? How did parents make the heart-rending decision to hand over their sons and daughters to people who were usually total strangers? Was there time to say goodbye? Or did it all happen in a moment, with no chance to think; in a whisper, in a corner of the Hollandsche Schouwburg, the former Yiddish theatre in Amsterdam, where the Jews were rounded up and from where some, just some, of the children were smuggled out? And then, once they were in hiding, how were they treated? Were they loved and nurtured or were they seen as semi-servants, there on sufferance, and sometimes by virtue of payment, only? Would they be betrayed? What would happen if the money ran out?

It does not immediately strike one that this was only the beginning, that for so many of those children who did survive the war, their troubles often did not end, but rather intensified, with the liberation.

261

As several of them were to put it, 'My war began in 1945.' Henny, part of that remarkable study of such children by Diane Wolf, *Beyond Anne Frank: Hidden Children and Postwar Families in Holland*, was typical of those who were too young to remember or who repressed their recollections. She was five and a half when she went into hiding: 'Slowly your memory gets lost, somewhere on the road. You don't remember your parents afterwards, you don't remember your brother, the life which was. And you start something new.'[2]

When parents returned, if they returned, they came back as strangers. How can one suddenly say 'mother' or 'father' to a person one doesn't even recognise? How can one face for a second time the severing of the parental bond, which by now many children had formed with their 'hiding mother' and their 'hiding father', who were the only parents they remembered? Nor was it simple for biological parents to receive their children back. After the agony of parting from them they had almost certainly sustained numerous other losses, perhaps the destruction of their entire wider family, parents, siblings, all their kin, to say nothing of the horrors through which they themselves had passed. Then, if they managed to return and find their child, they may well have had no home, no job, no world to which to go back, except absences, haunted places and the struggle to cope with each day. Lore's experience of her parents was not untypical: 'I think they didn't want to ask me anything about anything, and I probably didn't volunteer anything because I didn't know if they wanted to know anything. So they busied themselves with the work at hand. My father went to work, my mother went to work, I went to school. When we came home, we had dinner and we went to sleep and we got up.'[3] Parent–child relationships with real warmth and contact were sadly rather the exception than the rule.

Wolf's unexpected finding is that those children who stayed with their foster families sometimes had it easier. But that, as she firmly demonstrates, cannot justify the struggles which a single returning parent, having lost his or her spouse, or other surviving Jewish relatives who wanted to bring up a niece or nephew, had to go through to reclaim their or their family's children. The Commissie voor Oorlogspleegkinderen, the Commission for War Foster Children, created immediately after the liberation, had a majority of Christian members and a Christian chair; sadly and unhelpfully, there was little understanding or sympathy for the plight of the Jewish community. To many on the committee these children were Dutch first and Jewish second; some members held very negative views of Judaism. The description of a girl named Caroline K noted that 'she [was] typically Jewish – sneaky',[4] while a social worker's report contained the following assessment of the returning parents of another hidden child: 'Weak character, superficial, they spoil their children. They look unpleasant, they speak like a travelling salesman. When they visit the foster parents, they can't help but do business with the Canadian soldiers living there.'[5] It was to this committee that a survivor had to prove his or her suitability as a parent before being allowed to reclaim his or her own child or niece or nephew. Other motives were clearly mixed in with legitimate concern for the welfare of the children. A document dated 1946, discovered near Paris in 2005 and which carried the approval of Pope Pius XII, declared that Jewish children were only to be returned to the Jewish community 'as long as they had not been baptised'.[6]

But the suffering of the children derived primarily from the broken relationships, and often broken people, with whom they had to live. Furthermore, a child could not be expected to emerge from hiding as if all at once that other world had suddenly ceased to exist. Some children loved, and were deeply loved by, their hiding parents and now faced a second heart-rending parting, this time when they were older and acutely conscious of what was happening to them. Other children had been hidden in spaces in which they could scarcely move, where silence by day, fear by night and the total absence of love were their reality for years. In the outer world such an experience may come to an end, but in the inner landscape of the mind and heart it never goes away.

As I read Diane Wolf's remarkable book a deep anguish filled me, yet I also experienced a puzzling and disturbing sense of connection. I found myself wondering where it came from; after all I have never lived a single day other than amidst the privileges of freedom. Then I began to realise. I am not, of course, a hidden child; but, like many others, I have a child in hiding within me. Maybe that is why I read the work with such sorrow and compulsion. For my world changed suddenly when I was five and my mother died and, soon afterwards, the family left Scotland. The green hills and loch-side paths of my childhood vanished in the labyrinths of London. And, however good, however protected the subsequent life to which I was taken, and I was given love and encouragement in deep measure, there remains somewhere within me a child in mourning, seeking memories it cannot find, searching for a relationship which offers only the embrace of silence for ever, confused by the ineluctable attempt to conceive myself as someone other, at least the child of someone other, whom basically I never knew but to whom I owe my life and half my character and temperament, and many of my interests and loves.

Then it strikes me that there is an ancient tradition of such, in some way hidden, children. After all, who was the first 'hidden child'? Was it perhaps Moses, twice parted from his mother, once to be entrusted to the mercies of the Nile and once to be returned to Pharaoh's daughter, whose royal home, like the shelter of strangers, offered at once eternal parting and the only hope of safety? What impact did it have on Moses' identity and values? Was this maybe the secret of his faithfulness to his people, what led him to forsake both foster family and palace for the fortunes of a tribe of slaves whom he was to lead for forty years, yet from whom he was always separate, and by whom he was never really loved or understood?

*   *   *

Several times during the course of my walk I found myself taken to task for waxing lyrical about light. 'But what of the dark?' I was asked; didn't I feel burdened by the darkness which had dwelt, and perhaps still lingered, in the places through which I was walking?'

From the outset it was my aim to reflect on both, the light and the dark, on what obscures the light of the spirit as much as on what causes it to burn, and on what enables societies to conduct themselves in an enlightened rather than in a benighted manner as well as what prevents them from doing so.

The ninth of the ten plagues with which God is described as

punishing Egypt in the book of Exodus is darkness. The darkness was so deep, says the Torah, that: 'No man could see his brother, nor could anyone rise up from his place for three days' (Exodus 10:22–3). A penetrating Hasidic interpretation understands the latter situation not as the result, but as the cause of the former: it wasn't due to the darkness that 'no man could see his brother', but rather because no man saw or cared about his brothers and sisters that there was such a deep darkness across the land of Egypt in the first place.[7] Perhaps the most important lesson I have learnt from my walk concerns that issue of being able to see, hear and have regard for our brothers and sisters. Unless we are able to listen to each other's stories, take account of each other's humanity and act to defend each other's basic dignity, not just if, but most especially when, we belong to different faiths, national backgrounds or social groups, there will be darkness across our land. We may not live today in countries where children have to be hidden from their persecutors, though there are still many places like that across the globe, but we most certainly do live in a world where much of one another's humanity remains concealed from us, unless we truly listen, unless we expressly search it out.

Yet it strikes me, as I reflect on the question, that there is another aspect to darkness. It should not be understood solely as representing the bad. For darkness is also the womb of thoughts and deeds, of life itself. After all, the Bible relates how it was out of darkness that God first created light. It was not when God observed the light alone, but when God saw both 'evening and morning', the alternating rhythm of dark and light, that God 'saw that it was good'. There are times when we need and even long for the dark, when we pull the blanket over our head and seek comfort and respite in keeping out life's constant intrusions so that we can rediscover ourselves in that warmth and privacy once again.

I don't know if this can be translated into the political or historical domain, but at an inner, personal level, light and dark work in partnership within us. The real issue may therefore be how we use our darkness. What breeds in the inner recesses of the self when our consciousness broods over it, just as God's spirit once hovered over the face of the unlit deep? What do we make of our ignorance and unknowing? Is that darkness the source and womb of creativity, leading to the desire for knowledge and insight? A rabbinic interpretation of the verse from Ecclesiastes '*yitron ha'or mehachoshech*', translates it not as the plain meaning would seem to suggest – 'the benefit of the light over the dark' – but rather as 'the benefit of the light is *because of* the dark' (Ecclesiastes 2:13). Does what happens in our inner darkness lead us towards light; is there a natural generosity there, an openness to what we don't yet know or understand? Or is it only the abode of anxiety and fear, generating prejudice and reinforcing ignorance? If so, how can love reach it, bringing self-confidence, curiosity and the readiness to engage creatively with light and life?

The Talmud employs a remarkable euphemism when it refers to someone who is blind: it calls such a person *sagi nahor*, 'of great light'. This description of a blind person is not just a way of hiding a harsh reality beneath a deceptively optimistic phrase. It expresses a challenging potentiality: can the creative darkness to which we must all regularly return within our hearts and minds become the source of insight and wisdom? Can we turn our blindness as individuals and societies into light? If so, we will be able to bring darkness and light together as the true partners they have the capacity of becoming. For no place is so dark that light is incapable of penetrating it:

> Even the darkness is not too dark for you
> But the night shines as the day,
> The darkness is even as the light. (Psalm 139:12)

*   *   *

❖ I've been writing since before the early hours and now it's getting light, time to say the dawn prayers. Mitzpah is fast asleep on the bed; I wake him for our morning rituals. He and I are in this adventure together and we've shared most things on this journey; I say *birkot hashachar*, the morning blessings, as I take him out each day for his first pre-breakfast stroll. Later, when I put on my *tefillin*, my phylacteries, to recite the Shema, the meditation on God's oneness, he rolls over, expecting me to sit down next to him, tickle his tummy and incorporate him in my devotions. I have to admit that I sometimes oblige; after all, perhaps his (relative) innocence is more acceptable before God than my many words.

I must express my appreciation for that rascal of a black-and-white dog who has shared my wanderings, adventures, prayers and, on occasion, dinner over these last twenty days. I don't think he's put a paw seriously wrong (though both he and I still have a day to go) and he's been a wonderful companion. He's come a long way since that unforgettable occasion when I took him on the tube in the rush hour for the first time to accustom him to the noise and crowds of inner-city London. The carriage was full and everyone was squeezed tightly together. Despite the over-crowding people made a fuss of Mitzpah and stroked his head. All was going well until the young woman next to me suddenly called out in a loud voice, and I quote her exact words: 'Who just touched my arse?' Silence descended instantly throughout the carriage. Mercifully, the very next moment Mitzpah licked her hands and, realising who the culprit was, she burst into a fit of laughter.

This time, that dog has caused me neither trouble nor embarrassment – so far . . . I wonder if he would say the same about me.

I look at Mitzpah sleeping in the armchair in my study as I reread these words and feel a degree of love I do not understand. Somehow his presence makes me feel safe in my day, my life. I like to have him next to me when I pray; only thus can I fully express the depth of my gratitude for this great partnership of existence here on earth, God, all living being, my life, that fragment of it which is me.

Mitzpah features wonderfully in the film. Joe has even captured his crazy habit of spinning madly round and round in joyous abandon and Guy has set the scene to a piece of Hasidic music which makes it look as if the dog is dancing. My favourite compliment following the premiere is that I should apply for an award as best supporting actor. Poor Mitzpah, I take him with me to the cinema on that first occasion, though I'm not sure what dogs are actually able to see on the big screen.

Puzzled by hearing his name spoken repeatedly, but realising it isn't me who's calling him, for after all we're sitting right next to one another, and alarmed by the barking of a dog who sounds remarkably like himself, he eventually decides to answer back, to the delight and amusement of everyone present.

From Mitzpah's Blog

I had a horrible, horrible day. To start with I had a bad tummy-ache, because daddy didn't bring enough of my usual food. Then they went and took me to the vet. Daddy says it's so that we can go back home to London. But I don't see how going to the vet gets one any nearer England.

First they put some medicine on my neck. Next they gave me an injection. Then, a hundred times worse, they stuck something up my backside to see if I had a temperature. They even filmed it too. It was so humiliating! Doesn't anyone understand that animals too have a sense of dignity? I'm so pleased it was very expensive; that'll stop daddy ever doing it again.

But afterwards I got a present to make up for it all.

Love from a very upset Mitzpah

PS I don't think much of Amsterdam; all those trams and bicycles don't leave much space on the crowded pavement for a dog to walk, let alone run and have a bit of fun.

Day Nineteen – To Rotterdam and Hoek van Holland

I set out early for the Central Station to catch the train to Schiedam. Guy, Joe, Anna and I are due to meet up with friends from England who've come specially to join us for the final day's walking on the Continent. Sadly I haven't enough time to visit the flower market and am obliged to leave my habit of orchid collecting for another occasion. I buy two tickets and one dog pass (which saves me a substantial fine later in the day), queue for a much needed cup of coffee and board the train. I have little idea that this is to prove the most difficult walking of the entire journey and that for the first time I'm going to feel frightened.

Strangely, I had the opportunity to repeat the identical journey seven months later. I'd been asked to teach at a Jewish Studies conference near Amsterdam and decided not to rush home that same night. Instead, I booked myself into a hotel and arranged to travel back the next day by boat. I found myself staying almost exactly opposite the Hollandsche Schouwburg, built at the end of the nineteenth century as a theatre and place of entertainment, but turned by the Nazis into the main deportation centre for the Jews of Amsterdam. A sign outside invites the passer-by to pause and reflect: one hundred and four thousand Dutch Jews perished, many of them sent from this very place to Westerbork in the north of the country and from there onwards to death camps in the east. It was from here that men and women of the Resistance, among them many students, smuggled out babies and small children and took them to safe hiding places throughout the country.

I quietly recited the Kaddish. Next morning, without a compass to tell me which direction was east, I stood by the window facing the Schouwburg as I said my prayers.

*   *   *

❖   The final day's walking takes me from Rotterdam to Hoek van Holland, along the last twenty-five kilometres of that particular branch of the Rhine.

Grace, our youth worker, and Yoav, who runs our programmes for students, join me; I greatly appreciate their presence. First of all they are good company; secondly they turn my thoughts, which have been focused so strongly on the past, to the future. The light must be carried forward, not simply for the sake of memory, but for children, for the young, for hope. Eric from the synagogue's walking group, the Trekkies, joins us too, with a friend. More experienced at long-distance walking and more sensible than I, they bring equipment for all seasons. (Actually I do have waterproof trousers in my rucksack; it's just that it never occurrs to me to put them on until it's too late.) We're quite a merry band.

But I soon begin to feel guilty about the efforts they have all made to come. The weather turns from a troubling grey to light, then moderate, and finally lashing rain driven by a vicious cold wind. We follow bicycle lanes out of town, heading towards a path along the top of a dyke which runs right through to the Hoek. 'In Holland,' says Guy, as we discover that this route is less romantic than its equivalents in Germany and ajoins the motorway for several kilometres, 'cycling is a serious mode of transport, not a pleasure sport.'

We finally emerge from the city and its suburbs into open country. Our path is now right alongside the huge grey river, on which pass ocean-going ships. Mercifully, the violent wind blows from behind us, pushing us forcibly inland and blasting us onwards with such power that our speed increases considerably. If we had wings and could have flapped them, the last twelve kilometres would have passed in a couple of minutes. By now the rain has soaked through my trousers and boots. Grace and Yoav make the sensible decision to go back, though it's not at all clear where they will find shelter. Eventually, they tell me later, they reached a station and took the train. I'm greatly relieved when I learn of this. I hesitate, beginning to feel seriously cold, but Eric points out that from where we are now the only possible direction is onwards. The sole way to keep warm is by walking as fast as my feet will carry me. This I'm forced to do and, backed by the driving wind, keep up an extremely rapid pace. I rush on ahead, desperate to reach the Hoek; as soon as I stop moving I shiver uncontrollably. My boots are full of freezing water and for the first time since I set out from London I want this to be over. Meanwhile Mitzpah, born for the wet Welsh hills, thinks both the terrain and the weather wonderful. He rushes along the dyke path, stops for a stick, ignores the rain, enjoys his day. I make my sodden way with the roaring wind behind me and am more relieved that I care to admit when, just short of the town, I see the film crew and their warm car. A café, a cup of tea, and I begin to feel safe once again. I take out the towel and rub down the sopping dog; Mitzpah loves this attention and even raises his paws, each one in turn, for me to dry beneath his legs. I change into fresh trousers, socks and shoes. Eric and his friend bravely make it all the way to the station at the Hoek where we soon join them. Big puddles gather on the floor from the rainwater dripping off our clothes.

All of a sudden we see a man running, ambulances, a helicopter. Scarcely beyond our view a tragedy has taken place in the estuary. A boat has been struck by a huge wave and has sunk in the violence of the storm. Five men have disappeared into the freezing water and a major search and rescue operation is underway. Later we hear that three of them have been taken from the icy water alive. But two, including the captain, are still missing. The port authorities decide to try to raise the tug from the riverbed in the hope that it might contain an air bubble sufficiently large for them to have survived.

It was not until the Saturday night after my return to London that I was able to speak to the mayor's office in Hoek; I learnt that the two poor men had been drowned. The body of one of them had been washed ashore many miles up the coast; the other had not been found. I wrote at once to both their families; I felt connected to their fate.

Months afterwards I was sitting in comfort in the train from Amsterdam, looking out for the path along which I had walked, sodden and miserable, that November day, when a man took his place opposite me and smiled: 'Don't worry, your bags are not in my way.' He smiled again, 'I just saw the title of the book you're reading.' Warming to him, I explained that the volume, called *Sacred Trash*, was about the discovery of centuries of old documents, bills of lading, business correspondence, marriage contracts, previously undiscovered poems by famous authors, holy texts, in the attic of the Ben Ezra Synagogue in the old city of Cairo. 'It reminded me of the film *Out of the Ashes*,' he responded. 'You see, you had your finger over part of the word, so I read "*Sacred Ash*". I'm from Rwanda,' he added and smiled once again with a beautiful, gentle smile. Our peoples have much in common, we agreed.

'Maybe we can learn from the Jews how to find the capacity to be strong and carry on,' my companion observed. 'Some Rwandans want to move forward and rebuild their lives. Others say that everyone they knew and loved has been killed, so they just don't know what to do.'

His words made me think of a conversation from the previous night. 'I was born here in 1942,' said a woman who'd been hidden in Holland as a young child, as we were driving through a familiar district of Amsterdam. 'This area used to be a kind of Jewish socialist commune.' I looked out of the car window at the rows of houses and didn't dare ask her what had happened to her parents. 'Yes; that's how it used to be. But it's all gone now.'

'There are those who say, "We must build for the future," and those who say, "It's all been over for a long time now," ' the son-in-law of another hidden woman told me that same day.

My new friend continued: 'I was in a camp for three months. Luckily it was surrounded by UN soldiers; we begged them not to abandon us. We were fortunate. But for all that time we weren't allowed to leave the precincts, all five thousand of us. It was far too dangerous.

'Yes, they say Rwanda's a beautiful country, the land of a thousand hills. You even get snow on the highest mountains. There isn't much natural gas or oil, but the soil is very fertile and you can grow everything there. I don't know if I'll go back. Many Rwandans don't want to return because they're certain they'll come across the people who murdered their fathers and mothers and then they'll be killed because those types don't want any witnesses.

'Rwandans are tired. They talk about the past, but nobody admits to any guilt. Nobody's prepared to say that anything was their fault. That's why no one can make plans for the country's future.

'My name is Seraphim,' he says. He smiles, and gets off the train at Delft. I feel strangely alone after he's gone and ponder the contrast between his gentle, noble presence and the indescribably terrible events through which he has been made to live. Has he family? Has he got friends still in Rwanda? Is he lonely here in these flat, cold northern lands? I hadn't even asked.

He had found me through our shared histories and I am grateful to him for his generosity.

Later, after we've passed through Schiedam, I watch the landscape carefully. Surely this must be where we crossed the tracks and made our way on to that freezing coastal path? Or perhaps it was here? I'll never know exactly. How different it all looks today; the sun shines, a foal lies on a heap of hay and flicks his tail at the train, sheep graze in the meadow between the inn where I changed my sodden clothes and the harbour station, the estuary is beautiful and calm. As I walk towards the ship an arrowhead of geese flies overhead.

*　　*　　*

❖   I call Ivo at the mayor's office; he's due to show us where a statue is shortly to be placed in commemoration of the children who came with the Kindertransport, then take us to the fortress at the sea's edge where the Dutch Queen and her Government hid in May 1940 until the Royal Navy could ferry them to safety. Had they fallen into enemy hands the disaster of the Dutch defeat and its effect on morale across the Continent would have been even greater. However, we are none too eager for a prolonged walking tour; none of us have the heart for much further exposure to the elements.

There has been a miscommunication and Ivo doesn't realise we're expecting to meet with him today. He's not in his office. But when I reach him on his mobile he drops everything and comes to join us immediately. Within five minutes he's calling out to us in the terminal with smiles and greetings. I find this amazing. As a host on behalf of

273

his town he has put aside everything else to look after us. He is charming.

He takes us in his car to the site on a busy road right next to the sea where the monument will be erected. He explains that they had at first thought to place it by the railway tracks in the port; after all, the children had come here by train from Berlin, Prague, Vienna and many other destinations. But the sculptor had felt that what was most important was the sea. The waves represented at once hope and separation. Across them lay safety in Britain, at least for the time being. Yet those very waters were to part the children from their families, most of them for ever. It seems fitting that as we listen to this explanation we are blasted by the winds and shiver in the storm.

Inside we talk about the Kindertransport and the fate of the Dutch in the war. Ivo had limited opportunity of learning about the war directly from his grandparents. But the years of occupation, the 'winter of hunger' in 1944/5, these subjects have interested him deeply and he has done much research. He refuses to allow us to buy him a coffee and instead insists on treating the lot of us.

Since he is so hospitable, I tell him a story on the subject which still moves me even though I must have read it twenty times. Sidney Bloch recounts it in his book *No Time for Tears*. He and his brother are staying with their uncle near Newcastle; the year must be 1940. His uncle is a deeply religious and strictly observant man, the sort of person who never locks his door so that no poor person will feel too embarrassed to come in for a meal. One day Sidney gets home and finds him on the phone. 'No, it's really urgent; I must have the cash today.' His uncle is borrowing money; later they go out together and collect sums of between five and twenty pounds from many different people. Then they go to a furniture store, buy all the essential items for fitting out three homes with the basic necessities and help to load their purchases on to a truck. It follows their tram to three empty houses on the outskirts of the town. Soon a grocery van arrives with large bags of provisions which they also help to unpack and install in each of the homes. It isn't until the next day that Sidney discovers what the exercise has all been about. They go down to the docks where the last boat carrying refugees from Holland arrives. His uncle simply approaches three families and tells them in a mixture of English and Yiddish that they are expected. He takes them to the houses which he has carefully equipped and stays with them until a member of the local refugee organisation arrives.

'Do you really know any of them?' Sidney asks his uncle afterwards with great curiosity. 'I know they're refugees,' he says, 'I don't need to know anything else about them.'[1]

It took his uncle ten years to repay the loans. Soon afterwards he died.

*   *   *

On the beach at Hoek van Holland, in a raging storm, almost as far downriver as it is possible to walk towards where the Rhine meets the North Sea, Guy asks me what I've learnt from this journey. I have an immediate answer: 'How important it is to be able to hear and honour the stories of others, to listen not only to one's own heart but also to the heart of the other.' On this the sensitivity of individuals and the moral health of nations depend.

I think of the philosopher Emmanuel Levinas, who survived the Holocaust because he was captured in France as a soldier and therefore treated not as a Jew but as a prisoner of war. A student of Martin Heidegger, he saw in his teacher's embrace of Nazism not just a personal moral failure but an indictment of the entire Western philosophical heritage. If a serious thinker could be so incapable of distinguishing between good and evil, then the entire intellectual tradition on which he drew must somewhere be at fault. Ethics, Levinas therefore maintained in his seminal teaching after the war, must be 'first philosophy' and the essence of ethics is our immediate and unlimited obligation towards the other, towards our neighbour. Our entire life is not adequate to answer to our responsibility towards the person next to us. God is not revealed to us in this world through some miraculous disclosure, but in the face and presence of those who come towards us.

Guy then adds the words, 'now that the walk is over'. But it is not. It never is. Not even this stage is over until we walk from the Kindertransport memorial at Liverpool Street Station back to the synagogue in Finchley. And the walk continues far beyond that. Mitzpah most certainly agrees. For a fortnight after our return home I see his paws twitch in his sleep; in his dreams he's still running along the banks of his Rhine. I too, months later, am still walking, on a journey to myself, to the history of my family and people; on a journey towards other peoples also and towards trying to understand what enables societies to be tolerant and open, or what causes them to turn towards exclusion and hate. So long as we live, none of us is ever finished either with the light or with the dark.

*   *   *

❖   Before setting off for England we return briefly to Rotterdam, to the home of Rabbi Albert Ringer and his wife. Albert has sent me maps, train timetables, advice about how long each part of this day's walk will take. He has arranged a small gathering at his home where we can meet a few members of his congregation. We arrive wet, weary, dirty, and in dribs and drabs; a less appealing group of guests would be hard to imagine. Albert and his wife Aviva aren't in the least bit phased. Mitzpah receives food and water. We say the blessing over home-baked bread, followed by hot soup, smoked salmon rolls, coffee, tea. There is no agenda; we simply chat.

Sometimes we remain ignorant of what will develop out of a human contact till much later in the relationship; on other occasions we realise at once that a friendship is being born. That is how I feel talking to Albert. With a broad smile he tells me how he has become a rabbi later in his life. Everyone has stories here in Holland, he explains; everyone is a child of survivors. But you can't create a community only on a graveyard; you have also to think of the future. I can only imagine that with their compelling warmth, he and his wife nurture a very special congregation.

Poor people; even after we leave for the ferry they haven't truly seen the back of us. We are soon obliged to return. Stena Line, who sail the ferries between the Hoek and Harwich are prepared to allow us to embark, but not Mitzpah. They explain that due to the operation to search for the missing sailors they cannot know exactly when the ferry will depart; it might be soon or it might be in six hours' time or more. If we board, we'll be free to wander round the ship but the dog will have to go to the kennels and it simply wouldn't be fair for him to be cooped up in a cage for an indefinite period of time. This all makes perfect sense; I thank them and add my prayers that the men should soon be found alive.

But it isn't so easy to come up with alternative plans. The storm is so bad (and apparently has still not reached its peak) that ports and airports are shutting across the country and all along the Channel coast. We think on our feet and soon realise that the only route home is by car. Mitzpah seems to understand and visibly rejoices; he hadn't wanted to board the ship and had been tugging us away from the terminal with his anxious tail tucked tight between his legs. Once again he will be able to cross the sea in the comfort of the back of a car.

We return to Rotterdam and knock for the second time on Rabbi Ringer's door: please can we have the keys to our rented car back? I'm reminded of my grandfather's love of the Talmudic phrase *gam zu letovah* – 'this too is for the best'. Earlier we had been disappointed that the car-rental company was closed and that it had been impossible to return the vehicle. We had trespassed further on the good rabbi's kindness, asking him to drive it round the corner next morning and drop back the keys. Now access to that car has become our salvation.

On our long, late-night drive through Belgium into France a big bag of food and drink prepared by the Ringers sustains us. There are some things for which it's simply impossible to say a big enough thank you.

I call Nicky from the car and tell her of the change of plan: 'Don't meet me tomorrow in Harwich. Can you kindly pick us all up in Calais instead?' A last-minute booking on Eurotunnel saves us for the second time on this adventure.

At two in the morning we're still searching for accommodation in Lille.

From Mitzpah's Blog

I didn't like the first half of the walk today. We had a motorway on one side with lots of noisy lorries. On the other side were fields with sheep. I tried to get away from all the traffic but my daddy wouldn't let me off the lead. All I wanted was to play with those sheep. I'm sure they would have enjoyed it too; after all, I expect they're also bored most of the time.

Later we finally got on to a path by the river. I loved it because I could run as much as I liked. But my daddy was upset by the wind and the rain. I don't understand: if human beings are so clever why don't they have a proper coat of hair like we do? I've always thought those clothes were a stupid waste of money. The only advantage is that if humans didn't need wool there wouldn't be so many sheep for me to chase.

Actually I quite like getting wet and muddy because afterwards I get dried with a warm towel and then I can jump with my dirty paws on to the most comfortable chair. It's my way of saying, 'Hello, this is me.' What could be wrong with that?

Love,

Mitzpah

Day Twenty
Back to London and Shabbat at Home

When Guy, Anna and Joe did eventually discover a hotel on a business estate on the edge of the town, I decided that it was simply too late and too expensive to pay for the decent bed the place had to offer us, and slept, with Mitzpah for company, in the car. I did however have the temerity to ask if I could have breakfast inside; nothing can replace good muesli and strong coffee at the start of a day, with a quiet half-hour to read or write.

Joe dropped us off at the station before delivering the hired car back to the company, this time permanently. He soon rejoined us and an hour later we were on the fast train to Calais Fretun. There Mitzpah, spotting Nicky waiting on the platform, bounded up to her in swift leaps, the entire back half of his body rocking from side to side with the overjoyed swinging of his tail. He jumped up and licked her face over and over again. I, of course, had to wait for the cameras to be in place before giving her my hug.

I have to admit that I don't remember many details of the journey home after that meeting. I recall taking the wrong turning off the A13 so that we ended up driving past Highbury Corner, but it proved a reasonably quick route back to Finchley in the end. Soon I was parking the car in our driveway just like at any other time; we were home and it was over.

❖ Mitzpah and I actually arrived back on Friday about an hour and a half before Shabbat, in other words with just sufficient breathing space to pull out the wettest, dirtiest clothes and prevent them from souring the holy Sabbath by slowly going mouldy in the bottom of the rucksack. There was just time enough, too, to stuff newspaper in my boots in what I, of little faith, presumed to be the vain hope of drying them out in time for Sunday's perambulations. 'You'll see,'

279

said Nicky, 'they'll be fine.' She was right; and just as well too, as there was to be plenty more liquid sunshine, this time of the uniquely British variety, for them to keep at bay.

My body was home; but it has taken much longer for my thoughts to come back. One small symptom of this is that as soon as the Sabbath was over I was on the phone to Europe. First I called Ivo in Hoek van Holland to ask after the missing sailors. Next, I can't recall exactly any more, I spoke to or emailed Renata von Trott. Over the next few days I called Dr Ries in Koblenz, Rachel Heuberger in Frankfurt and my new friends in Cologne. My pretext was that I wanted to make sure that I'd properly thanked everyone who'd helped me. But the deeper reason was that I didn't want these relationships to end. I didn't want the walk to be finished.

One night I dreamt about my grandparents. I found myself walking slowly through the downstairs rooms of the house in Hodford Road which they bought soon after the end of the war and where they lived until almost the end of their days. I had't been inside it for almost twenty years, since Nicky and I began our married life there in the upstairs flat, before moving out a few weeks later when the house was finally sold. There was the lounge with the two big armchairs; no one but my grandparents ever sat in them, he in his and she in hers, never alternating. There were the shelves of pot plants which we assiduously watered whenever they went on holiday. There were the windows which overlooked the small rockery with the honeysuckle on one side where the blackbirds built their nest and where once the local cat killed all their fledglings and left their bodies in the grass. There was the dining-room, dark with its heavy shelves of books and deep oak furniture; here we used to gather for dinner on Friday night with guests who were almost always, like our own family, refugees. It seemed to me as if the far side of this room, where my grandfather's heavy desk stood, extended all the way to Frankfurt, as if it traversed in its length the mystery of all those books with their intriguing titles: *Denk ich an Deutschland in der Nacht* ('When I think of Germany in the night') – a line from a poem by Heine; *Kinder der Nacht* ('Children of the Night'), dedicated to my grandfather in small, neat handwriting by Otto Frank, the father of Anne; *Dying We Live* and numerous other volumes. I walked through the room and out into the hallway where the big trunks lay covered by cloths to make them look tidy, with their labels still on them, their histories never fully unpacked. The day we were eventually obliged to clear them away, when my grandparents needed a live-in carer and we had to empty out the spare room, we discovered my great-grandfather's dress clothes cut in the style of the mid-nineteenth century. We threw away armful after armful of old papers, but I now remember that among them were copies of *Aufbau*, the newsletter of the German-Jewish community after the Holocaust, and perhaps other important journals. I know exactly why we had to get rid of those endless piles of dank and yellowing papers, but I have a doubt inside me now: perhaps there was some fragment of history in what we consigned to the bonfire at the end of that huge garden which we shall never be able to reclaim.

How familiar everything was about that house, the decades since I saw it last vanished into nowhere. I never thought that it would all be gone for ever, or that my heart would one day long for it.

*   *   *

Just as I'm about to complete this manuscript and with it end another dimension of this journey, I receive an unexpected email from Rachel Heuberger. 'I believe this will be of interest to you,' she wrote. German Radio has been digitising its archives and among the materials now made available is a recording of my grandfather's address at the rededication of the Westend-Synagoge in 1950.

I use the mouse to place the arrow on the blue, underlined text and prepare to listen to the static which is bound to impair this sixty-year-old soundtrack. But instead my grandfather's voice rings out, clear, vibrant and unfaltering, on what must have been among the most emotionally and spiritually challenging occasions of his entire career:

'*Mah Tovu Ohalecha Ya'akov mishkenotechah Yisrael*: How goodly are your tents, O Jacob; your dwelling places, O Israel.'
Respected Congregation, dear friends, it is with these words, the

words of a non-Jewish seer of ancient times, that pious Jews until this very day enter the House of God. The words ring with a special solemnity in our ears and hearts at this hour, as we see before us this ancient house of God in its restored glory.

But you will not find it difficult to understand that for me personally my joy at seeing this house is mixed with painful memories. I am marking a reunion with this synagogue after an absence of more than eleven years.

My friends, before me stands the memory of the solemn dedication of this very synagogue almost exactly forty years ago. Then too it took place in the days immediately prior to our New Year's festival, which is also for us a day of judgement, and which precedes the Day of Atonement.

When, after a long absence, I walk through the streets of Frank-furt . . . Is this the ancient free city, the city where kings were crowned and kaisers elected? Is this the great and wealthy city, the city which was the birthplace of such a man as Goethe?

What judgement from heaven has descended upon this, and count-less other, German cities! Shattered and shaken, one walks through the old, no longer recognisable streets and squares. In the hollow grey frames of the broken windows dwells terror and from above the clouds look through.

But by sheer effort, driven by the will to live and to create, the German nation is rebuilding its country and its fatherland. And, what is of incomparably more significance morally, the best among the Germans are endeavouring to make reparation for the monstrous wrongs they did, or allowed to be done, to the Jewish People.

This synagogue stands as fine testimony to that will to make good. But, my friends, only the future can prove, only the future can show, whether the spirit in which this synagogue has been so beautifully rebuilt is a genuine and enduring spirit, whether today's celebration will have been no more than a hollow ceremony or the summons to a new and better Germany.

We hope, indeed we trust, that if the people in whose hands Germany's fate lies today do not forget, but are mindful of what once was, and remember also what then followed, the freedom and unity of all layers of society, all religions and all denominations throughout Germany will be ensured.

'Do not forget,' these words apply to us Jews too. Do not forget, but do forgive.

Therefore let the words with which the approaching Day of Atonement calls out to us form the conclusion of this brief address: *Shalom, shalom larachok velakarov amar Adonai* . . . Peace, peace, to the far off and to the near, says God, the God of us all.

Amen.

I can as little comment now as I could speak then, when I first saw that verse in the Westend-Synagoge: 'I shall not die, but I shall live . . . '

From Mitzpah's Blog

I'm so happy that I was able to travel home by car. Humans don't know what it's like to be shut up in a tiny cage for hours. This way I could stretch out all night on the back seat. Daddy slept there too, which meant there wasn't quite as much space as I would have liked.

But the best part of the journey was when mummy met us at a railway station. I was so happy to see her again. Mind you, *she* doesn't feed me pieces of bread and croissant under the table as often as daddy does.

I'm so proud that I have my own passport. They used a special machine to scan me before we were allowed to get on the train back to England. I saw a big sign about the Borders Agency; is it just for border collies like me?

Now I'm back in London it feels a bit strange. I miss the walking and running for hours and hours every day. I hope we can plan something exciting soon.

Shabbat Shalom,
Mitzpah

Day Twenty-Two
From Liverpool Street Station to the Synagogue

Coming home has initially been a culture shock for Mitzpah. For one thing, he arrived back at Amberden Avenue to find the house occupied by another border collie. It was only John's dog Pippin, a long standing friend of his. But it's one thing to have a visitor and quite another to discover that precisely when you've temporarily moved out, she's decided to move in.

However, the two of them seem to be getting on reasonably amicably, with only the odd bark and show of teeth at mealtimes. For poor Mitzpah the issue is rather the bewilderment of being back here: What's happened to my long walks? Where's that big river gone, along which we were playing so merrily for so many days? Where are my new friends and their strange machines which show pictures which look very much like me? Poor dog, he'll need at least three or four hours of serious walking every day and some new crazy project to look forward to.

Today at least he has his wish. We set off by tube for Liverpool Street Station, where, by the Kindertransport Memorial, we begin our final stretch of this particular journey, back through London to the synagogue. We only have time to hear a brief outline of the events leading up to the decision by Britain in the days following Kristallnacht to accept ten thousand Jewish children into this country. Hermann, himself one of these 'Kinder', who has come specially to address us at the start of today's walk, emphasises that it was a unique act of generosity; the United States did not do likewise, nor did any other country. He notes the role played by the Quakers and the close cooperation between them and Jewish relief organisations. But most of all he focuses on the courage and heroism of the parents. When Hermann stresses the fact that Britain agreed to accept children, but not their parents, I cannot help but think of the crueller side of this act of generosity. A place on the Transport entailed severing perhaps the closest of all relationships, the bond between parent and child. I know of at least one of the Kinder for whom it took decades to appreciate that what his parents had done in sending him off without them to a faraway land was not an act of abandonment but a deed of selfless love. Two thirds of these fathers and mothers would never see their children again.

I recently spoke to a hidden child who survived the war in Brussels. No one explained to him afterwards why the visits of his mother had become increasingly rare and then stopped. 'Why did she leave me?' he asked himself and wondered for years what terrible thing he must have done wrong to merit such punitive treatment. Finally he plucked up the courage to ask one of his surviving relatives why his parents had abandoned him.

'But they never abandoned you,' he was told. 'They loved you; they adored you; you were the most important person to them in the whole world.'

'Then where are they?' he asked, his heart filling up with sudden joy.

'They were murdered.'

When he related this conversation to me many decades later he told me that he could still feel that swing from anguish to joy and then to utter pain. 'I hate surprises,' he said, 'even good ones. You never get over it; you never recover.'

Most, but not all, of the children travelled by boat from Hoek van Holland to Harwich and from there to Liverpool Street Station, where they waited in great trepidation to discover who it would be with whom they would depart to a strange home and a totally unfamiliar routine. Most of them, Hermann tells us, made something of their lives; they gained professional qualifications, established successful careers and more than repaid this country for taking them in. But some, he reminds us, were not able to overcome the trauma which shattered their child-hood; they lived out their lives in dank bed-sitting rooms, lonely and depressed. Still, in 1988, the year of the first Kindertransport reunion, Margaret Thatcher wrote a letter to the Kinder in which she expressed her gratitude for the contribution these 'children' had made to the life and creativity of Britain.

We walk together, Nicky, Libbi, Mitzpah, Pippin and I, and at least fifty members of our community. I am moved by how many people join us. The Trekkies, our synagogue's valiant and well-practised walking group, have prepared an excellent route and we pass underneath several of central London's busiest roads along the banks of canals. Ducks, swans, canoes, narrow boats – who would have thought we were in the middle of one of the world's greatest cities? Sheva, Racheli's dog, even decides that conditions are just right for a swim and has to be coaxed back out of the water. We pass King's Cross, St Pancras, Euston; soon we are standing outside the Royal Free Hospital where Mossy, Libbi and Kadya were all born. I have witnessed both dying and birth in this hospital. I've sat quietly by many bedsides, trying to be inwardly silent, listening and praying with life. I've helped to straighten the limbs of the dead and stood in the presence of the departing soul. But I also rushed out on her very first morning on earth to buy the teddy bear which still sleeps on Kadya's bed every night.

We choose the dog-friendly option back from here, which is also the muddiest path across the Heath. The rain decides that it too mustn't miss out; it generously accompanies us almost to the very last footfall. I'm touched when, along the last third of the route, down through Big Wood and up over the North Circular, several families come to meet us with their children, to walk together, to say hello, simply to share our path for a few minutes. When we do reach the synagogue there are still more people, including more children, to welcome us home with hot cups of tea.

I realise once again that this light which I have helped to bring from a different era, a past in which I have become more and more deeply immersed over the previous weeks, really belongs to the future.

I remembered the promise I made a few days before I set off:

❖ Yesterday I donned a builder's hard hat and boots and was shown round our new synagogue building. I had seen it before; it was already exciting then, but it was in nothing like the state I saw it now. It was possible to visualise the shape and size of every space and room, where the windows were, where the doors were being fitted, what it would look like to sit and face the Holy Ark. It was even possible to imagine where people might congregate and chat (both during and after the service), where children would gather and play and where, perhaps, we could arrange seats at small tables for coffee.

Most exciting of all was the light. It poured through from skylights into the places where we will pray, reminding me of Rabbi Milton Steinberg's words of appreciation on the day he first left hospital after recovering from a serious heart attack:

> As I crossed the threshold the sunlight greeted me . . . The sky overheard was very blue, very clear and very, very high. Not, I thought, the *shamayim*, heaven, but *shemei shamayim*, a heaven of heavens . . . And everywhere in the firmament above me, in the great vault between the earth and sky, on the pavements, the buildings – the golden glow of sunlight. It touched me, too, with friendship, with warmth, with blessing. And as I basked in its glory there ran through my mind those wonderful words of the prophet about the sun which someday shall rise with healing on its wings.[1]

I thought of my friend Paul, may his memory be for a blessing, who worked so hard to begin the process of creating our new synagogue and who dreamt that the foundation stone would be laid during his chairmanship (over ten years ago).

But most of all I thought of the future. Where are the children's toys going to be kept? How long will it take before there are crisps all over the floor? When will our first wedding be? Not the first *chuppah* to take place on these premises – though that in itself is very exciting and still uncertain because there's something of a competition on to see who will book the earliest date – but rather, when will the first couple who meet while chatting here in this foyer choose to celebrate their marriage on precisely that very same spot?

I realise that I've been so preoccupied with the past while preparing for my walk from Frankfurt, with history, with the Holocaust, with voices calling out in hope or warning, that I've half forgotten about the future. Light, after all, doesn't consist of memorial lamps alone; it is there to bless the present and the future with God's illumination.

What a future it can be – and what joy, and sense of responsibility, the thought of it brings! May the light in our new home, the sunlight which flows through skylights and windows, the light in our hearts, the light we bring from our history, the light of Torah and learning, the radiance of God's presence, shine on the children's games and the fine print of Talmudic commentaries alike, on our own community and our neighbours of different faiths with whom I hope we will share a peaceful and creative future.

Then I thought of the grandfather of the Bar Mitzvah boy who told me that he had survived Auschwitz-Birkenau and spoke to me of how it felt, having passed through the gates above which were sadistically emblazoned the laconic, deceitful words *Arbeit Macht Frei*, to stand in freedom once again before the open doors of the Holy Ark and sing the words, '*Shema Yisrael* – Hear, O Israel, the Lord our God, the Lord is one.'

*   *   *

I decided not to leave the torch switched on at the back of our old synagogue; it was sure to get lost in the anticipated chaos preceding our move. Instead I brought it back home with me that Sunday afternoon and plugged it into a socket in our dining-room. There it remained for five months, shining like a blessing on the picture of Nicky and me at our wedding.

When would we finally be able to move into our new synagogue? For over a year the builders had been ahead of schedule and on budget, an almost unheard of achievement. Then came a month of snow, followed by weeks of waiting: would the work be completed by the beginning of March, or on the first day of spring, or would we have to wait a further ten days until just before the festival of Passover? It would be foolish to send out invitations for an opening ceremony which we would only find ourselves having to postpone. Eventually the lighting of the *Ner Tamid* was fixed for early April, on a date which proved to be just three days after we took possession of the building.

That night we gathered in the dimly lit synagogue. As the light was transferred from the torch to the new *Ner Tamid* Jackie sang the same words to the same melody she had chosen when the torch was first switched on in Frankfurt: 'God is my light and my salvation' (Psalm 27:1). I recall very clearly the moment when the brass bars of the Eternal Lamp above me began to glow, reflecting in a radiance of orange and gold the hidden light concealed within them. I turned the torch off and at once feelings of relief and emptiness flowed simualtaneously through me, leaving me in tears.

This journey, so deeply important to me, was now seemingly over. Henceforth that torch would lie in the bottom of some drawer; no doubt it wouldn't be long before I'd even forgotten where it was. I felt as if I had switched off a part of myself, a light which I was deeply unwilling to relinquish. Yet I also felt that something of the inexplicable depth and complexity of the past had been transferred to the new – its suffering, its courage, its wisdom and its hope.

At the beginning of each Day of Atonement, even before the intoning of the opening *Kol Nidrei* meditation with its surging and searing melody, the Ark is opened, two Torah scrolls are taken out and carried in almost total silence around the synagogue. The quiet is broken only by the low chanting of the seven times repeated verse *Or zarua latsaddik ulyishrei lev simchah*, 'Light is sown for the righteous and joy for the upright in heart' (Psalm 97:11). I can still remember the first time I heard my teacher Rabbi Louis Jacobs sing those words when I was a boy. Even then I felt a sense of awe which drew me towards them: where was this hidden light, what was its nature, with what part of myself, and I trusted instinctively that every person had such a faculty, would I be able to see it?

Slowly through the subsequent years I began to realise that these thoughts were addressed to the same concerns as the unanswerable questions concerning the origin of the soul and the essence of creation. These inscrutable mysteries, as compelling as they are unfathomable, have long held a power over me from which there is no release. During the course of my life they have only grown in intensity: where is that hidden light, which, according to rabbinic teaching, God once sowed so that it illumined the entire earth, but concealed almost immediately afterwards? The traditional answer is that God stowed it away for the righteous in the world to come. But surely it is also present here in our everyday reality, garbed within all forms of life, closeted behind the ribcage of our body, burning secretly within the chambers of the heart. There are encounters with goodness and courage, experiences of beauty and wonder, which render that light visible so that it shines like the loadstar in the vast night sky. Such moments of illumination, however rare and however fleeting, reveal a truth so compelling that we cannot bear the thought of being parted from it. Henceforth that is our guide across the always uncharted and sometimes lonely landscape of our life. Inevitably there are long stretches of time when everything around us, and even the very vitality within us, seems to be muffled in silence and encompassed in darkness. But then the voice returns, singing quietly, '*Or zarua*, a light has been sown . . . ', and the eternal flame, which had never been extinguished, becomes visible to us once again.

❖ Mitzpah sits in my study, curled up in the armchair which he has made his own, and watches me with his big, steady eyes, alert to my every mood and move. Twice recently when I've taken him with me to synagogue meetings and he's been lying on the floor, half asleep and half looking up to check what's going on, the person sitting next to me has commented, 'There's so much love for you in those eyes.' It's mutual; we're bound together in this bond of life. I too am always eager for the voice which says, 'Walk!'

From Mitzpah's Blog

Tell that man to stop wasting time on his stupid computer and take me on my next adventure. I'm waiting, and I'm bored.
    Love,
    Mitzpah

Notes

INTRODUCTION

1 Georg Salzberger, *Erlebnisbericht*, 1960, unpublished, in the archives of the Jewish Museum in Frankfurt-am-Main

2 Georg Salzberger, *Leben und Lehre*, p. 111

FINAL PREPARATIONS

1 Aharon Appelfeld, *The Story of a Life: An Extraordinary Memoir of Survival*, translated by Aloma Halter, p. 101

2 from the pamphlet issued by the British Foreign and Commonwealth Office on 20 November 2008, on the occasion of the unveiling of a plaque to commemorate British diplomats who helped to rescue victims of Nazism

3 Georg Salzberger, *Erlebnisbericht*, op. cit.

DAY ONE – IN FRANKFURT: LIGHTING THE TORCH

1 Georg Salzberger, *Erlebnisbericht*, op. cit.

2 Georg Salzberger, *Leben und Lehre*, op. cit., p. 49 and following, '*Meine ersten Amtsjahre*'

3 Moses Mendelssohn, *Jerusalem, or On Religious Power and Judaism*, translated by Allan Arkush, Introduction and Commentary by Alexander Altmann, p. 78

4 ibid., Introduction, p. 3

5 ibid., p. 79, a footnote in which he quotes with approval Mr Iserlin's opinions in the issue of *Ephemerides* of October 1782

6 ibid., p. 45

7 ibid., p. 135

8 quoted in Alexander Altmann, *Moses Mendelssohn: A Biographical Study*, p. 517. I have translated *Verkündingung* as 'herald' rather than 'manifesto'.

9 Moses Mendelssohn, *Jerusalem*, op. cit., p. 93

10 Georg Salzberger, *Erlebnisbericht*, op. cit.

11 in a letter to Eugen Rosenstock, 25 August 1924, included in *Franz Rosenzweig: His Life and Thought*, presented by Nahum Glatzer, pp. 134–5

12 Address on the Opening of the Freies Jüdisches Lehrhaus in Frankfurt, 1920, in *Franz Rosenzweig: On Jewish Learning*, edited by Nahum Glatzer, p. 98

13 *Franz Rosenzweig, On Jewish Learning*, op. cit., pp. 56–8

14 Michael Brenner, *The Renaissance of Jewish Culture in Weimar Germany*, p. 80

15 Alexander Altmann, *Moses Mendelssohn: A Biographical Study*, Jewish Publication Society, Philadelphia, 1973, p. 569

16 Gotthold Ephraim Lessing, *Nathan der Weise*, Act III, Scene 7, my own translation

17 in *The Cultural Writings of Franz Rosenzweig*, edited and translated by Barbara E. Galli, Syracuse University Press, Syracuse, New York, 2000, p. 108

18 ibid., p. 111

19 quoted by Kurt Duewell in 'Jewish Cultural Centres in Nazi Germany', in *The Jewish Response to German Culture*, edited by Jehuda Reinharz and Walter Schatzberg, pp. 299–300

20 Michael Brenner, op. cit., pp. 216–17

DAY TWO – FROM FRANKFURT TO MAINZ

1 taken from www.dpcamps.org/dpcampsGermanyWo-Z.html

2 Lore Geminder, 'Keine Wintermäntel, Frankfurter Rundschau, 29 August 1945', in Eva Kolinsky, *After the Holocaust*, pp. 163–4

3 Kolinsky, op. cit., pp. 111–12

4 taken from www.dpcamps.org/dpcampsGermanyWo-Z.html

5 Kolinsky, op. cit., p. 123

6 Monica Kingreen, 'Von Frankfurt in das KZ Dachau, die Namen de rim November 1938 deportierten Maenner', in Monica Kingreen (ed.), *'Nach der Kristallnacht': Jüdisches Leben und antiJüdische Politik in Frankfurt am Main 1938–1945*, p. 67

7 ibid., p. 57

8 ibid., p. 56

9 Georg Salzberger, *Erlebnisbericht*, op. cit.

10 Jean Amery, 'On the Necessity and Impossibility of Being a Jew', in *At the Mind's Limits*, translated by Sidney Rosenfeld and Stella P. Rosenfeld, p. 86 & p. 100

DAY THREE – FROM MAINZ TO BINGEN

1 Paul Tillich, *Dynamics of Faith*, pp. 57–60

DAY FOUR – FROM BINGEN TO BACHARACH, AND BACK TO FRANKFURT

1 Heinrich Heine, *The Rabbi of Bacharach* (translated by E. B. Ashton), p. 15

2 ibid.

3 Rachel Heuberger, *Aron Freimann und die Wissenschaft des Judentums*, p. 78

4 ibid., p. 101

5 ibid., p. 165, my translation

6 'Wiederweihe des ersten jüdischen Gotteshauses in Frankfurt am Main', report in the *Frankfurt Rundschau* for 12 September 1945, quoted in Eva Kolinsky, *After the Holocaust*, op. cit., pp. 164–5

DAY FIVE – FROM BACHARACH TO ST GOAR

1 Gershom Scholem, 'Franz Rosenzweig and His Book *The Star of Redemption*', in Paul Mendes-Flohr (ed.), *The Philosophy of Franz Rosenzweig*, p. 21

2 *Franz Rosenzweig: His Life and Thought*, op. cit., pp. 95–6

3 Address on the Opening of the Freies Jüdisches Lehrhaus, 1920, in *Franz Rosenzweig: On Jewish Learning*, op. cit., p. 98

4 quoted in *Franz Rosenzweig: His Life and Thought*, op. cit., p. 107

5 extracts from this correspondence are published in *Franz Rosenzweig: On Jewish Learning*, op. cit., pp. 109–18

6 ibid., pp. 123–4

7 Gershom Scholem, op. cit., pp. 40–1

8 Marc Cioc, *The Rhine: An Eco-Biography*, p. 39 & p. 45

9 Hölderlin, 'Hymns and Fragments', quoted, in translation, in Marc Cioc, op. cit., p. 8

10 Mark M. Anderson, 'Ludwig Börne begins his professional career', in Sandler L. Gilman and Jack Zipes (eds), *Yale Companion to Jewish Writing and Thought in German Culture 1096–1996*, p. 130b

11 Ludwig Börne, Letter from Paris (1832), in ibid., p. 130b

12 Georg Salzberger, *Leben und Lehre*, op. cit., p. 94

13 quoted in Mary Rosenberg (ed.), *Heinrich Heine: Jüdisches Manifest*, Hugo Bieber, p. 263

14 quoted in Hugo Bieber and Moses Hadas, *Heine: A Biographical Anthology*, p. 430

15 Heine, 'Postscript to the *Romancero*, Paris, 30 September 1851', in ibid., pp. 424–5

16 ibid., p. 426

17 Exodus 1:8 and Talmud Sotah 11a

18 Heinrich Heine, 'Religion and Philosophy in Germany', 3, Conclusion, in Hugo Bieber and Moses Hadas (eds), op. cit., p. 331

DAY SIX – FROM KOBLENZ TO SAFFIG

1 Kadya Molodovsky, 'Prayers', translated by Kathryn Hellerstein, in *Four Centuries of Jewish Women's Spirituality: A Sourcebook*, edited by Ellen M. Umansky and Dianne Ashton, pp. 154–5

2 Harold Sapperstein, in *Rabbis in Uniform*, edited by Louis Barish, p. 224 and following

3 Nils Roemer presents a more complex and ambivalent picture of Dr Illert in his many references to the latter's role in his book *German City, Jewish Memory: The Story of Worms*, arguing that he 'reinvented himself in the postwar years as the cemetery's rescuer who had safeguarded the remains of the synagogue and the archives'. See there p. 151 and following.

SHABBAT IN KOBLENZ

1 Markus Roentgen, 'Abgeschlossene oder unabgeschlossene Vergangenheit', in *Lebendiges Zeugnisses*, periodical published by Bonifatiuswerk der deutschen Katholiken, Panderborn, 56th year, 2001, p. 288

2 Marcus Gryglewski, quoted in Einst und Jetzt, *Then and Now: On the History of the Dresden Synagogue and its Community*, p. 98, my translation

3 Jeremy Crang, 'Victor Klemperer's Dresden', in *Firestorm: The Bombing of Dresden*, 1945, edited by Paul Addison and Jeremy A. Crang, p. 90

DAY EIGHT – FROM MARIA LAACH TO REMAGEN

1 Midrash Vayikra Rabbah 31:4

DAY NINE – FROM REMAGEN TO BONN

1 W. Gunther Plaut, *Unfinished Business: An Autobiography*, pp. 127–8
2 from Ephraim of Bonn's Hebrew account of the York Massacre incorporated in Joseph haCohen's sixteenth-century chronicle *Emek Habakhah (Valley of Tears)*, published in Neubauer and Stern's *Hebraeische Berichte ueber die Judenverfolgungen waehrend der Kreuzzuege*, Berlin, 1898, and translated in Cecil Roth, *A History of the Jews in England*, Chapter 2
3 Shalom Spiegel, *The Last Trial: On the Legends and Lore of the Command to Abraham to Offer Isaac as a Sacrifice*, translated by Judah Goldin, pp. 148–9. I've added the quotation marks in the last line of each stanza, to emphasise that these words are direct citations from the Torah.
4 *Encyclopaedia Judaica*, entry for 'Bonn'

DAY TEN – FROM BONN TO COLOGNE

1 Lore Salzberger-Wittenberg, *Himmel und Erde*, pp. 44–9
2 Hugo Gryn, *Chasing Shadows: Memories of a Vanished World*, p. 257
3 Angela Merkel, speech on 16 October 2010
4 Thilo Sarazin, *Germany is Doing Away with Itself*, quoted in the *Daily Telegraph*, 13 January 2011
5 quoted by Russell A. Berman in 'Multiculturalism Uber Alles', in *Defining Ideas*, A Hoover Institute Journal, 13 December 2010
6 ibid.
7 included by Mendelssohn in a footnote to *Jerusalem* in which he refers to his earlier work *Dreams of a Friend of Mankind*, from which the quote is taken. See Moses Mendelssohn, *Jerusalem, or On Religious Power and Judaism*, op. cit., p. 79
8 David Cameron, speech on 5 February 2011

9 Gary Younge, 'The multiculturalism the European right fears so much is a fiction', *Guardian*, 14 March 2011

10 *Dina demalchuta dina*, 'The law of the land is the law', see Babylonian Talmud Nedarim 28a *et al.*

11 The Count of Clermont-Tonnerre in a debate in the French National Assembly on 23 December 1789, in Paul Mendes-Flohr and Jehuda Reinhard (eds), *The Jew in the Modern World*, p. 104

12 debate at the Assembly of Jewish Notables, on 4, 7 and 12 August 1806, in Paul Mendes-Flohr and Jehuda Reinhard (eds), op. cit., p. 118

DAY ELEVEN – IN WUPPERTAL

1 Izzeldin Abuelaish, *I Shall Not Hate*, p. 196 & p. 192

2 Point 5 of the Barmer Theologische Erklärung – the Barmen Declaration of 31 May 1934

3 See Mishnah: Sanhedrin 4:5: 'The person who saves a single life is as if they had saved an entire world.'

4 Berthold Klappert and Guenther van Norden, *Tut um Gottes Willen etwas Tapferes*, pp. 13–14

5 Mishnah Avot 4:17

6 preamble of the Barmer Theologische Erklärung, op. cit.

7 Berthold Klappert and Guenther van Norden, op. cit., p. 14

8 Karl Barth, letter to Hesse, 30 June 1935, in Berthold Klappert and Guenther van Norden, op. cit., pp. 21–2

9 Johannes Rau, in Berthold Klappert and Guenther van Norden, op. cit., Introduction, p. 5

10 Berthold Klappert and Guenther van Norden, op. cit., p. 26

11 ibid., pp. 38–9, Notes 1 and 4

12 document from Stadtarchiv Wuppertal (ed.), *KZ-Kemna 1933–1934*, Wuppertal, 1984, on the site of Birkbeck, University of London, www.camps.bbk.ac.uk/documents/ec.shtml

13 Record of the One-Hundred-and-Fourteenth Day, Thursday, 25 April 1946, of the trial of major German war criminals at Nuremberg, on the website of the Nizkor project, www.nizkor.org/hweb/imt/.../tgmwc-12-114-10.shtml

14 Daniel Swift, *Bomber County*, p. 189

15 'The Bomber's Baedecker' – *The Guide to the Economic Importance of German Towns and Industries*, The Ministry of Economic Warfare, London, 1943

16 Joerg Friedrich, *The Fire*, p. 3

17 ibid., p.7

18 W. G. Sebald, *On the Natural History of Destruction*, p. 70

19 ibid., p. 29

20 ibid., p. 89

21 ibid., p. 10

22 ibid., p. 14

23 Daniel Swift, op. cit., p. 189

DAY TWELVE – FROM WUPPERTAL TO IMSHAUSEN

1 *Selected Poems of Else Lasker-Schüler*, translated by Audri Durschlag-Litt and Jeanette Litman-Demeestere, with a Preface by Yehudah Amichai, Preface, p. 10

2 ibid., Introduction, p. 36

3 first published 1903, then in the collection *Der Siebenter Tag*, 1905

4 *Selected Poems*, op. cit., Introduction, p. 25

5 Dagmar Lorenz, 'Else Lasker-Schüler becomes permanently exiled in Jerusalem', in *Yale Companion to Jewish Writing and Thought in German Culture 1096–1996*, op. cit., p. 565

6 quoted in *Selected Poems*, op. cit., Introduvtion, p. 28

7 ibid., pp. 98–101, translation slightly modified

8 ibid., pp. 222–7, translation adapted

9 ibid., pp. 206–7, translation adapted

10 ibid., Introduction, p. 11

11 ibid., p. 215

12 Dagmar Lorenz, op. cit., p. 567 & p. 564

13 Sebastian Haffner, *Defying Hitler: A Memoir*, translated by Oliver Pretzel, pp. 124–5

14 Clarita von Trott zu Solz, *Adam von Trott zu Solz, eine Lebensbeschreibung*, p. 182

15 Marie 'Missie' Vassiltchikov, *The Berlin Diaries, 1940–45*, p. 48

DAY THIRTEEN – FROM IMSHAUSEN BACK TO COLOGNE

1 Clarita von Trott zu Solz, op. cit., p. 320
2 ibid., p. 326
3 Gollwitzer, Helmut, Kuhn, Kaethe and Schneider, Reinhold (eds), *Dying We Live: The Final Messages and Records of the Resistance*, translated by Reinhard C. Kuhn, Pantheon Books Inc., New York, 1956, p. 126
4 ibid., p. 129
5 ibid., p. 129
6 Klary Friedl, quoted in Marian Malet and Anthony Grenville, *Changing Countries: The Experience and Achievement of German-Speaking Exiles from Hitler in Britain from 1933 to Today*, p. 244

SHABBAT IN COLOGNE

1 Amos Oz, *A Tale of Love and Darkness*, p. 330
2 Kurt Duewell, op. cit., p. 298
3 Herbert Freeden, 'A Jewish Theatre under the Swastika', in *Leo Baeck Institute Yearbook, I*, 1956, p. 147
4 See Georg Mosse's comments on Hinkel in *German Jews beyond Judaism*, Indiana University Press, Bloomington and Hebrew Union College Press, Cincinnati, 1985, p. 79 and accompanying notes.
5 Herbert Freeden, 'A Jewish Theatre under the Swastika', op. cit., pp. 161–2
6 Herbert Freeden, *The Jewish Press in the Third Reich*, translated by William Templer, Berg, Providence and Oxford, 1993, p. 169
7 Kurt Duewell, op. cit., p. 305

DAY FIFTEEN – FROM COLOGNE TO DUISBURG

1 *The Jew in the Modern World: A Documentary History*, edited by P. Mendes-Flohr and J. Reinharz, op. cit., p. 28
2 ibid., p. 33
3 ibid., p. 35
4 Mendelssohn, *Jerusalem*, op. cit., as quoted in Julius Schoeps, 'Mendelssohn writes *Jerusalem*', in *Yale Companion to Jewish Writing and Thought in German Culture 1096–1996*, op. cit., p. 91
5 Georg Mosse, op. cit., p. 3

6 ibid., p. 4

7 Samson Raphael Hirsch, *The Nineteen Letters*, Feldheim Publishers, Jerusalem and New York, 5729/1969, p. 25

8 ibid., the 10th letter, p. 75

9 Samson Raphael Hirsch, *Commentary to the Torah*, Leviticus 19:18

10 Paul Mendes-Flohr, *German Jews: A Dual Identity*, p. 18

11 ibid., p. 46 & p. 48

12 ibid., pp. 35–6

13 Franz Rosenzweig's Address on the Opening of the Freies Jüdisches Lehrhaus, in *Franz Rosenzweig: On Jewish Learning*, op. cit., p. 98

14 Peter Brown, *Oskar Panizza: His Life and Works*, p. 30 (read on line)

15 Jack Zipes, *The Operated Jew: Two Tales of Anti-Semitism*, Note 9, p. 108

16 Peter Brown, op. cit., p. 30

17 Jack Zipes, op. cit., p. 52

18 ibid., p. 53

19 ibid., p. 59

20 ibid., p. 61

21 ibid., p. 63

22 ibid., p. 73

23 ibid., p. 74

DAY SIXTEEN – DUISBURG TO KLEVE

1 This section is based on Helmut Walser Smith's account in *The Butcher's Tale: Murder and Anti-Semitism in a German Town*

2 Mishnah Berurah on Shulchan Aruch: Orach Hayyim 472:11, Note 38

3 Wolfgang Krebs, *Jüdisches Leben in Kleve*, p. 23. The material about Kleve is based on this book.

4 ibid., pp. 106–7

5 In *The Penguin Book of Modern Yiddish Verse*, edited by Irving Howe, Ruth Wisse and Khone Shmeruk, p. 678

DAY SEVENTEEN – ACROSS THE BORDER INTO HOLLAND

1 Helga Krohn, 'Holt sie raus, bevor es zu spaet ist! Hilfsaktionen zur Rettung Jüdischer Kinder zwischen 1938 und 1940', in Monica Kingreen (ed.), op. cit., pp. 109–10

2 Vera Gissing, *Pearls of Childhood*, p. 155

3 Jacob Wasserman, *Mein Weg als Deutscher und Jude*, pp. 122–3, my translation

4 ibid., pp. 119–20

5 Diane Wolf, *Beyond Anne Frank, Hidden Children and Postwar Families in Holland*, p. 55, quoting Judith Miller, *One, by One, by One: Facing the Holocaust*

6 Miep Gies with Alison Leslie Gold, *Anne Frank Remembered*, p. 11

7 Diane Wolf, op. cit., p. 56 & p. 80

8 Louis Hagen, *Arnhem Lift: A Fighting Glider Pilot Remembers*, pp. 23–4

DAY EIGHTEEN – FROM LOCHEM TO AMSTERDAM

1 Diane Wolf, op. cit., p. 330

2 ibid., p. 173

3 ibid., p. 184

4 ibid., p. 120

5 ibid., p. 120, quoting from the work of Elma Verhey, *Kind van de rekening (Footing the Bill)*

6 ibid., p. 123

7 Rebbe Yitzhak Meir of Ger, *Chummash Peninei Hahasidut*, *Shemot*, p. 95

DAY NINETEEN – TO ROTTERDAM AND HOEK VAN HOLLAND

1 Sidney Bloch, *No Time for Tears, Childhood in a Rabbi's Family*, pp. 136–7

DAY TWENTY-ONE – FROM LIVERPOOL STREET STATION TO THE SYNAGOGUE

1 Milton Steinberg, quoted in *Jewish Reflections on Death*, edited by Jack Riemer, p. 135

Bibliography

Abuelaish, Izzeldin, *I Shall Not Hate*, Bloomsbury, London, Berlin, New York, Sydney, 2011

Addison, Paul and Craig, Jeremy (eds), *Firestorm, the Bombing of Dresden, 1945*, Pimlico, London, 2006

Altmann, Alexander, *Moses Mendelssohn: A Biographical Study*, Jewish Publication Society, Philadelphia, 1973

Amery, Jean, *At the Mind's Limits*, (translated by Sidney Rosenfeld and Stella P. Rosenfeld), Indiana University Press, in association with the United States Holocaust Memorial Museum, Bloomington and Indianapolis, 1980

Appel, Klaus, *Eines Morgens Waren Sie Alle Weg: Memoiren von Holocaust Ueberlebenden*, Switzerland, 2011

Appelfeld, Aharon, *The Story of a Life: An Extraordinary Memoir of Survival*, Penguin Books, London, 2006

Aris, Heinz-Joachim, Goldenbogen, Nora and Rossberg, Ingolf (eds), *Einst und Jetzt: Then and Now: On the History of the Dresden Synagogue and its Community*, Goldenbogen, Dresden, 2001

Barish, Louis (ed.), *Rabbis in Uniform*, Jonathan David, New York, 1962

Bieber, Hugo and Hadas, Moses, *Heine: A Biographical Anthology*, Jewish Publication Society of America, Philadelphia, 5717/1956

Bloch, Sidney, *No Time for Tears: Childhood in a Rabbi's Family*, William Kimber, London, 1980

Brenner, Michael, *The Renaissance of Jewish Culture in Weimar Germany*, Yale University Press, Newhaven and London, 1996

Brown, Peter, *Oskar Panizza: His Life and Works*, Peter Lang, New York and Bern, 1983

Brumlik, Micha, *Kein Weg als Deutscher und Jude*, Ullstein Taschenbuchverlag, Munich, 2000

Chazan, Robert, *God, Humanity, and History: The Hebrew First Crusade Narratives*, University of California Press, Berkeley, Los Angeles, London, 2000

Chazan, Robert, *In the Year 1096: The First Crusade and the Jews*, Jewish Publication Society, Philadelphia and Jerusalem, 5755/1996

Cioc, Mark, *The Rhine: An Eco-Biography 1815–2000*, University of Washington Press, Seattle and London, 2002

Dresdner Hefte, Beitrage zur Kulturgeschichte, 106: Gottes Häuser, Dresdner Kirche im Wandel, Dresden, 2011

Elon, Amos, *The Pity of It All: A Portrait of Jews in Germany 1743–1933*, Penguin Books, 2004

Epstein, Jon and Jacobs, David, *A History in Our Time: Rabbis and Teachers Buried at Hoop Lane Cemetery*, Leo Baeck College, London, 2011

Evans, Richard J., *In Hitler's Shadow: West German Historians and the Attempt to Escape from the Nazi Past*, Pantheon Books, New York, 1989

Feinberg, Annette, 'The Janus-Faced Jew: Nathan and Shylock on the Postwar German Stage', in *Unlikely History: The Changing German–Jewish Symbiosis, 1945–2000*, edited by Leslie Morris and Jack Zipes, Palgrave, New York and Hampshire, England, 2002

Fermor, Patrick Leigh, *A Time of Gifts: On Foot to Constantinople – From the Hook of Holland to the Middle Danube*, John Murray, London, 2004

Freeden, Herbert, *The Jewish Press in the Third Reich*, translated by William Templer, Berg, Providence and Oxford, 1993

Freeden, Herbert, 'A Jewish Theatre under the Swastika', in *Leo Baeck Institute Year Book*, 1, 1956, Institute for the East and West Library, pp. 142–62

Friedländer, Hugo, *Interessante Kriminalprozesse von kulturhistorischer Bedeutung, 1911–1921, Band 1*, S. pp. 67–89

Friedrich, Joerg (translated by Alison Brown), *The Bombing of Germany 1940–1945*, Columbia University Press, New York, 2008

Bibliography

Fritzsche, Peter, *Life and Death in the Third Reich*, Belknap Press of Harvard University Press, Cambridge, Massachusetts and London, England, 2008

Galli, Barbara (editor and translator), *Cultural Writings of Franz Rosenzweig*, Syracuse University Press, Syracuse, New York, 2000

Gies, Miep with Gold, Alison Leslie, *Anne Frank Remembered*, Corgi Books, London, 1988

Gilman, Sandler L. and Zipes, Jack (eds), *Yale Companion to Jewish Writing and Thought in German Culture 1096–1996*, Yale University Press, Newhaven and London, 1997

Gissing, Vera, *Pearls of Childhood*, Robson Books, London, 1988

Glatzer, Nahum, *Franz Rosenzweig: His Life and Thought*, Schocken Books, New York, second (revised) edition, 1961

Gollwitzer, Helmut, Kuhn, Kaethe and Schneider, Reinhold (eds) *Dying We Live: The Final Messages and Records of the Resistance*, translated by Reinhard C. Kuhn, Pantheon Books Inc., New York, 1956

Grenville, Anthony and Malet, Marian (eds), *Changing Countries: The Experience and Achievements of German-Speaking Exiles from Hitler to Britain from 1933 to Today*, Libris, London, 2002

Gryn, Hugo with Gryn, Naomi, *Chasing Shadows: Memories of a Vanished World*, Viking, London, 2000

Haffner, Sebastian (translated by Oliver Pretzel), *Defying Hitler: A Memoir*, Phoenix, London, 2003

Hagen, Louis, *Arnhem Lift: A Fighting Glider Pilot Remembers*, BCA London, NY, Sydney, Toronto, 1993

Heine, Heinrich (translated by E. B. Ashton), *The Rabbi of Bacharach*, Schocken Books, New York, 1947

Heuberger, Rachel, *Aron Freimann und die Wissenschaft des Judentums*, Max Niemeyer Verlag, Tuebingen, 2004

Heuberger, Rachel, *Rabbiner Nehemias Anton Nobel, die Jüdische Renaissance in Frankfurt am Main*, Societätsverlag, Frankfurt, 2005

Hirsch, Samson Raphael, *The Nineteen Letters*, Feldheim Publishers, Jerusalem and New York, 5729/1969

Horovitz, Rabbiner Dr Markus, *Frankfurter Rabbinen, mit Ergänzungen von Rabbiner Dr Josef Unna*, 'Ahva' Co-op Press, Israel, 1969

Howe, Irving, Shmeruk, Krone and Wisse, Ruth, *The Penguin Book of Modern Yiddish Verse*, Viking Penguin Inc. New York, London and Canada, 1987

Jospe, Alfred (ed.), *Studies in Jewish Thought: An Anthology of German-Jewish Scholarship*, Wayne State University Press, Detroit, 1981

Kingreen, Monica (ed.), *'Nach der Kristallnacht': Jüdisches Leben und antijüdische Politik in Frankfurt am Main 1938–1945*, Campus Verlag, Frankfurt and New York, 1999

Klappert, Bertold and van Narden, Guenther (eds), *Um Gottes Willen Tuet Etwas Tapferes: Karl Immer im Kirchenkampf*, Neukirchner Verlag, Neukirchen-Vluyn, 1989

Kolinsky, Eva, *After the Holocaust: Jewish Survivors in Germany after 1945*, Pimlico, London, 2004

Krebs, Wolfgang, *Jüdisches Leben in Kleve*, Verlag für Kultur und Technik, Norbert Luetzenkirchen, Kleve, 2004

Lasker-Schüler, Else, *Selected Poems* (translated by Audri Durschlag-Litt and Jeanette Litman-Demeestere, with a Preface by Yehudah Amichai), Green Integer, Los Angeles and Kobenhaven, 2002

Lessing, Gotthold Ephraim, *Nathan der Weise*, in *Lessings Werke*, Stuttgart, 1874

Levin, Bernard, *To the End of the Rhine*, Sceptre, Sevenoaks, fourth impression, 1991

Low, Alfred D., *Jews in the Eyes of Germans from the Enlightenment to Imperial Germany*, Institute for the Study of Human Issues, Philadelphia, 1979

Magee, Byron, *Wagner and Philosophy*, Penguin Books, London, 2000

Mendelssohn, Moses, *Jerusalem, or On Religious Power and Judaism* (translated by Allan Arkush, with an Introduction and Commentary by Alexander Altmann), Brandeis University Press, University Press of New England, 1983

Mendes-Flohr, Paul (ed.), *The Philosophy of Franz Rosenzweig*, published for Brandeis University Press by University Press of New England, Hanover and London, 1988

Bibliography

Mendes-Flohr, Paul, *German Jews, A Dual Identity*, Yale University Press, Newhaven and London, 1999

Mendes-Flohr, Paul and Reinharz, Jehuda, *The Jew in the Modern World: A Documentary History*, Oxford University Press, New York and Oxford, 1980

Mendes-Flohr, Paul (ed.), *Martin Buber: A Contemporary Perspective*, Syracuse University Press and the Israel Academy of Sciences and Humanities, Jerusalem, 2002

Mosse, Georg, *German Jews beyond Judaism*, Indiana University Press, Bloomington and Hebrew Union College Press, Cincinnati, 1985

Plaut, Gunther W., *Unfinished Business: An Autobiography*, Lester and Orpen Dennys, 1981

Reinharz, Jehuda, and Schatzberg, Walter (eds), *The Jewish Response to German Culture from the Enlightenment to the Second World War*, published for Clark University by the University Press of New England, Hanover and London, 1985

Riemer, Jack (ed.), *Jewish Reflections on Death*, Schocken Books, New York, 1976

Robertson, Ritchie, *Jewish Thinkers: Heine*, Grove Press, New York, 1988

Roemer, Nils, *German City, Jewish Memory: The Story of Worms*, Brandeis Uiversity Press, Massachusetts, 2010

Rollins, William and Zohn, Harry (eds), *Men of Dialogue: Martin Buber and Albrecht Goes*, Funk and Wagnalls, New York, 1969

Rosenberg, Mary (ed.), *Heinrich Heine: Jüdisches Manifest*, Hugo Bieber, New York, 1946

Rosenzweig, Franz, *On Jewish Learning*, edited by Nahum Glatzer, University of Wisconsin Press, Wisconsin and London, 1955

Salzberger, Georg, *Leben und Lehre*, Verlag Waldemar Kramer, Frankfurt-am-Main, 1982

Salzberger, Georg, 'Erlebnisbericht', a deposition on life in Frankfurt under the Nazis, unpublished manuscript in the Jewish Museum in Frankfurt, 1960

Salzberger-Wittenberg, Lore, *Himmel und Erde*, Kramer, Frankfurt-am-Main, 1966

Sebald, W. G. (translated by Anthea Bell), *On the Natural History of Destruction*, Modern Library, New York, 2003

Sorkin, David, *The Transformation of German Jewry 1780–1840*, Wayne State University Press, 1999

Sorkin, David, *Moses Mendelssohn and the Religious Enlightenment*, Peter Halban, London, 1988

Spiegel, Shalom, *The Last Trial: On the Legends and Lore of the Command to Abraham to Offer Isaac as a Sacrifice* (translated by Judah Goldin), Jewish Lights Publishing, Woodstock, Vermont, 1993

Swift, Daniel, *Bomber County: The Lost Airmen of World War Two*, Hamish Hamilton, London, 2010

Taylor, Frederick, *Dresden, Tuesday 13 February 1945*, Bloomsbury, London, Berlin, New York, 2005

Tillich, Paul, *Dynamics of Faith*, Perennial Classics, HarperCollins, New York, 2001

Vassiltchikov, Marie 'Missie': *The Berlin Diaries, 1940–1945*, Pimlico, London, 1999

von Trott zu Solz, Clarita, *Adam von Trott zu Solz: Eine Lebensbeschreibung*, Lukas Verlag, Berlin, 2009

Waldman, Mark, *Goethe and the Jews: A Challenge to Hitlerism*, Putnam, New York and London, 1934

Walser Smith, Helmut, *The Butcher's Tale: Murder and Anti-Semitism in a German Town*, Norton, New York and London, 2003

Wasserman, Jakob, *Mein Weg als Deutscher und Jude*, Deutscher Taschenbuch Verlag, Munich, 1999

Wolf, Diane L., *Beyond Anne Frank: Hidden Children and Postwar Families in Holland*, University of California Press, Berkeley, Los Angeles and London, 2007

Zahl Gottlieb, Amy, *Men of Vision: Anglo-Jewry's Aid to Victims of the Nazi Regime 1933–1945*, Weidenfeld and Nicolson, London, 1998

Zipes, Jack (translator and editor), *The Operated Jew: Two Tales of Anti-Semitism*, Routledge, New York and London, 1991

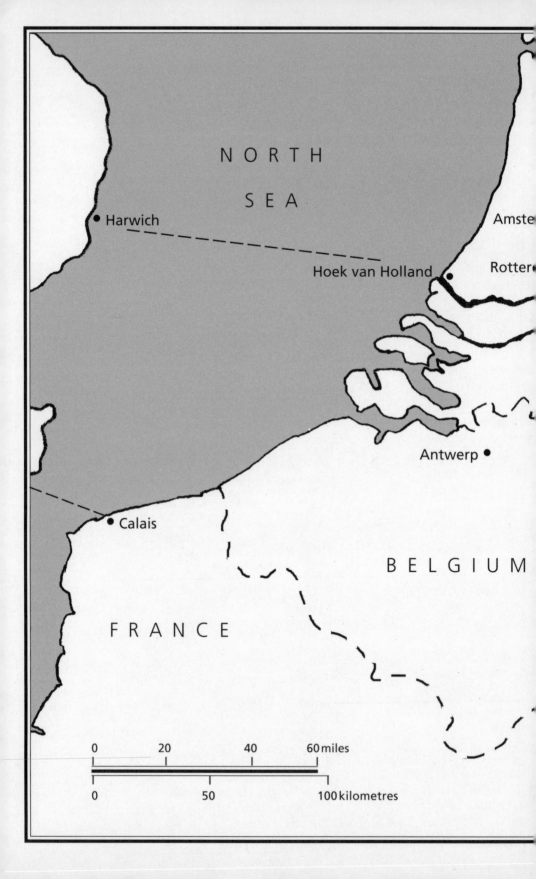